RETHINKING THE FRENCH CLASSROOM

> In the face of a backlash against multiculturalism, this volume offers professors concrete strategies for teaching difference and diversity at all levels of the French classroom, as well as tools to promote their programs on campus.
>
> Colette Trout, Ursinus College (emerita)

This volume investigates how teaching practices can address the changing status of literature in the French classroom. Focusing on how women writing in French are changing the face of French studies, opening the canon to not only new approaches to gender but to genre, expanding interdisciplinary studies and aiding scholars to rethink the teaching of literature, each chapter provides concrete strategies useful to a wide variety of classrooms and institutional contexts. Essays address how to bring French studies and women's and gender studies into the twenty-first century through intersections of autobiography, gender issues and technology; ways to introduce beginning and intermediate students to the rich diversity of women writing in French; strategies for teaching postcolonial writing and literary theory; and interdisciplinary approaches to expand our student audiences in the United States, Canada, or abroad. In short, revisiting how we teach, why we teach, and what we teach through the prism of women's texts and lives while raising issues that affect cisgender women of the Hexagon, queer and other-gendered women, immigrants and residents of the postcolony attracts more openly diverse students. Whether new to the profession or seasoned educators, faculty will find new ideas to invigorate and diversify their pedagogical approaches.

E. Nicole Meyer (Ph.D. University of Pennsylvania) is Professor of French and Women's and Gender Studies at Augusta University, USA. She publishes on a wide array of topics including contemporary French and Francophone women's autobiography, Flaubert, and French for specific purposes. Her current book project is *Fractured Families in Contemporary French and Francophone Women's Autobiographies*.

Joyce Johnston (Ph.D. Indiana University-Bloomington) is Professor of French, Associate Dean of Liberal and Applied Arts, and Director of the Division of Multidisciplinary Programs at Stephen F. Austin State University, USA. She has received multiple teaching awards including Stephen F. Austin State University's Teaching Excellence Award. She is the author of *Women Dramatists, Humor, and the French Stage: 1802–1855*.

RETHINKING THE FRENCH CLASSROOM

New Approaches to Teaching Contemporary French and Francophone Women

Edited by E. Nicole Meyer and Joyce Johnston

NEW YORK AND LONDON

First published 2019
by Routledge
52 Vanderbilt Avenue, New York, NY 10017

and by Routledge
2 Park Square, Milton Park, Abingdon, Oxon OX14 4RN

Routledge is an imprint of the Taylor & Francis Group, an informa business

© 2019 Taylor & Francis

The right of E. Nicole Meyer and Joyce Johnston to be identified as the authors of the editorial material, and of the authors for their individual chapters, has been asserted in accordance with sections 77 and 78 of the Copyright, Designs and Patents Act 1988.

All rights reserved. No part of this book may be reprinted or reproduced or utilised in any form or by any electronic, mechanical, or other means, now known or hereafter invented, including photocopying and recording, or in any information storage or retrieval system, without permission in writing from the publishers.

Trademark notice: Product or corporate names may be trademarks or registered trademarks, and are used only for identification and explanation without intent to infringe.

Library of Congress Cataloging-in-Publication Data
A catalog record for this title has been requested

ISBN: 978-1-138-36993-1 (hbk)
ISBN: 978-0-367-02346-1 (pbk)
ISBN: 978-0-429-40000-1 (ebk)

Typeset in Bembo
by Taylor & Francis Books

CONTENTS

List of contributors   viii
Acknowledgments   xii

Introduction   1
E. Nicole Meyer and Joyce Johnston

PART I
Exploring Identities/Exploring the Self: French Literature and Women's Studies in the Twenty-First Century   9

1 Why Teach (French) (Women's) Literature?   11
  Eilene Hoft-March

2 Fractured Families: Program Growth through Innovative Teaching of French and Francophone Women's Autobiographies   19
  E. Nicole Meyer

3 Worldwide Women Writers and the Web: Diversity and Digital Pedagogy   27
  Alison Rice

4 "Representing the Self": Contemporary French Lit Meets the Twenty-First-Century Student   35
  Dawn M. Cornelio

PART II
New Beginnings, New Horizons: Women Writers in Beginning and Intermediate French Classes   43

5 Teaching French and Francophone Women Authors Online   45
Sage Goellner

6 Integrating Women's Voices and Contemporary Cultural Materials through E-journaling   53
Elizabeth Berglund Hall

7 Linking Beginner and Advanced Language Learners through Images of Women   61
Joyce Johnston

8 Building Bridges from Language to Civilization through Gisèle Pineau's *Un Papillon dans la cité*   68
Natalie Edwards and Christopher Hogarth

PART III
Colonial and Postcolonial French Women Writers: Teaching Diversity on Shifting Ground   77

9 Peoples, Authors, Protagonists: Teaching Francophone Women Authors through Gender Identity Themes   79
Laurence M. Porter

10 Incorporating Oceanian Women Writers into the Francophone Literature Classroom   87
Julia L. Frengs

11 Making the Case for French Studies: Strategies for Teaching Gendered Multiculturalism in Contemporary French Literature   95
Rebecca E. Léal

12 Teaching Algeria through the Lens of Feminism   103
Florina Matu

13 Teaching Hélé Béji, Postcolonialism, and the Arab Spring: Perspectives from Baudrillard, McClintock, and Giroux   111
Eric Touya de Marenne

PART IV
Interdisciplinary Approaches to French Studies   119

14 Breaking Down Jail and Cross-Divisional Walls: Teaching Simone de Beauvoir and Existentialist Writers in the Twenty-First-Century French and Criminal Justice Classroom   121
Araceli Hernández-Laroche

15 Francophone Women Writers outside the French Classroom: An
    Integrated Approach to Exploring Women's Voices   128
    Shira Weidenbaum

16 Pushing Boundaries: A Feminist Interdisciplinary Approach to Team
    Teaching French and American Women's Lives during World War II   135
    Courtney Sullivan and Kerry Wynn

17 Women Novelists and the Music of Paris   143
    Arline Cravens

18 Introducing or Expanding Queer Content in the Contemporary
    Francophone Classroom   150
    CJ Gomolka

Index   *159*

CONTRIBUTORS

Dawn M. Cornelio (Ph.D. University of Connecticut) is Professor of French Studies at the University of Guelph. Her research focuses on contemporary French women's writing and the theory and practice of literary translation. Her literary translations have been read at international festivals around the world and have appeared in *Contemporary French and Francophone Studies*. She is currently creating a critical website analyzing the work of Chloé Delaume and translating Delaume's novel, *Certainement pas*, into English for publication. She has been awarded the Distinguished Professor Award for Excellence in Teaching by the University of Guelph Faculty Association (2007–8), the Award for Excellence in Teaching by the College of Arts (2006–7), and the Teaching Excellence Award by the Central Student Association (2005–6).

Arline Cravens (Ph.D. Washington University) is Assistant Professor of French at Saint Louis University, where she teaches courses on French women writers of the nineteenth and twentieth centuries, as well as courses on the representation of music in French literature of the nineteenth and twentieth centuries. Her primary research focuses on women writers of the nineteenth and twentieth centuries, and the role of musical aesthetics and gender theory in their fiction. She has published on the role of music and the feminine ideal in George Sand and has had articles accepted for publication and forthcoming on Marie D'Agoult and Virginie Despentes.

Natalie Edwards (Ph.D. in French from Northwestern University) is Associate Professor in French at the University of Adelaide, Australia. Her research focuses on late twentieth- and twenty-first-century life writing in French, particularly by women writers. She has published two books on French and Francophone women's autobiography: *Shifting Subjects: Contemporary Francophone Women's Life Writing* (2011) and *Voicing Voluntary Childlessness: Narratives of Non-Mothering in French* (2016). She has also co-edited seven volumes on Francophone women's writing. She has won several teaching prizes, including a national Australian Award for University Teaching and the University of Adelaide's premier teaching award. She is currently the Society for French Studies UK's International Visiting Fellow 2018–19.

Julia L. Frengs (Ph.D. University of Maryland) is Assistant Professor of French at the University of Nebraska-Lincoln, where, in addition to French-language courses, she teaches courses on the cultures and literatures of the French-speaking world. Her research focuses on French-speaking Oceania, women's writing, representations of the body, and environmentally engaged literatures of French expression. Her latest articles have appeared in *Interculturel Francophonies* (2017) and *Romance Notes* (2016). Her monograph, *Corporeal Archipelagos: Writing the Body in Francophone Oceanian Women's Literature* was published in 2017.

Sage Goellner (Ph.D. University of Wisconsin-Madison) is Assistant Professor of French in the Department of Liberal Arts and Applied Studies at the University of Wisconsin-Madison. Her areas of research are nineteenth-century French literature and women authors. She is currently completing a book project on haunting in nineteenth-century Orientalist literature.

CJ Gomolka (Ph.D. University of Maryland) is Assistant Professor of Modern Languages (French) at DePauw University. His main areas of research and publication are sexuality and gender in nineteenth- and twenty-first century French and Francophone studies. His current book project investigates the intersections and negotiations between the French Republican tradition of universalism and contemporary articulations of queerness in the Francophone world including chapters on the *transpédégouine* movement, the podcasts *Homomico, Gouinement lundi*, and *Les Couilles sur la table*, the emergence of queer studies in France, as well as Brahim Nait-Balk's *Homo dans la cité*.

Elizabeth Berglund Hall (Ph.D. University of Wisconsin-Madison) is Assistant Professor General Faculty at the University of Virginia. She is co-author of a fifth-semester French-language textbook, *Textures: Pour approfondir la communication orale et écrite* (forthcoming). She has published articles on French and Francophone women in such journals as *Dalhousie French Studies, Romanic Review, Nottingham French Studies*, and *Women in French Studies*, and is first editor of a forthcoming volume on Hélène Cixous (*Cixous after/depuis 2000*). She is a collaborator on a multidisciplinary project for the use of e-portfolios in the language classroom.

Araceli Hernández-Laroche (Ph.D. University of California Berkeley) is Associate Professor of Modern Languages and Assistant Chair of Languages, Literature and Composition at the University of South Carolina Upstate. She is the past-president of the South Carolina Chapter of the American Association of Teachers of French. She publishes on Mediterranean studies, existentialism, and explores the intersections of colonialism and world wars in the works of French, Italian, and North African writers. Her research and teaching areas also include feminist writers, the Global South, migration, literary and cultural translation, and service learning. Araceli serves on various boards and volunteers with immigrant advocacy groups.

Eilene Hoft-March (Ph.D. University of California Berkeley) is Professor of French and Milwaukee-Downer and College Endowment Association Professor in Liberal Studies at Lawrence University, Appleton, Wisconsin. She teaches French, Gender Studies, and Freshman Studies and will soon be contributing to Lawrence's new Global Studies program. Her research focuses on twentieth- and twenty-first-century life writing in French with recent publications on Catherine Clément, Marie Darrieussecq, and Hélène Cixous. In her time at Lawrence University she has received the Young Teacher Award and the Excellence in Teaching Award.

Christopher Hogarth (Ph.D. Northwestern University) is Lecturer in French at the University of South Australia. He holds a Ph.D. from Northwestern University and specializes in

African and African diasporic writing in both French and Italian. He is the editor of *The Contemporary Francophone Intellectual* (2014) and has published on authors such as Fatou Diome, Marie NDiaye, and Ken Bugul. He has published several pedagogical articles on topics such as autobiography in the language classroom and short-term study-abroad programs.

Joyce Johnston (Ph.D. Indiana University-Bloomington) is Professor of French, Associate Dean of Liberal and Applied Arts, and Director of the Division of Multidisciplinary Programs at Stephen F. Austin State University, where she has also served as coordinator of the gender studies interdisciplinary minor. She is the recipient of multiple teaching awards including Stephen F. Austin State University's Teaching Excellence Award and Indiana University's Teaching Excellence Recognition Award. She has authored several articles on nineteenth-century women playwrights and her monograph, *Women Dramatists, Humor, and the French Stage: 1802–1855*, was published in 2014.

Rebecca E. Léal (Ph.D. University of Iowa) is Assistant Professor of French at Elmhurst College, where she directs the French program and teaches all levels of language and culture as well as faculty-led study-abroad courses in Europe, the Caribbean, and North Africa and professional development workshops for K-12 educators. Her research focuses on multiculturalism in twentieth-century France, with particular attention to postcolonial migration as well as the use of popular cultural productions as pedagogical documents in the French-language classroom.

Florina Matu (Ph.D. University of Alabama) is Assistant Professor of French at St. Edwards University where she teaches a variety of French and culture courses including Francophone media, Francophone and Hispanic Caribbean literature, and Francophone Africa. Her research focuses both on teaching the Francophone world as well as women writers of the Maghreb such as Maïssa Bey and Faïza Guène.

E. Nicole Meyer (Ph.D. University of Pennsylvania) is currently Professor of French and Women's and Gender Studies at Augusta University, Georgia, having chaired their Department of English and Foreign Languages. Previously, she taught the full gamut of French courses and chaired at the University of Wisconsin-Green Bay. She publishes on a wide array of topics from French and Francophone women's autobiography to Flaubert, French for specific purposes, service learning, contemporary French cinema, and nineteenth-, twentieth-, and twenty-first-century French and Francophone literature. Her current book project is *Fractured Families in Contemporary French and Francophone Women's Autobiographies*. Among her teaching awards are Augusta University Scholarship of Teaching and Learning Fellow 2016–17, University of Wisconsin System Teaching Scholar, 2004–5, Advanced Online Teaching Fellow, 2013–14, Creative Approaches to Teaching Award, 2004, and Teaching at Its Best Award, 1998.

Laurence M. Porter (Ph.D. Harvard) is Oberlin College Affiliate Scholar in Comparative Literature and has taught a vast array of courses ranging from French literature to African studies, from Latin American and Caribbean studies to women's studies. He has received the Dean's Medal of Excellence from the College of Arts and Letters and the Distinguished Faculty Award from Michigan State University, and was awarded the 1998 National Endowment for the Humanities Senior Fellowship for University Teachers. In addition to editing and contributing to multiple Modern Language Association volumes on approaches to teaching, and his encyclopedia on Gustave Flaubert, he has published numerous articles on nineteenth-century French literature, including on approaches to teaching Victor Hugo, Gustave Flaubert, West African folktales, Francophone women authors of Canada, and Francophone Caribbean authors.

Alison Rice (Ph.D. University of California Los Angeles) is Associate Professor of French and Francophone literature and film at the University of Notre Dame, where she is presently Director of the Institute for Scholarship in the Liberal Arts. Her research explores women writers of the Maghreb and she is the author of *Time Signatures: Contextualizing Contemporary Francophone Autobiographical Writing from the Maghreb* and *Polygraphies: Francophone Women Writing Algeria*.

Courtney Sullivan (Ph.D. Texas-Austin) is Professor of French at Washburn University in Topeka, Kansas. Her research focuses primarily on representations of courtesans in nineteenth-century French film and popular culture as well as depictions of the demi-mondaine in contemporary film. She is the author of *The Evolution of the French Courtesan Novel: From de Chabrillan to Colette* (2016). She is currently working on representations of the Creole *quarteronne* in nineteenth-century Francophone literature.

Eric Touya de Marenne (D.E.A., Université de Paris IV, Sorbonne; Ph.D., University of Chicago) is Associate Professor of French at Clemson University. His research and teaching interests include nineteenth- through twenty-first-century French and Francophone literature and culture and interdisciplinary approaches to literature, art, media, theory, culture, economics, ethics, and society. He is Chevalier dans l'Ordre des Palmes Académiques and received the John B. and Thelma A. Gentry Award for Teaching Excellence in the Humanities in 2012. His most recent publications include *Francophone Women Writers: Feminisms, Postcolonialisms, Cross-Cultures* (2011) and *The Case for the Humanities: Pedagogy, Polity, Interdisciplinarity* (2016).

Shira Weidenbaum (Ph.D. Yale University) is a tutor of French and Humanities and Faculty Development Coordinator at Quest University Canada in Squamish, British Columbia. Her research focuses on religious propaganda in the sixteenth century. Her article on the use of the dialogic genre in *Discours Familier* by Pierre Regis appeared in *Les Etats du dialogue à la Renaissance*, and she has forthcoming articles on *Les Dialogues rustiques* and *Le Pacifique*.

Kerry Wynn (Ph.D. University of Illinois-Urbana Champaign) is Associate Professor of History and Director of the University Honors Program at Washburn University. She is the author of "'Miss Indian Territory' and 'Mr. Oklahoma Territory': Marriage, Settlement, and Citizenship in the Cherokee Nation and the United States," in *Moving Subjects*, edited by Tony Ballantyne and Antoinette Burton, and "Civilizing the White Man: American Indian Elites Define Citizenship in Oklahoma," in *Representation and Citizenship*, edited by Richard Marbeck.

ACKNOWLEDGMENTS

Nicole would like to express gratitude to my son, Max Papadopoulos, who has brought me so much joy every day of his life, and to my parents, Richard and Ilse R. Meyer. While I miss their physical presence, they live in my heart. In addition, others who have helped in innumerable ways are Joyce Johnston, who listened and then jumped on board when I gushed about a cool project we could write and edit together. Her positive attitude, no matter what the challenges may be, is inspiring to all that meet her. Working with her has been a pure pleasure throughout. Personal thanks go to Women in French colleagues, who have become wonderful colleagues, collaborators, and friends. In particular, Annabelle Rea invited me to join, Mary Anne Garnett's belief sustained me, Cathy Nesci's simple acts of kindness when my parents died will never be forgotten. In addition, I would like to express thanks to Lucienne Frappier-Mazur, Gerald Prince, and the late Frank Bowman for their wonderfully inspiring questions and guidance, Susan Stanford Friedman, longtime Director of the Institute for Research in the Humanities, Dale Bauer, former director of Women's and Gender Studies, and to the University of Wisconsin-Madison Libraries for their generous support of my research. Gratitude also to the Office of Faculty Development and Teaching Excellence, the Office of Experiential Education, and Dr. Skip Clark, past Dean of Pamplin College, all of Augusta University.

Joyce would like to express sincere gratitude to Stephen F. Austin State University, the Department of Languages, Cultures, and Communication, the Division of Multidisciplinary Programs, and to the Stephen F. Austin State University Research Enhancement Program whose grant supported this work. Working with E. Nicole Meyer is a privilege and a joy. Her meticulous, imaginative work is equaled only by her passion for teaching French and Francophone women's writing. Personal thanks go to my colleagues in languages at Stephen F. Austin State University, who set the bar for teaching excellence so high. Special thanks to Mae and Zach who bring light to my life with both love and silliness. My most heartfelt gratitude goes out to my husband, Ryan, who has been a constant source of support and encouragement for over two decades.

We would both like to thank Geivonna Little, James Stingley, Ethan Fatheree, and Allison Boyle for their assistance through this process. In addition, we are grateful to Women in French and the current president, Cecilia Beach. We both wish to thank the conferences that gave a home to our pedagogical panels, especially to the Rocky Mountain Modern Language

Association (and to Arline Cravens who presented the need) for their continued support of Women in French pedagogy tables. Other conferences which have supported some of the authors' pedagogical presentations of teaching women in French are the Modern Languages Association, the Nineteenth-Century French Studies Association, the College Literature Association, and the Midwest Modern Languages Association. We would like to thank the wonderful Routledge team, in particular Jenny Abbott, Louise Peterken, and Dawn Preston, with whom it was a great pleasure to work.

INTRODUCTION

E. Nicole Meyer and Joyce Johnston

Several principles anchor this volume. Teaching matters. Teaching French and Francophone women's texts (in the largest possible sense of the word) matters. Creative strategies engage students to ask deeper, more meaningful questions. And, finally, the better we teach, the easier it will be to recruit and retain students in French, an embattled language in the States, despite its cultural, literary, and linguistic prominence across the world. This volume investigates how teaching practices can address the changing status of literature in the French classroom. Focusing on how women writing in French are transforming the face of French studies, opening the canon to not only new approaches to gender but to genre, expanding interdisciplinary studies, and aiding scholars to rethink the teaching of literature, each chapter provides concrete strategies useful to a wide variety of classrooms and institutional contexts.

Our volume addresses first and foremost a number of critical issues facing not only French professors, but humanities on the whole. Why is it important for our students to study Francophone women, their writings, their images, and their lives? Why is it essential for us to understand their voices within context? Why does the use of French language and culture need to be included in the humanities? Universities aim to prepare a new generation of students for unknown professional and personal adventures. Ironically, while an understanding of other cultures, languages, and perspectives is crucial to achieving this aim, language requirements in many institutions are threatened or already eliminated. In the face of a backlash against multiculturalism, our volume offers professors concrete strategies for teaching difference and diversity at all levels of the French classroom, as well as the tools to promote their programs on campus. Today's French instructors must be prepared to teach outside of the French classroom. We are challenged to reinvent how we teach along with what we teach. In studying women's voices which are often silenced, not only can we better understand immigration, religion, and political institutions of the Francophone world, we can engage in analyzing or even producing our own narratives in courses that engage students both to critically think at a deeper level and to articulate their thoughts in French.

Second, this text focuses first on the "How" – the practical aspects of teaching French and Francophone women. How do we best bring our students to appreciate stories of and by Francophone women as we motivate them to explore uncomfortable questions of trauma, marginalization, and the scars of a colonial past? How do we teach minority or LGBTQ+ voices without preaching? And how do we deliver all of this to students who are not native speakers of French? The essays within offer proven lessons, activities, and other strategies from a variety of institutional contexts, from small colleges, to large universities, from the online classroom to the lecture hall. We share innovative ideas for collaboration with other disciplines, service learning, and outreach courses designed for non-traditional students. The chapters in this volume offer award-winning teachers' approaches to tackle head-on the question of how to sell women's and gender studies and French studies to our students and our institutions by providing examples of how to incorporate contemporary events, important critical theories, the newest technology, and interdisciplinary approaches into our instruction and curricula.

The first section of this book, "Exploring Identities/Exploring the Self: French Literature and Women's Studies in the Twenty-First Century," addresses teaching French and gender in the twenty-first century. Our focus is to attract students to French programs through cutting-edge pedagogy and approaches for teaching subjects which instructors avoided decades ago: trauma, incest, and suicide to name a few. These essays underscore the importance of teaching diversity to increasingly more diverse student audiences. Several essays present particularly cogent arguments defending the humanities, our own discipline, and their essential role in every student's education.

In "Why Teach (French) (Women's) Literature?" Eilene Hoft-March offers a compelling case for why French studies and women's studies are crucial to student learning, and thus to a university's success. Twenty-first-century students must learn to read narratives that emerge from unfamiliar cultures and from identities seen as different or marginalized. Through a nuanced discussion of contemporary texts such as Marie Darrieussecq's *Clèves*, Marie Nimier's *La Reine du silence*, and Hélène Cixous *Osnabrück*, Hoft-March nimbly presents a series of questions exploring interpretive and human activity, the autobiographical creation of self, and language's intersection with cultural context. Hoft-March frames the teaching of women's literature as a means to motivate students to evaluate their own narratives, past, present, and future; to oblige them as best one can to experience difference(s); to teach them to use their (and others') words powerfully and sensitively; to teach them to resist unevaluated propositions; and to encourage them to act responsibly, even justly. E. Nicole Meyer builds upon the creation of self-narrative through a course focused on the narration of childhood, and the narrator's relation to her family in the autobiographies of Colette, Ken Bugul, Marguerite Duras, Nathalie Sarraute, and Annie Ernaux, in "Fractured Families: Program Growth through Innovative Teaching of French and Francophone Women's Autobiographies." Meyer incorporates current student interests through discussions of self-narration by considering selfies, tattoos, films, and other representations of present-day traumas. The effective use of interdisciplinary lenses to ask compelling questions and explore other cultural perspectives and practices both opens students' minds while drawing them to our classroom. The difficulty of voicing what has previously remained silent (e.g., incest, domestic violence, ageing, and Alzheimer's disease), as well as the complex linguistic, geographical, and other divides that shake the lives of the writers analyzed in the course, inspire students to both deeper reflection and further study in a course taught either in French, in translation, whether face to face or online. The next chapter builds upon innovative pedagogy through further use of the web. "Worldwide Women Writers and the Web: Diversity and Digital Pedagogy," by Alison Rice, offers ideas for fusing traditional literary study with multimedia technology through "Francophone Metronomes," a website she designed, featuring filmed interviews of 18 living authors of various ages who come from locations as different as Algeria and Bulgaria, Senegal and South Korea. Rice offers practical suggestions for teaching Francophone women's texts in tandem with online testimonies included in her website in intermediate and advanced courses and demonstrates how instructors can enhance their students' ability to discuss multilingualism, multiculturalism, and literature as a response to the human experience. In Chapter 4, "'Representing the Self': Contemporary French Lit Meets the Twenty-First-Century Student," Dawn M. Cornelio discusses a third-year literature course entitled "Representations of the Self," which prompts students to extend their study of autofiction to create their own first-person narrative in French. Students develop new perspectives towards so-called "taboo" subjects (i.e., eating disorders, suicide, and incest). Cornelio discusses her innovative course within the context of her Canadian institution's revamped French studies curriculum designed to enhance recruitment and retention.

The second section of the volume, "New Beginnings, New Horizons: Women Writers in Beginning and Intermediate French Classes," focuses on how emphasizing Francophone women's lives and writing in beginning and intermediate courses can enhance recruitment and retention efforts. Given that many French professors teach students whose first exposure to French comes at university, we cannot miss our chance to entice beginners to continue their study of the language and its cultural products. When we introduce students to women writers and gender issues in beginning and intermediate French courses, they are motivated to continue their French studies based on interest in both content and language. Essays in this section demonstrate how to incorporate technology and pedagogical innovations such as online pedagogy, content teaching in early classes, collaborative learning, and e-journaling with the dual goal of promoting language acquisition and spawning interest in the study of Francophone women.

Agreeing with Cathy N. Davidson that the sciences and technology cannot thrive without a corresponding flourishing of the humanities, Sage Goellner considers the ways in which online education can provide a new space to rethink the teaching of French and Francophone women authors through the use of digital archival material to create a survey of both famous (Colette, Simone de Beauvoir) and lesser-known women authors from the Middle Ages to the present. In "Teaching French and Francophone Women Authors Online," Goellner offers ideas for a beginner-level course taught in English in an online environment which will attract an oft overlooked audience – those taking courses away from campus – to French studies. By promoting access, interpretation, analysis, and synthesis of texts by authors from Christine de Pisan to Assia Djebar, Goellner shows how instructors can use ideas from her course to attract traditional and non-traditional continuing studies students while emphasizing the importance of exploring a diverse array of perspectives and voices. In "Integrating Women's Voices and Contemporary Cultural Materials through E-journaling," Elizabeth Hall presents an innovative teaching tool, the interactive e-journal, through which third-semester French-language students compile interactive, online journals as they further develop their understanding of French and Francophone culture. Hall describes student collaboration through online groups, and also suggests different journal topics through which students discover Francophone women's perspectives on their own terms. The incorporation of cultural material such as short stories by Monique Proulx and stained glass artwork by Marcelle Ferron into the intermediate classroom introduces diverse perspectives and minority points of view into the curricula through this creative project. The following chapter creates links of another kind. Joyce Johnston's "Linking Beginning and Advanced Language Learners through Images of Women" demonstrates how to link a beginner-level language class with an advanced literature and film class through the study of the representation of women in François Ozon's film *8 Femmes*. The film serves as a perfect springboard for beginners to explore female film icons such as Catherine Deneuve and Isabelle Huppert, while advanced students hone their film-analysis skills. Johnston discusses how advanced students can lead beginners in class discussions regarding symbolic use of color and cinematic typing of women. Such an approach gives advanced students leading activities ownership of their French program while enticing beginner students to further their own French study. Upper-intermediate language classes form the focus of the following chapter. "Building Bridges from Language to Civilization through Gisèle Pineau's Novel *Un Papillon dans la cité*" offers an engaging format for an upper-intermediate class focused on both civilization and women's expression. Award-winning professors Natalie Edwards and Christopher Hogarth present their highly successful intermediate course in which students improve their language skills through a study of Gisèle Pineau's novel *Un Papillon dans la cité*. By using each of the five chapters from Pineau's work as a springboard for corresponding units, Edwards and Hogarth offer students a departure point to discover Francophone civilization. Units in question focus on French departments and regions overseas, French colonial and postcolonial legacy, immigration, religion, political institutions, and gender equity.

Colonial and postcolonial concerns—literary and cinematic voicing of the Francophone world—reveal the difficulties of integrating different cultural approaches to sexuality, gender, and race into our toolkit. Our third segment, "Colonial and Postcolonial French Women Writers: Teaching Diversity on Shifting Ground," proposes practical pedagogical strategies to address these challenges through an examination of the vast French-speaking world, from Oceania to the Maghreb to contemporary France and beyond. Faculty increasingly face the challenge of teaching diversity in the face of the current backlash against multiculturalism. How can we teach without preaching, invite respectful discussion, and avoid essentialist clichés? We propose innovative approaches to teaching contemporary events, voicing postcolonial theoretical concerns, and articulating systems of power, discourse, and marginalization.

This section opens with Laurence M. Porter's "Peoples, Authors, Protagonists: Teaching Francophone Women Authors through Gender Identity Themes." Between 1946 and 1962, good and great literature by Francophone women flourished. During the protracted period when Francophone women still did not have equal access to political power, they nonetheless became able to imagine the exercise of such power, and to dramatize it in their fictions, which they presumably hoped foreshadowed positive social change. Porter proposes studying others' experiences and values through fictional protagonists as imagined and depicted in a social context by women authors from the target cultures. Rather than aiming to "cover everything," the course introduces students to the wide varieties of postcolonial feminist writing. In "Incorporating Oceanian Women Writers into the 'Francophone' Literature Classroom," Julia Frengs offers us a guide for teaching Oceanian texts. Literature emanating from French-speaking Oceania (French Polynesia, New Caledonia, Vanuatu, Wallis, and Futuna) is an understudied and oft mislabeled body of literature, and thus already complicates the composition of syllabi when planning introductory courses on the cultures and literatures of the "Francophone" sphere. Frengs's agile consideration of "canon" and of the term "Francophone world" frame her discussion of the difficult decisions regarding choice of texts and course structure that one faces in designing general undergraduate "Francophone" literature courses which include the Oceanic region (and women of the Oceanic region). Frengs's activities that facilitate student interaction include a Pinterest discussion board, podcasts, and students taking on leadership roles during discussions. She considers how instructors can teach students to engage with texts in ways that allow women authors to successfully communicate their multiple, nuanced messages while avoiding a dissemination of stereotypical, exoticized views of the indigenous societies of the Pacific in regards to the treatment of women.

Rebecca Léal focuses on the use of different genres and media to teach the gendered melting pot of contemporary France within the smaller private college context. Léal adapts her multimedia materials to intermediate-language-level "bridge courses," and to English-language courses, such as first year seminars, comparative Franco-American relations courses, or world literature in translation. In the third chapter of this section, "Making the Case for French Studies: Strategies for Teaching Gendered Multiculturalism in Contemporary French Literature," Léal demonstrates how topics such as the evolution of immigration, family resettlement policies (*Inch'Allah dimanche*), and Harki refugees (*Leïla*) offer a wealth of possibilities for exploring diversity issues in France today. The following chapter narrows the focus to Algeria, a focus of many Francophone study programs across the U.S. "Teaching Algeria through the Lens of Feminism" by Florina Matu suggests several thought-provoking approaches to the study of cultural diversity of Algeria and socio-political and cultural effects of colonialism and postcolonialism on the literary and cinematic map of Francophonie. Through a study of works such as Maïssa Bey's *Bleu blanc vert*, Leïla Aslaoui's *Coupables*, and Gilles Pontecorvo's *The Battle of Algiers*, students examine how female characters articulate or express problems of identity and resistance, gender roles and family dynamics, sexuality and difference, marriage and womanhood while becoming familiar with theory such as feminism, postcolonialism, socio-criticism, and psychoanalysis. Matu offers concrete examples of reading guides, activities, and assessment tools, as well as approaches which help students free themselves from the abundance of stereotypes associated with Algerian culture. The section closes with an astutely argued chapter of ways of approaching the Arab Spring in our curricula. In "Teaching Hélé Béji, Postcolonialism, and the Arab Spring," Eric Touya de Marenne focuses on teaching recent historical events in the Maghreb through the work of Tunisian author Hélé Béji, and through intersections with contemporary literary theorists such as Jean Baudrillard, Anne McClintock, Henry Giroux and bell hooks, among others. Over the past 30 years, Béji has written books and essays on the subjects of decolonization, cultural pluralism, feminism, dialogues between East and West, and the problems of democratization in Tunisia's postcolonial era. Touya de Marenne's teaching of Hélé Béji's *Désenchantement national* (1982), *Nous, décolonisés* (2008), and her more recent articles on the Arab Spring (2011–13) develops new pedagogical strategies by expanding theoretical and interdisciplinary perspectives on colonial and postcolonial concerns and issues pertaining to historical and civic progress. In so doing, Touya de Marenne problematizes and expands the interdisciplinary nature of French studies in ways that encourage student reflection.

The final series of chapters examines how to adopt these new pedagogical strategies within expanding interdisciplinary contexts. In "Interdisciplinary Approaches to French Studies" we push the boundaries of what formerly was the French discipline, beyond French literary and cultural studies of the past. Chapters within this section offer the reader ideas for developing new courses and new approaches to teaching French through a variety of disciplinary lenses and within a variety of curricular contexts. From teaching works in translation to team teaching, we propose means to attract and engage students who otherwise might not be exposed to French studies or to the lives and works of French-speaking women. Interdisciplinary connections, be they of criminal justice, history, music, or queerness, enhance our teaching of French through the incorporation of other disciplines and voices.

Araceli Hernández-Laroche presents an award-winning service-learning, cross-divisional honors course on the study of torture and terrorism from a global perspective in "Breaking Down Jail and Cross-Divisional Walls: Teaching Simone de Beauvoir and Existentialist Writers in the Twenty-First-Century French and Criminal Justice Classroom." In an age of increasing "glocal" diversity, criminal justice majors (and many others) can better serve increasingly non-English-speaking communities if they gain proficiency in French or another world language. This course, which Hernández-Laroche co-teaches with a criminal justice professor in an active-learning classroom, prompts students to consider French existential literature alongside sociological and criminal justice theory. Simone de Beauvoir's *Le sang des autres* as well as her highly visible engagement against state-sponsored torture during the Algerian War feature prominently in the course through discussions of how French and Francophone women shaped ethical debates in the course of war-torn conflicts on both sides of the Mediterranean during world wars and decolonization. In "Francophone Women Writers outside the French Classroom: An Integrated Approach to Exploring Women's Voices," Shira Weidenbaum underscores that in recent years, specialists in French and Francophone literature have begun teaching more and more outside of French programs in general education classes or at institutions where no French major or minor exists. Thus, we increasingly seek new ways to bring Francophone women writers to a non-specialist audience. Weidenbaum demonstrates how French women writers can be meaningfully included in broader courses presented to non-specialist undergraduates. The notion of public and private voices grounds an exploration of Francophone women's writings, taught in translation, alongside works by women from other parts of the globe. Weidenbaum offers ideas for teaching diverse voices from often unlikeable or problematic women characters in texts such as Marie Vieux Chauvet's *Amour* and Irène Némirovky's *Jezebel*, juxtaposed with Margaret Atwood's *Penelopiad*. Team teaching provides another means of crossing disciplinary boundaries in Chapter 16. "Pushing Boundaries: A Feminist Interdisciplinary Approach to Team-Teaching French and American Women's Lives during World War II," by Courtney Sullivan and Kerry Wynn, describes the response to a lack of awareness about women's history and about World War II in France and underscores the importance of studying French women's writings. To this end, Sullivan and Wynn's course explores women's roles during World War II in French and American fiction, film, autobiography, and history. The course, co-taught by the French and history faculty, investigates World War II representations of women as agents or victims of change—the overarching theme grounding all assignments. Drawing upon diverse sources to examine women's memories of their own experiences, as well as their portrayal in popular culture, this course provides a model for an innovative interdisciplinary approach, bringing the complexity of French women's experiences to an expanded audience.

From the literary-musical milieu of the Parisian salon to the twentieth-century music hall, Arline Cravens's course, "French Women Novelists and the Music of Paris," leads students on an exhilarating exploration of writers, musicians, and the representation of music in French literature by women. Cravens invites students to discover icons such as George Sand as well as those from twentieth-century "jazz fiction." In her chapter, Cravens describes how to introduce students to an interdisciplinary conception of the arts, emphasizing how women writers and musicians, often marginalized during their own time, played a vital role in aesthetic evolution during recent centuries. Her suggestions for lectures, resources for videos and music performance, writing activities, and student presentations allow French instructors to expand their literary-musical teaching repertoire, and to thus appeal to a wider audience. Our volume concludes with CJ Gomolka's "Introducing or Expanding Queer Content in the Contemporary Francophone Classroom," which opens French studies toward an inclusive pedagogy necessary to our future success. Since the 1990s, academic interest in queer studies has been generative of existential conversations on college campuses for both queer- and non-queer-identified students who question the "define and confine" techniques of cultural and political heteronormativity. Often, and for a variety of reasons, Francophone classrooms miss important opportunities to include past and current discussions concerning queerness in the Francophone world, even when these discussions offer ideal opportunities for interdisciplinary and inclusive pedagogy. In his chapter, Gomolka offers concrete approaches and strategies that prove instructive for those interested in introducing or expanding queer content in their Francophone classrooms. In addition, he proposes structures, methods, and engaging resources that serve as a short *entrée* into the historical dimension of queer studies in France.

We believe the variety of essays contained in this volume will offer our reader concrete ideas for how to approach twenty-first-century issues in an engaging and sensitive manner. To examine the words of diverse Francophone women, whose texts mark the scars of oppression by male domination and colonized suppression, yet celebrate and foreshadow social change, introduces students to the possibility of social change and to a radically new conception of what makes a literary text great. The canon of the great authors that dominate high school curricula and many university general education programs is not dead, but enriched.

PART I

Exploring Identities/Exploring the Self: French Literature and Women's Studies in the Twenty-First Century

1

WHY TEACH (FRENCH) (WOMEN'S) LITERATURE?

Eilene Hoft-March

Those of us who have for a long time loved, learned, and taught literature may have forgotten that the value of humanistic literary training, so self-evident to us, needs to be made explicit and compelling to our students, not to mention our colleagues, our administrators, and the general public. The lists of reasons for deep study of literature—and they are legion on the internet if not always in university libraries—are most often invoked nowadays to ward off implicit or explicit critiques emerging from comparisons with other disciplines deemed more "useful" (read: "leading to a well-paid job"). Do biologists or economists have to explain the need for the knowledge and practices of their fields? Do they need to contend with a popular image of useless cultivation, redolent with elitism? Majoring in literature appears to the uninitiated as a sweatless endeavor that brings no material benefits neither to the nascent literata nor to the people with whom she engages. I suspect that the disciplines perceived to exist in a higher order of intellection have become associated with improvements to our physical, material lives and, therefore, appear more germane to our shared welfare. The biologist and the economist are seen to engage in a pragmatic and laudable enterprise because it is considered profitable for the able practitioner and for society more generally—probably in that order.[1]

What defenders of the humanities, and particularly of literary studies, need to argue more cogently is, above all, what is or should be common to most or even all disciplines in the development of intellectual skills. The student with a French major, like the student with a chemistry major, should be able to identify a problem, approach it with curiosity, and find ways to interrogate it. She should learn to sift through complex systems, discriminating among what is crucial, contextual, and insignificant. She should be able to widen the focus, that is, to project on a mega-level, and, conversely, to dial down the focus and trawl for significant minutiae. She should be able to identify causal relationships, patterns, anomalies, ambiguities, and contradictions. From this, she should develop skills of recall and prediction, and should imagine or perhaps even implement strategies of avoidance, prevention, adoption, or invention. These are the benefits that accrue to a mind educated to be agile and productive, whether one reads data sets or Proust.

But, there needs to be more in this line of argumentation. For if all disciplines when fully deployed can promise an apprenticeship in the intellectual skills already outlined, this still doesn't offer a compelling argument for literary training above all others; a nimble mind would easily grasp as much. If we pursue the notion that the main product of higher education is the well-trained mind, we must and do have further, more sophisticated skills to tout, especially for the person trained linguistically and culturally, skills that, far from being quaint or obsolete, are absolutely vital to the world in which we live.

Why Study Literature?

In her eloquent argument for an education in the humanities, *Not for Profit: Why Democracy Needs the Humanities*, Martha Nussbaum has a chapter entitled "cultivating imagination," in which she endorses disciplines that teach literature and the arts. She begins by reviewing the work of the renowned child analyst, Donald Winnicott, who claimed that developing imagination was vital to a child's successful engagement with others and with the world. Imagination, in this view, is an effective mental tool capable of breaking the formidable grip of narcissism: through imagination we are not so narrowly focused on or driven by self-interest. We are more motivated by curiosity, by openness to novelty and even to the unknown, by the capacity to forget self and take risks—all of the qualities needed at some point to help move individuals and societies forward.

I would extend this notion of imagination to include breaking out of the reflexive and thoughtless (in the neutral sense) practices that can occupy human existence. A fundamental reason that animals have brains in the first place is literally to plan our next moves—otherwise, we could survive quite nicely as philodendrons or heliotropes—rooted in place and responding with patent reflexivity to our immediate environment. Imagination requires us to focus on difference, change, and contingency; it develops a more nimble or nuanced responsiveness to that which we know less well. It also nudges us into some degree of fearlessness about the unknown.

As to learning to respond to unfamiliar situations, literary texts offer complex accounts of other humans' activities, sometimes even in the form of long narratives that can function as thought experiments in being human. These thought experiments provide low-stakes opportunities to examine—sometimes even from within a character's consciousness—experiences we may have never had ourselves, decisions we have possibly never been obliged to make, consequences we may not have had to endure, and emotions we need to feel vicariously only. This imaginative participation gives us a useful theoretical experience, a bank of knowledge that can be as extensive as is our reading experience, a proficiency in human affairs that may be used to serve in our real-world interactions.[2]

It is important to acknowledge that a reader's imaginative participation through literature is not always bent toward escape: reading fiction, poetry, or theater can certainly provide a form of respite for many from the lucrative, goal-driven work day. Escapism can be both a motive for and an effect of reading literature. However, to understand this as literature's sole function should be recognized and called out as extremely limited. We should be reminding sceptics that the reading of literature provides, like our primal dreams and nightmares, an emotional and intellectual testing ground for how or how not to live our lives. Furthermore, with such weighty consequences at stake, we should be arguing for developing wide-ranging but discriminating reading experiences, especially in an age flooded both with minimalist texts and yet fewer opportunities to ponder complex situations and responses to them.

For this reason, I would advocate mightily for being very explicit to students (on syllabi, in assignments, and in class discussions) about the development of imagination and the heuristic powers conferred by the study of literature. Our questions should lead students to understand the pertinence of literature to the art of making sense of humans, not just making sense of texts.[3] Let us be unequivocal in making those connections; let us ask those questions and ponder them at length. For instance, what is to be gleaned from so unfamiliar a protagonist as Marie Darrieussecq's sow-like woman in *Pig Tales*? What does it mean for us that the figurative meanings assigned to this pig-woman by others transform her literally? How does our own rationalizing transform our understanding of the world and our engagement with it? Another example: what, if anything, do we have to learn from a dystopia such as Elsa Boyer's *Beast*? How close are we to the novel's civilization of hybridized statesmen (part animal, part machine, part human) who wield precarious but extensive political sovereignty? What would it take to plunge our own human culture into the enslaved and impoverished conditions depicted in the book? What would happen if we compared these fantasies to Charlotte Delbo's witness to an otherwise unfathomable experience in Auschwitz-Birkenau? What moral dilemmas and failings are we obliged to consider with the knowledge of its historic occurrence through her courageous account in *Auschwitz and After*? Or perhaps more accessibly, what do we have to learn about the potent combination of anger at, love for, and grief over an absent parent that emerges so tentatively and so lucidly in Marie Nimier's *Queen of Silence*? How do we construct and live by our own narratives about origins and destinies? These questions may sound simplistic but in fact they focus on training readers to interpret human behaviors in a human context and to identify structures that advance or impede human action.

Having made this point to our students, we must go one step further in our arguments: being able to make sense of human beings is an invaluable (read also: commodifiable) ability.[4] While such training doesn't generate large data sets, create algorithms, or engineer things or processes, it gives ample practice in understanding human values, in analyzing human problems, and in positing human solutions; these are the foundations for communications, negotiations, teamwork, and leadership. Show me a career that a college graduate would hanker after that doesn't require that kind of expertise and I will eat this essay.

Why Study Literature in French?

In some not-so-distant past, educators were comfortable with the term "foreign" language as a way of distinguishing other-language learning from the "language arts" programs that trained American youngsters to understand and manipulate their native tongue according to accepted usage. At some point, no doubt as a means to demystify the notion of other languages as exotic, mysterious, and resistant to understanding, let alone mastery, we ceased to insist on the "foreign"-ness of other languages. I suspect this was mostly designed to be a positive and affirming development in the formulation of the aspirations of higher education to prepare students to engage in a globalized and accessible world. I have a nagging concern, however, that some slippage has also occurred here: that "languages" have merely become versions of the phenomenon of human language itself, much of it handily reduced to the *lingua franca* of this early part of the century—English. Add to the perception of English as a linguistic passkey to the world the fact of our (the US's) relative geographic insularity and the often insufficient and rudimentary levels of foreign-language education being taught in most public schools, and you create the prejudices against foreign-language programs with which we are only too familiar. Foreign-language programs in public K-12 schools are rapidly evaporating, leaving the task most often to those institutions that can boast an elite education, which brings us back to the association of our discipline with impracticality if not pretentiousness. Of equal concern is that graduate programs, even exclusive ones, are moving away from any foreign-language requirement as part of their doctoral programs.[5] One unfortunate consequence of this scale-back in language study is that high-level administrators and colleagues in other disciplines are increasingly less likely to have experienced the value of deep training in at least one additional language. We few defenders of the discipline need to articulate the transferrable intellectual benefits that foreign-language study imparts.

An opening gambit could be to review language's immense and irrefutable power to capture minds, to redirect energies and resources, and ultimately to have real impacts. Marketing experts, charismatic leaders, politicians, and teachers, to name a few, all use language with some if not all of these goals in mind. Popular examples abound and should be used to good effect: we live in a world where coined terms and language shifts signal where public attention is focused (think "Black Lives Matter," "digital natives," "opioid epidemic," among many current linguistic time capsules). To pursue one example: the expression "fake news" (speaking in 2017) has stirred up the citizenry in this country across the political spectrum. It has revealed the nature of some of the deep distrust in the functioning of the body politic, at one end of the spectrum characterizing profound skepticism of the press's ability to remain neutral and fair, at the other end, generating a responsive distrust of those who claim distrust of the press. In some respects, these polarized responses shouldn't even belong to a specific political stripe. In our own time, the phrase "fake news" will surely be associated for some time with the early presidency and pugilistic administrative style of Donald Trump, as well as his lack of appreciation of certain news organizations. To be sure, the phrase already resonated with a long-established phenomenon of viralized stories and comments that, intentionally or not, misinformed the public. However, the relaunch of this expression should be further associated in the minds of American citizens with the first amendment of the Constitution and, perhaps most importantly, must be understood in the context of a democracy that ideally understands its proper functioning to be based on having access to relatively reliable truths, whether through the press or through other public exchanges. Whatever the personal or political motives of the speaker(s), the references and extended meanings of such a phrase demand thoughtful, critical evaluation to comprehend its potency and to respond to it knowledgeably. To Google-translate those words into any other language risks short-shrifting and thus misconstruing all the socio-historical connotations and debates that are packed into that two-word American phrase as it is presently employed. As with our language and our culture, so with other languages and cultures—and so we must argue.

Connotation and context can, of course, be made somewhat accessible to attentive non-speakers of a language. More difficult to convey are those aspects that not only defy accurate translation but also begin to shape expression and even cognitive experience. Colleagues and students alike who fail to see the purpose of extensive training in a foreign language would do well to be reminded of the tight connections between language and thought, and between a specific language and the thought it makes possible. (And I don't mean quoting the old chestnut about Inuits and designations for snow.) For starters, the fact that French retains a considerable Latinized vocabulary results often in a precision useful in making fine distinctions and in expressing complexity. It has the added benefit of increasing comprehension of technical vocabulary in English, especially in the liberal professions. Stylistically, French has a penchant for using the abstract rather than real, empirical, or affective experience (as does English more typically); human experience of the world is consequently categorized differently between the two languages. And even the slight preference in French for witticisms and word play call upon a linguistic agility far less required or even useful in an American social context. Guiding students to appreciate the distinctive power of French and to recognize the language's ability to exceed the literal are specific ways in which to train students to anticipate the unfamiliar, including but not limited to, different cultural paradigms in order to make better sense. Acquiring these more sophisticated linguistic skills prepares the serious language and culture student with the reflex not to make mono-cultural assumptions and to remain open to unexpected meanings.

To this end, at least some of the literary texts we study with advanced students should give them a sense of a different universe that starts at the level of language. I can't think of a better example of contemporary prose more reliant on word play, creative syntax, figures of speech, and allusions than Hélène Cixous's writing. That she is a polyglot (French, English, German, perhaps more) with deep philosophical interests and Catholic reading tastes only adds to the meanings to be gleaned from her extensive and reverberating oeuvre. Her book-length writings might look to the unwary like novels or, given the (apparently) personal events they are built on, like autobiography. However, the writer's scrupulous attention to language, to the act of putting words to paper, even to language as the crux of many an event of the heart or mind, obliges readers to focus, likewise, on the effects of language.

Rather than assign to students one of Cixous's essays, I would choose a work situated about mid-stream in her (still) prodigious writing career, *Osnabrück* (1999). In that book, the author famously decides to write about her mother, Eve Cixous, having previously acknowledged only her deceased father, Georges, as the inspiration and impetus for her writing. In either case—mother or father—Cixous ratifies language's super-human capacity to link us in meaningful and sustainable ways to someone or something beyond ourselves, regardless of our "real" (physical, historical, geographic) circumstances. If she chooses Eve, it is in some respects to harness the mother's death-resistant force, her remarkable and ever-lasting "survivance": "She has neither beginning nor end. She is a three-letter formula: E, V, E. She is breve-ity itself as are the words for all infinite things: sea, sky, yes, no. God. Stop" (48). Eve exceeds her paltry one-syllable designation; likewise, she will exceed the attempts to narrate her, but without exhausting language's virtual possibilities. The writer says on the book's last page: "I can't write this book. Neither begin nor end it. Not yet" (230). And the author will literally spend at least 15 more writing years wavering over what language to use to embody and sustain her mother, demonstrating over and again the boundlessness not only of language but of human relationship.

A second feature of Cixousian language on display in this book is the author's ability to speak idiosyncratic truths even in the shared ordinariness of human existence. For instance, the writer mimes Eve's distinctive modes of expression and her peculiar idiolect. Sometimes this emerges in a "transcription" of a baggy, convoluted monologue that snarls in grammatical ambiguities, lost trains of thought, and sudden deviations into insignificant detail. But this non-history expresses a form of homage and filial devotion and, better still, exemplifies language's shimmering semantic possibilities. Clearly, the Cixousian apple hasn't fallen far from the tree: in her own right, the writer delights in multiple direct objects after a single transitive verb, in breathlessly punctuation-free sentences, and in undecidable antecedents. Consistent with Eve's special concoction of German-Jewish-Algerian-French, Cixous permits herself colorful phrasing from her mother tongues, not to mention sparks of neologism in such terms as "la tombalité"/"tombness" (18) and "l'engouevernement"/"fervoregime" (87).

For her part, Eve's blandest pronouncements are sometimes deceptively resonant with important human issues. Eve says "je suis terre à terre"/"I am down-to-earth/I go from land to land" (44), a statement that identifies the mother as pragmatic and blunt (Eve goes to market, preaches thrift, cooks meals, polices eating, vacuums vigorously); she is the unapologetic and unimaginative Hausfrau. But baked into this simple declaration is also a tacit, shared human history: Eve has followed a perilous refugee's itinerary from one inhospitable land to the next. The European Holocaust and the Algerian expulsion echo in her sentence.

And Osnabrück, her native city, doubles as the Eden that turned her out but also the "promised land" on which Eve sets her sights, suggesting both attachment to her native land and an unceasing wandering away from and toward this foreign place. In this manner, Cixous models richly connotative language, the kind that ignites imaginative thought and expands meanings. She also demonstrates how human systems of meaning don't solely or even consistently operate on principles of digital decisiveness: a thing, its opposite, and many variants can sometimes hold equally true in the realm of human sense making.

Relatedly, Cixous reminds us not only how humans make sense of the world, but how humans make sense of humans. For example, a single run-on sentence describes the highly finessed rapport of writer and mother:

> [I] have always lived accompanied by a mother stranger to my desires so dissociated from my events so associated with my movements and who always leads me to keep quiet and therefore write that is to speak noiselessly soundlessly, so that I address her without her hearing and yet she understands me behind her back.
>
> *(47)*

The passage represents an intimacy between two very unlike people, their separate lives nevertheless nested one within the other. Eve's foreignness obscures from her crucial elements of the daughter's life, such as her, the daughter's desires, her writing, the events important to her including Eve [*événement*] herself. Possibly and oppositely, Eve is the silent accomplice to the writer as well as the unconscious object of her apostrophe. This arrangement stands as a tacit accord between the two women. These moments in Cixous's texts, delicately teased out in words, remind us that language—spoken and written—is the medium with which we most often broker, sustain, damage, or undo relationships and responsibilities, and not only the human variety. Could the careful use of language be any more important than that?

Why Study Women's Literature in French?

To add "women" as a defining disciplinary category redoubles and extends the task already begun through the study of literature and foreign language: that is, to initiate the hard conceptual work of acknowledging the alterity (from oneself, from one's culture) of another's identity, their experience, their self-expression, their integration into or exclusion from different forms of community—and all of this may be further inflected by the more general circumstances of history, culture, and class. A crucial first step in understanding a person, a system, or a problem is developing the habit of holding off on assumptions and being amenable to some manner of paradigm shift.

Darrieussecq's 2011 novel *Clèves* demonstrates well the deleterious effects of making unevaluated socio-cultural judgments. The book also offers a good entry point into issues of gender and sexuality for sophisticated college-age readers. Their recent histories as children make them particularly apt at recognizing the comic ingenuousness of the pre then post-pubescent protagonist, Solange. Through her interior monologue, this otherwise taciturn character spends much of her mental energy on what her culture says, or more often doesn't, about gender identities and relationships, verbal and physical expressions of love, and human sexuality. As the narrative unfolds, it becomes clear that Solange has emerged into the adult world unequipped by family, friends, her cultural milieu, or even literature itself to distinguish between figurative and literal language about "love" or to understand culturally determined and gender-variant sexual practices. As a direct result, she acts in ways that will result in her community's strong indictment of Solange as a social and sexual outcast. If readers, unlike Solange, can anticipate the outcome, we are also invited not to judge her as grotesquely pathetic (a rejectable other), but as the logical product of a social environment devoid of conversations for and among adolescent girls—not to mention full-grown women—in a fully glossed language of desire. This shifts the problem from that of an isolated individual to that of a deeply flawed but remediable human system.

On this point of thinking otherwise, we need to be explicit about the breadth and vibrancy brought to our field through Francophone texts. The wealth and range of culture from the Caribbean, Oceania, the Maghreb, West Africa, and Québec provide even more compelling arguments to learn French and to access Francophone cultures. Many of the questions that face world leaders and organizations both international and national are frequently represented and extensively examined in this burgeoning literature: the status of women, postcolonialist practices, reduced or misused resources, warmongering, immigration, poverty cultures, religious challenges, and so on. In a century that will see 9 billion inhabitants populating the planet's receding surfaces, the opportunities for contact with others and for (mis)understandings will spike accordingly. And so, let us also teach Assia Djebar, Aminata Sow Fall, Fatou Diome, Maryse Condé, Anaïs Barbeau-Lavalette. It gives us our best chance at training our students to anticipate and work within human and humane systems that will allow them and the others they will encounter to thrive with dignity.

Coda

I have taken the risk of stating what is surely self-evident to my colleagues in the profession. These arguments, however, remain far from obvious to colleagues outside our field, the very people who also inculcate education values in our students and advocate for programs that support them. It behooves us to ensure that our faculty and administrative colleagues, not to mention our students, understand the urgent need for the kinds of thinking we actively cultivate. Finally, we need to make abundantly clear that our ultimate goal isn't to clone ourselves—though a few more French teachers to refresh our numbers will always be welcome—but rather to build the ranks of people who are curious and imaginative, empathic and engaged, adventurous and effective.

Notes

1 The STEM (Science, Technology, Engineering, Mathematics) Education Coalition has, among its "General Principles," the following statement: "STEM education is closely linked with our nation's economic prosperity in the modern global economy; strong STEM skills are a central element of a well-rounded education and essential to effective citizenship" (p. 1, www.stemedcoalition.org/wp-content/uploads/2012/04/Note-STEM-Education-Coalition-Core-Principles-2012.pdf, cited on August 17, 2017). That such education is linked to prosperity is perhaps easier to imagine than links to effective citizenship.
2 Speaking of the effects of an education that includes a firm and wide foundation in the humanities, Touya de Matrenne says that these academic fields "give access to the narrative imagination of different individuals and cultures around the world, and stimulate students' critical thinking, significantly widening their perspectives and awareness of the human condition. They enable them to escape the limits of the individual's presence" (99).
3 Todorov sharply criticizes the academy in France for having eviscerated literature of its principal purpose: "the tendency to refuse to see literature as a discourse on the world is a dominant position [in the university]" (33). He expresses the hope that literature will regain its status as "thought and knowledge of the psychic and social world we inhabit," saying further that "the reality literature

aspires to understand is quite simply (although nothing could be more complex) human experience" (72–3).
4 Madsbjerg, trained as a philosopher and political scientist, argues that quantitative analysis is often at pains to describe correctly "human" problems. He champions what he calls "sensemaking," a humanities-based interpretive art that captures crucial information overlooked in quantitative evaluation: "this kind of thinking trains our minds to synthesize all types of data, to explore without need of proving or disproving a narrow hypothesis, and to engage empathically with the particularities of a given world" (xx). He also claims "if the hardest—and most lucrative—problems of the coming century are cultural, then these are the very skills we need to be celebrating" (168) and, of course, cultivating.
5 I freely admit that a foreign-language reading exam that requires only a modicum of language training and a bilingual dictionary scarcely achieves the linguistic acumen I am advocating here.

References

Boyer, Elsa. *Beast*. P.O.L., 2015.
Cixous, Hélène. *Osnabrück*. Des femmes, 1999.
Darrieussecq, Marie. *Clèves*. P.O.L., 2011.
Darrieussecq, Marie. (Linda Coverdale, trans.). *Pig Tales*. New Press, 1997.
Delbo, Charlotte. (Rosette C. Lamont, trans.). *Auschwitz and After*. Yale University Press, 1995.
Madsbjerg, Christian. *Sensemaking: The Power of the Humanities in the Age of the Algorithm*. Hachette, 2017.
Nimier, Marie. *La Reine du silence* [*The Queen of Silence*]. Gallimard, 2004.
Nussbaum, Martha. *Not for Profit: Why Democracy Needs the Humanities*. Princeton University Press, 2010.
Todorov, Tzvetan. *La Littérature en péril* [*Literature in Peril*]. Flammarion, 2007.
Touya de Marenne, Eric. *The Case for the Humanities: Pedagogy, Polity, Interdisciplinarity*. Rowman & Littlefield, 2016.

Optional Reading

Vinay, J.P. and J. Darbelnet. *Stylistique comparée du français et de l'anglais* [*Comparative Stylistics of French and English*]. Didier, 1958.

2

FRACTURED FAMILIES

Program Growth through Innovative Teaching of French and Francophone Women's Autobiographies

E. Nicole Meyer

Why does it seem that a devotion to close reading and thinking must always be justified?[1] Time and again, students, academics, and administrators are questioned about the value of studying literature and/or literature by women and/or literature written in French. The essential skills we teach, those of asking interesting questions, incorporating diverse and fresh perspectives, creating intersections with a plethora of disciplines and life issues that impact us all, seem devalued in our current society. While creativity and innovation are frequent buzzwords of many a university mission statement, the power of the humanities somehow gets swallowed by a strong yet rather myopic appreciation of the sciences. Just as studying calculus can add interesting perspectives to literary research and has proven invaluable to my own analysis of literature, recent studies compellingly argue that the humanities deserves a primordial place in the academy.[2] They permit us to ask the "big" questions, reconfigure and redefine the boundaries of power and knowledge in ways that further all knowledge, including that of social and other scientists. While this imbalance of value for what we do dates far back, it currently permeates decision making at all levels of the academy and society, often hidden behind mostly unsubstantiated arguments that what we do does not pay, or is simply useless fluff.

Why read? Why analyze texts and other cultural products of our society? Why prioritize creative thought and expression as well as an appreciation of the imagination? Why teach our students to express deep thought through writing, in French, no less? In a 1929 interview with Viereck, Einstein stressed the importance of imagination above knowledge, for the latter is limited, while imagination is not. "I am enough of the artist to draw freely upon my imagination," states Einstein. "Imagination is more important than knowledge. Knowledge is limited. Imagination encircles the world" (117). A year later, John Dewey stressed the importance of imagination in his *Democracy and Education*: "Only a personal response involving imagination can possibly procure realization even of pure 'facts.' The imagination is the medium of appreciation in every field. The engagement of the imagination is the only thing that makes any activity more than mechanical" (132). Dewey warns against neglecting imagination, for without it, "achievement comes to denote the sort of thing that a well-planned machine can do better than a human being can, and the main effect of education, the achieving of a life of rich significance, drops by the wayside" (132). Currently, however, Einstein's and Dewey's warnings go unheeded as education stresses "STEM-based knowledge—theories from science, technology, engineering and math, and the abstractions of 'big data'— [and thus] alternative frameworks for explaining reality have been rendered close to obsolete" (Madsbjerg, ix). Christian Madsbjerg, Martha C. Nussbaum, Helen Small, Eric Touya de Marenne, Peter Brooks, Hilary Jewett, and others strongly argue for the inherent value of the humanities which permits us to ask the "big" questions, reconfigure, remap, and redefine the boundaries of power and knowledge. In their approaches, which encompass literary studies, philosophy, political theory, law, science, physics, and mathematics, these authors exemplify the training and discipline of close reading that underlie the practice of quality literary analysis and which prove invaluable to the multiple scientific and humanistic disciplines they discuss. The course described below not only helps teach students the art of persuasion, it also promotes breadth, depth, and the ability to change, all skills invaluable to the working world. Touya de Marenne's argument soars when revealing how art, music, creativity, and other humanistic approaches have been and can be integrated into the analysis and creation of scientific inquiry. After all, as Einstein states, the "most outstanding thinkers in the scientific domain were also very creative people influenced by their interests in the arts" (75).

More importantly, foreign languages, literatures, and cultures, postcolonial, feminist, and gender studies open our students' minds to difference. These areas address essential issues of tolerance and inclusion in their own daily lives. Studying a multiplicity of perspectives, of races and classes enables the reader of the works included below to cross boundaries, transcend academic disciplines, and to appreciate the sense of "infinite responsibility toward the other," to cite Touya de Marenne (121).[3] In short, asking significant questions, interrogating women's narratives, and exploring other cultural perspectives and practices opens our students' minds in ways that redefine "use" and "usefulness" and provide rich significance to the lives of those who do so.[4] Teaching courses which are useful in these last ways is one of the secrets to building successful French programs, in my experience.

Why Fractured Families?

Just as social connection unites many if not all of the aforementioned issues, (often fractured) family links narrator to her childhood and to her autobiographical narration of that past. The French and Francophone women's contemporary autobiographies that I teach reveal diverse fissures, be they matriarchal, linguistic, geographic, or other structures that crumble under pressure, incest, or cultural divides. The difficulty of voicing what has previously remained silent (e.g., incest, rape, and other incidents of domestic violence) permeates the books I teach. Cracks that were always there, hidden, deep, waiting to quake, shake the lives of the writers I analyze as well as those of their families, whether it be suicide, incest, adultery, violence, or simply a hurtful word, glance, or action. Such fractures matter to me and to the university students I teach.

My course, "French and Francophone Women's Autobiography," focuses on notable autobiographies from the twentieth century.[5] The course addresses the problems raised when women use words to describe or define themselves, with an emphasis on the various forms and rhetorical strategies they employ. Readings include Colette, Simone de Beauvoir, Ken Bugul, Marguerite Duras, Nathalie Sarraute, and Annie Ernaux, as well as critical readings by Heilbrun and others.[6] Whether taught in French, English, face to face, or online, the course begins with a variety of exercises, questions, and the generation of short self-narratives to create connection within the group that forms the class. These can range to a questionnaire and circulating exercises exploring student interests to "two truths and a lie." This simple task requires the students to introduce themselves by stating three simple phrases describing themselves. The class then votes which one of the sentences is false. The latter exercise begins the exploration into what is true, what is fiction, and how our personal prisms color our own life stories. Sharing a childhood disagreement with a sibling helps us understand that multiple narrations of single events proliferate, especially when others such as a parent are brought into the story. Colette's *Break of Day* provides ample discussion on the relation of fiction and non-fiction in the writing of one's life story.

Theory permeates the course as well, from Carolyn Heilbrun's *Writing a Woman's Life* to other theorists such as Margaret Homans, Sidonie Smith, and Cathy Caruth. The inclusion of theory varies depending on the abilities of students. At my current university, less is more. However, in class discussions, I model theoretical approaches. A few chapters from Heilbrun and carefully chosen quotes for each autobiography as well as a brief introduction of the author works best. Philippe Lejeune's definition of the autobiographical pact as "a retrospective account in prose that a real person makes of his own existence stressing his individual life and especially the history of his personality" (14) deserves study of the four delineated aspects (form of narration, subject, situation of the narrator, and the position of the latter). Before commencing focused study of the autobiographies, further discussion encompasses the notion of authenticity, intended public, literary quality, etc., but also the nature of a woman's life story—do events or rhetorical strategies that are exclusively feminine exist? What is the significance of transforming life or *a* (woman's) life into text?

In the case of Colette, in-class discussion assignments center on the relationship of Colette with her mother, the notion of "model" and what her mother represents to the narrator, Colette's unique definition of true friendship, and the role of nature and natural cycles (day/night; birth/death; ageing and potential loss of desirability). We discuss the purpose of the fictional characters Hélène and Vial, and the love triangle that is thus created and controlled by Colette. Throughout the course, carefully chosen quotes and images of the authors are shared through the syllabus, in-class discussion questions, and paper topics. For each of the four paper assignments, at least one choice focuses on the author's stylistic choices. For Colette, I ask "what is the role of the textual interruptions such as letters and breaks in the text?" Indeed, the innovative incorporation of her mother's voice through letters, an intriguing use of mirroring, the challenge of being patient, and the play of absence and presence of "my subtle companion" as well as of writing in her daily life bring rich interpretation to the words: "It's not too much to be born and to create each day" (139). Through writing (oft at night), she creates herself and thus takes control of and rewrites her story.

Marguerite Duras's presentation of self is also frequently mediated through complex relations with others, in particular family and lovers. In our current age of selfies, Twitter-soaked communication, and an endless fascination both with one's own self and that of others, hybrid ways of telling a woman's stories through images emerge. How do Duras's words create fixed images? Considering the immediacy of the selfie offers a new way of looking at Duras's representation of the self in her autobiographical *The Lover* (1984) and her "rediscovered 1945 wartime journal," *La Douleur* (1985), translated as *The War: A Memoir*. As the reader dives into the autobiographical cracks, voids, and silences of *The Lover*, it becomes clear that the complex dance of pronouns (I/she) in the narration, compounded by the predominance of violent and sexual images, rapid substitutions between brother(s) and lover, and the mother's absence while being present in that absence reveal much about the "moi profond" of the young narrator. In addition, Duras's narrative gaps disclose much about the function of re-membering the past, forgetting, and keeping silent painful events that nonetheless peek through the fissures of this fascinating work.

From the opening paragraph, absences abound. "One day, I was already old, in the entrance of a public place, a man came up to me" (3) opens the text, immediately suggesting gaping holes—one day (so many have passed) she stands in a public place and an unnamed man approaches her, pointing out her crevassed, devastated face (3). This image that only the narrator "sees" points to the passage of time, the transition from private to public figure, and to traumatic ("*brutal*," 4) events that the narrator soon points out as having been silenced ("of which I have never spoken," 3), skirted around (to use Mary Lydon's term). The language of the opening paragraphs focuses on the surface, the exterior, rather than Duras's interior "I" promised by Lejeune's autobiographical pact.

First entitled *The Absolute Image, The Lover* originally was designed to include actual photographs collected by Duras's son (Spear 27). In her *Autobiographical Tightropes*, Leah Hewitt stresses the importance of the "absolute image," the imaginary photograph of the young girl's meeting with le Chinois (the Chinese man) (112). The fixed non-verbal object, a photograph, was never taken (Hirsch 146), and remains thus always absent. At the same time, it points to an important moment in time, "one day" that will change her life forever, as she distances herself from the closed circle of family, enters the limousine, and crosses the Mekong River. This movement (opposite of the stasis suggested by a photographic moment in time) brings her closer to writing the suppressed memories which bubble often below the surface of the pages of *The Lover*, and which clearly relate to her unnaturally "aged" face. The following phrase immediately precedes the introduction of that absent image of crossing the Mekong: "My face ... It's scored with deep, dry wrinkles, the skin is cracked ... I have a face laid waste" (4–5).[7]

Lacerated, destroyed, broken skin and face suggest but do not name the violent unspoken events that precipitate them. Behind closed doors, during the night, "the childkiller of the night, of the night of the hunter" (6) causes fear and her own desire to kill her elder brother, tear away "that black veil over the light, from the law which was decreed and represented by the elder brother" (7). Again and again, Duras describes the violence of the elder brother without directly delineating the nature of his actions. Is it possible that the assassin of the night hunted his sister and incested her? The word "incest" is never written in *The Lover*, yet many elements suggest it. In addition to her older brother's violent nature, the family's closed circle holds many unspoken secrets which seem to penetrate her lovemaking with le Chinois, causing role reversals suggestive of incest. Violence seems present throughout many of Duras's memories. Her brother's violence, his reign of terror over the family suggests it strongly. Issues of power and control infiltrate this work and provide interesting contrasts with the dynamics of Colette's work.

For those interested in space, place, and narrative, the battle between closed, dark spaces and those occasional open, liquid-filled moments of cleansing will fascinate them. Moreover, reading this work in tandem with *The War: A Memoir* exposes thematic, narrative, and other intriguing parallels and deepens the students' readings of the narrator's traumatic past, whether of her brother's sadistic violence which Claire Cerasi notes parallels that of the Nazis or, in *The War*, of her agonizing wait for her husband's return, dead or alive, from the camps. She imagines her husband (and her) dying in dark, deep trenches. His return as a frail, corpselike stranger being helped up the stairs in the dark incites her wordless shrieks (54). Questions cease, and 17 days of desperate desire for fecal resemblance to that of a human, and the return of the ability to eat dominate the text. Her identity merges with that of her husband to the point that she too cannot eat during this time. "My identity was displaced" (63).[8] Fear spreads and obscures, and reminds this reader of oral testimonies of the Holocaust (see that of Ida Fink discussed in Langer, vi). Distance and time permit Duras to throw light onto these "hidden" periods that she has buried (8), publishing both texts decades after. The difficulty of narrating such massive lived material and pain and the dangers of silence is palpable when reading these works.

Two other unique ways of deepening students' understanding of narrative beyond that on the page prove enlightening. Firstly, after completing *The Lover*, students watch Jean-Jacques Annaud's 1992 film. They discuss the director's choices and how they affect story and interpretation in the filmed version. Secondly, at this point in the semester I arrange a panel of tattooed women to describe their tattoos, what they signify to them, and why they chose this "permanent" etching onto their skin. The intersection of the various stories told by the panel expand the notion of women's life story in delightful ways. In effect, the choice to mark their bodies reveals both to them and to the students the notion of empowerment, the ability to tell one's own story, and brings up fascinating discussions of writing/tattooing narrative whether onto a page or onto skin.[9] While it has only been mentioned by one student, the enforcing of tattooed numbers which scarred so many deported Jews deserves thought.

Fragmented body and narrative return in the Senegalese writer Ken Bugul's *The Abandoned Baobab*.[10] This powerful autobiography reveals a traumatic separation from mother and mother country, feelings of anger and abandonment as well as the narrator's struggles to assume her identity in a disintegrating society in which she seeks to reclaim her "lost" self before she can feel whole again in her home country. Re-membering the fragments of her body and past village life, violence, childhood, race, and postcolonial questions incite thought-provoking class discussions of this text.[11] All of the previous works relate to Sandra Gilbert and Susan Gubar's statement quoted on the course syllabus: "Women will starve in silence until new stories are created which confer on them the power of naming themselves" (in Heilbrun 33). Paper topics range from "relate the quotation that precedes the work ('The obliterated shall be remembered') to the text" to propose a reading of a specific paragraph or image (the amber bead being shoved into the child's ear) or perhaps analyze the role of women and gender in society as represented in this work.

Nathalie Sarraute's extensive examination of the multilayered discourses of childhood and youth in her autobiographical *Enfance* (*Childhood*) reveal the disembodied, fractured world of her family. As with the previous course texts, that which is not said, silenced gender, the traumas of childhood, and the quest for understanding oneself inspire wonderful class discussions. Born in Russia to Jewish parents in 1900, Sarraute spent her childhood traveling between her divorced parents and between Russia and France. The silences that speak to my students result from the numerous fissures caused by historical context (Jews and political dissidents being persecuted), the geographic and linguistic gaps exposed by Sarraute's inventive text, and the various verbal blows and other intense "traumas" of her childhood. Given the complexities of writing one's life, especially at the age of 83, the concise title, *Enfance*, provides a wonderful place to start our analysis. Lacking definite, indefinite, or a possessive article to indicate whose childhood is featured, this title aptly fits the gender-deprived text that follows. Questioning this deprivation of gender identity throughout, we examine how Sarraute further complicates the reading process. Not once does Sarraute use the pronoun "she" for the young girl nor for the genderless voices which open the autobiography and which question the possibility of remembering or evoking memories of childhood.[12] In addition, the notion of plot becomes difficult to capture in Sarraute's writing. After completing the work, I ask students to summarize the "plot" of *Childhood* in five to seven words. This incites a lively discussion of what is the essential import of this autobiography for each reader. In-class discussions also develop the disjunctions (linguistic and other) as well as a plethora of divisions within the autobiography.

Indeed, divisions proliferate in the young girl's early life: two parents separated by divorce and geography, two different countries (France, Russia), two distinct cultures and languages (French and Russian), but also the two languages that open and close the book, German and English. Further divides are represented by her three different first names, Nathalie, Natasha, and Tachok, displaying the easier affection of her father as well as her gender. Her mother's harsh phrases reveal a less warm approach to her daughter. The emotional disconnect between her mother and herself also exists between her and her stepmother. Indeed, stepparents and a stepsister divert attention from her parents and create further distance. While Nathalie is an exceptionally sensitive young girl, our contemporary students can relate to her complicated family life. Sarraute's *Childhood* resonates deeply with my students.

Another title intrigues us, that of Annie Ernaux's *Une Femme*. Translated into English as *A Woman's Story*, the original title's indefinite article "a" or number "one" opens the text to multiple readings. Is the story of a woman (universal, perhaps) or one woman (her mother)? The predominance of "my," "I", and the detailed description of the daughter's perceptions reveal that this is truly both her story and that of her mother. At the same time, the death of one's mother and the numbness of feelings processing the banal details surrounding any death truly is universal.[13] Here, Ernaux's direct, simple prose captures both her mother's voice and then the cruel loss of words due to Alzheimer's that follows. As the mother increasingly forgets words and gestures, this decline of a loved one as well as the inevitable role reversal as daughter cares for her mother provides much fodder for class discussion.

Just as Ernaux feels compelled to share her mother's story: "Isn't writing also a way of giving?" (90), the reader has difficulty putting the slim volume down until reaching the final white space on the page, following this brief, moving final paragraph:

> I shall never hear the sound of her voice again. It was her voice together with her words, her hands, and her way of moving and laughing, which linked the woman I am to the child I once was. The last bond between me and the world I come from has been severed.
>
> *(90)*

The course thus opens and closes with autobiographies that explore the bond between mother and daughter, however, so many universal questions are asked throughout, so many silences voiced. Whether taught online or face to face, whether in English or in French, the course entices new students to explore the autobiographies of women perceived to be different in so many ways. Yet, this course not only encourages new students to "try" French and Francophone autobiographies, it opens them up to explore their own inner selves. Each time I teach this course, at least one student lets me know they intend to write their own autobiography. Many enroll in the French program for further study. And, in our current academic climate, this is priceless.

Notes

1 Gerald Prince's "Talking French" questions the relation of the global situation and perceptions of the value of French study, reading, and culture in contemporary times, including the role of theory, "humanities crises, geographic changes and populist suspicions" and their effect on our profession. Most intriguing is his call to read closely and reexamine our practices, while remembering the importance of words to our world.

2 Richard Goodkin's book project *Connecting the Dots: The Calculus of Personality in French Fiction and Film*—developed during his Senior Fellowship at the Institute for Research in the Humanities,

University of Wisconsin—Madison proposes a fascinating reading integrating scientific and mathematical theories into a perceptive reading of literature ranging from Proust to Duras.
3   Transparent Language's blog states that Google makes a good case for foreign-language education "in a myriad of ways," including increasing empathy towards others, better understanding other perspectives, and improving critical thinking and thus making more informed decisions.
4   Bérubé and Ruth argue that our teaching profession is of great import and our attention to the human needs to be rewarded in academe.
5   I have included twenty-first-century texts by Annie Ernaux on occasion.
6   It goes without saying, however, that in English versions of the course, students read more than in the French versions of the course.
7   "J'ai un visage lacéré de rides sèches et profondes, à la peau cassée … J'ai un visage détruit" (10).
8   "Mon identité s'est déplacée" (79). My translation.
9   Smith's notion of autobiographers relying on a "trace of something from the past" (45) relates nicely to these discussions.
10 Due to the series editor's refusal to publish her work unless published under a pseudonym, Mariétou M'Baye uses the pseudonym Ken Bugul, which in Wolof means "personne n'en veut" (nobody wants it or her), a name given to a child of a woman who has suffered many stillbirths, in the hope that God will not desire this child and hence take away yet another (Magnier 153). See Meyer, 1999, 197 and Irène Assiba d'Almeida, 44–5.
11 See my article "Silencing the Noise, Voicing the Self: Ken Bugul's Textual Journey Towards Embodiment" for a reading of this wonderful work.
12 The perceived abandonment and actual separation from her mother does gender the young girl, however. "Je vous *la* laisse," proclaims the mother (258), and two pages later the child declares "j'étais déchirée" (260).
13 For a graduate course (or if your students are avid readers) I would definitely read this text in companion with that of de Beauvoir (see Meyer, 2002).

References

Annaud, Jean-Jacques, dir. *The Lover*. 1992.
Bérubé, Michael and Jennifer Ruth. *The Humanities, Higher Education and Academic Freedom: Three Necessary Arguments*. Palgrave Macmillan, 2015.
Bugul, Ken. *The Abandoned Baobab: The Autobiography of a Senegalese Woman*, trans. Marjolijn de Jager. University of Virginia Press, 2008.
D'Almeida, Irène Assiba. *Francophone African Women Writers: Destroying the Emptiness of Silence*. University of Florida Press, 1994.
Dewey, John. *Democracy and Education: An Introduction to the Philosophy of Education*. 1916. Unabridged classic reprint, 2015.
Cerasi, Claire. *Marguerite Duras de Lahore à Auschwitz*. Champion-Slatkine, 1993.
Colette. *Break of Day*. Farrar, Straus and Giroux, 2002. *La Naissance du jour*, 1928. Flammarion, 1984.
Duras, Marguerite. *L'Amant*. Les Editions de Minuit, 1984. *The Lover*, Harper Collins, 1986.
Duras, Marguerite. *La Douleur*. Gallimard, 1985. *The War: A Memoir*. Pantheon Books, 1986.
Ernaux, Annie. *A Woman's Story*. Seven Stories Press, 2003. *Une Femme*. Gallimard, 1987.
Goodkin, Richard. Connecting the Dots: The Calculus of Personality in French Fiction and Film. Unpublished Ms. http://humanities.wisc.edu/events/entry/richard-goodkin-1
Heilbrun, Carolyn. *Writing a Woman's Life*. W.W. Norton & Co., reprint ed., 2008.
Hewitt, Leah D. *Autobiographical Tightropes*. University of Nebraska Press, 1990.
Hirsch, Marianne. *The Mother/Daughter Plot: Narrative, Psychoanalysis, Feminism*. Indiana University Press, 1989.
Langer, Lawrence L. *Holocaust Testimonies: The Ruins of Memory*. Yale University Press, 1991.
Lejeune, Philippe. *Le Pacte autobiographique*. Seuil, 1975.
Lydon, Mary. *Skirting the Issue: Essays in Literary Theory*. University of Wisconsin Press, 1995.
Madsbjerg, Christian. *Sensemaking: The Power of the Humanities in the Age of the Algorithm*. Hachette, 2017.
Magnier, Bernard. "Ken Bugul ou l'écriture thérapeutique." *Notre librairie* 11(1985): 151–155.
Meyer, E. Nicole. "Silencing the Noise, Voicing the Self: Ken Bugul's Textual Journey Towards Embodiment," in *Corps/décors: Métaphores, parodies, orgies*, ed. C. Nesci, G. Prince, and G. Van Slyke. Rodopi, 1999, 191–199.

Meyer, E. Nicole. "Voicing Childhood: Remembering the Mother in Annie Ernaux's Autobiographies." *Journal of the Midwest Modern Language Association* 35. 2(2002): 33–40.
Prince, Gerald. "Talking French." *PMLA: Publications of the Modern Language Association of America* 131. 5 (2016): 1489–1494.
Sarraute, Nathalie. *Childhood*. University of Chicago Press, 2013. *Enfance*. Gallimard, 1983.
Smith, Sidonie. *A Poetics of Women's Autobiography: Marginality and the Fictions of Self Representation*. Indiana University Press, 1987.
Spear, Thomas. "Dame Duras: Breaking through the Text," in *Language and in Love Marguerite Duras: The Unspeakable: Essays for Marguerite Duras*, ed. Mechtild Cranston. Scripta Humanistica, 1992, 12–36.
Touya de Marenne, Eric. *The Case for the Humanities: Pedagogy, Polity, Interdisciplinarity*. Rowan & Littlefield, 2016.
https://blogs.transparent.com/language-news/2018/01/01/sorry-stem-google-just-made-the-case-for-more-foreign-language-education/. Accessed May 25, 2018.
Viereck, George Sylvester. "What Life Means to Einstein: An Interview." *Saturday Evening Post*. October 26, 1929: 17, 110, 113–117.

Optional Reading

Bate, Jonathan, ed. *The Public Value of the Humanities*. Bloomsbury Academic, 2011.
Beauvoir, Simone de. *A Very Easy Death*. Pantheon Books, 1985.
Brooks, Peter and Hilary Jewett, eds. *The Humanities and Public Life*. Fordham University Press, 2014.
Caruth, Cathy. *Unclaimed Experience: Trauma, Narrative and History*. JHU Press, 1996.
Clancier, Anne. "Réflexions autour de La Douleur de Marguerite Duras."*Revue française de psychanalyse* 4(1991): 1033–1036.
Criso, Rachael. "Elle est une autre: The Duplicity of Self in L'Amant," in *In Language and in Love, Marguerite Duras: The Unspeakable: Essays for Marguerite Duras*, ed. Mechtild Cranston. Scripta Humanistica, 1992, 37–51.
Jay, Paul. *The Humanities "Crisis" and the Future of Literary Studies*. Palgrave Macmillan, 2014.
Murphy, Carol J. "Duras's L'Amant: Memories from an Absent Photo," in *Remains to Be Seen: Essays on Marguerite Duras*, ed. Sanford S. Ames. Peter Lang, 1988, 171–182.
Nussbaum, Martha C. *Not for Profit: Why Democracy Needs the Humanities*. Princeton University Press, 2010.
Robson, Kathryn. *Writing Wounds: The Inscription of Trauma in post-1968 French Women's Life-writing*. Rodopi, 2004.
Small, Helen. *The Value of the Humanities*. Oxford University Press, 2013.
Solomon, Julie. "'J'ai un visage détruit': Pleasures of Self-Portraiture in Marguerite Duras's *L'Amant*." *Australian Journal of French Studies*. Jan. 1, 1997; 34, 1. 100–114.

3

WORLDWIDE WOMEN WRITERS AND THE WEB

Diversity and Digital Pedagogy

Alison Rice

"Francophone Metronomes" is a website of my own creation devoted to an unprecedented phenomenon of global diversity among women writers of French. It features filmed interviews conducted in Paris with 18 authors of various ages who come from locations as different as Algeria and Bulgaria, Senegal and South Korea. Some of these writers have long been renowned names in literature and theory, such as Hélène Cixous, Maryse Condé, Julia Kristeva, and Leïla Sebbar, while others, like Fatou Diome, Anna Moï, and Shumona Sinha, have only rather recently become acclaimed authors of publications in French. By placing the expressions of internationally recognized writers alongside those of lesser-known writers, and by bringing together the experiences of women with disparate itineraries, the project opens up to transnational comparative study of Francophone writers that is not limited to pre-established categories of literary analysis. The website also serves as a powerful pedagogical tool, in the classroom and beyond. Divided into chapters on topics ranging from feminism to immigration, the interviews contribute to fruitful discussion and exchange as they allow students to hear a chorus of eloquent voices explain their personal approaches to topics of particular pertinence to women from around the world who write in French today. Whether it is a question of second-year cultural studies courses or graduate-level classes in Francophone literature, teaching texts in tandem with the oral statements available on the website is a powerful way to get students involved in literary interpretation, as they examine how each author expresses herself and allows the rhythm of her idiosyncratic speech to shed light on the voices that come through in her written work.

The Person behind the Text: Image and Intonation

In the classroom, I often distribute questions for reflection specifically related both to the text we read and the portion of the filmed interview that relates to the text in question, but sometimes I prefer to project part of the interview spontaneously during the class session and see what comments emerge following the viewing. Students who encounter a writer like Fatou Diome as a person for the first time through the screen in the classroom setting often have impassioned reactions. They are deeply impressed with her way of speaking, with the way she varies her tone and carefully places her words, with the rhythm she adopts as she smoothly communicates her message. Most are drawn in by the joyfulness of her speech, even when the topics she addresses are serious, like the trials of immigration and the insults of racism. They find themselves attracted to her optimistic attitude, and they bring up their surprise at hearing her frequent laughter that is so sincere and heartfelt. While they certainly often detect the irony in her short stories, it is the combination of oral expression and body language contained in the interview that make them aware of other aspects of her humorous approach toward life. When we return to the text following our viewing, students perceive its content differently, and they find that their reading begins to flow in a manner influenced by the opportunity not only to hear the author as she speaks, but also to watch her as she moves in harmony with her words and employs her hands in eloquent gestures that complement her comments.

Putting students in contact with writers in this manner was one of the major motivating factors behind my desire to conduct this series of filmed interviews. I hoped to provide readers with a broader appreciation for these literary works that can be acquired through exposure to the individual behind the oeuvre. I had found that the opportunity to study first-hand in Paris during an academic year abroad with such thinkers as Hélène Cixous led me to approach their writing on a different level. At first, it was simply the chance to listen to them articulate their thoughts that had helped me to comprehend what were difficult concepts and turns of phrase for me, but soon I also had come to realize that all forms of interaction, and every type of exposure to the entire person in whose name a profound body of work was published, turned out to be helpful to my growing understanding of that corpus. I therefore filmed all of these contemporary women writers from elsewhere in a gesture that was intended to embrace their varying appearances and affirm their differing accents, as well as to make these voices accessible to others. The project was meant to celebrate this newfound diversity in Francophone literary creation.

Cultural Differences: Reading the Other

The inclusion of a variety of women writers in our French courses has obvious implications for the students in our classrooms in American universities. The questions of multilingualism and multiculturalism that find their way into these texts invite young scholars to reflect on their own linguistic and cultural identifications. One of the novels that students particularly relate to is Chahdortt Djavann's *Comment peut-on être français?* (How Can One Be French?), a text I teach in a fourth-year course titled "Making It: Minorities and Money" that focuses on the immigrant experiences of a variety of individuals from diverse backgrounds in France. Djavann's novel draws largely from the writer's own experience to relate the difficulties she encountered upon her arrival in the French capital city as a solitary young woman who had never studied French. Prior to exposing them to the interview with the work's author, I ask my students to closely examine a passage that evokes the immense differences between two women who meet in Paris.

> Everything about Julie that Roxane didn't understand, she chalked up to the word "French" and everything about Roxane that Julie didn't understand, she chalked up to the word "Iranian" ... for the two women one thing was certain: when you were Iranian, you weren't French, and when you were French, you weren't Iranian.
>
> (90)[1]

In their textual analyses, students hone in on the words within quotation marks that are meant to encapsulate the beings they describe: "Iranian" and "French." They note that these terms are indicative of the way some people perceive others as embodying absolute otherness. Some students articulate their understanding that each protagonist assumes that what she finds to be inscrutable about the other is necessarily attributable to her different national origin. While these students criticize the rush to judgment that is encapsulated in this immediate assumption, they nonetheless understand that when people know close to nothing about another culture, they are wont to chalk up all unusual attributes to differences due to a foreign origin. If Roxane happened to be a very unusual Iranian, Julie would be making a mistake in jumping to the conclusion that Roxane's behavior was representative of others from her homeland. This is the danger of establishing an equivalence between what might be individual idiosyncrasies and characteristics common to an entire population.

Their study of this passage with its emphasis on the cultural connotations that are caught up in each of these national designations leads well into a pair of questions about the French language itself, a tongue whose apprenticeship this text focuses on in unusual and refreshing detail. I ask students to respond to the following in an in-class writing exercise: "Roxane makes a distinction between her native Persian tongue and French. She affirms that the latter is 'the language of precision, intransigence, exactitude' (106). Are you in agreement with this understanding of French? How has your experience with French differed from and resembled Roxane's?" These queries inspire a lot of animated discussion. Students relish the opportunity to talk about their own experiences with French. They usually mention the difficulty they face when it comes to grammatical details that are indeed "intransigent," at least according to their contact with it in the classroom. Some who are more proficient in French claim that the tongue is not always quite as precise as English, since they have sought in a bilingual dictionary the equivalent of a particular English term in French and found only a circumlocution to refer to the same object or phenomenon. Other students find that a similarity exists between the French way of life as they understand it and the French use of language, both in oral and written forms. In their analyses, they point out that French society often valorizes slowing down and savoring a moment in ways that elude many Americans; they claim that the use of the language follows a parallel path and includes longer descriptions than the concise, to-the-point style that characterizes most texts in English. Those who have been exposed to canonical French writers like Marcel Proust then establish a contrast between the long sentences that are found in his work and the less complicated sentences and grammatical structures that make up the writings of contemporary women writers, especially those who, like Chahdortt Djavann, learned the French language later in life.

Learning the Language: From Text to Screen

In discussions focusing on *How Can One Be French?*, students like to rehearse Roxane's struggle to learn the gender of all nouns and they tell similar stories of their own battles with the notion of assigning a gender to inanimate objects or ideas when nothing similar exists in their native tongue. Spanish speakers explain that gender wasn't as tough for them to understand, of course, but they mention that sometimes the genders are different in French and that this discrepancy throws them off. Some students evoke their personal learning styles, emphasizing the disparity that exists for them between understanding a written text and comprehending spoken words in French. Others bring up a comparable distinction between expressing themselves orally and writing in French; there are those who experience greater ease with oral expression, while others have more natural talent for written production. A large percentage of students affirm their admiration for the beauty of the language, emphasizing its aural impressions on them and confirming that it was this musicality that inspired them to learn it. This choice to study French in the American academic setting stands out in contrast to the necessity of becoming fluent in the tongue that characterizes the immigrant's ordeal in Chahdortt Djavann's text. The principal protagonist has no alternative but to learn the language if she hopes to make it in the French capital city, but she is nonetheless smitten with the culture and the city within which she finds herself. In fact, she admits that she dreamed of living in the French capital long before she arrived there. In like manner, American students are quick to say that the French lifestyle holds a special fascination for them.

After they have had a chance to contemplate cultural and linguistic questions in *How Can One Be French?*, students are eager to consider what the author confirms in the filmed interview on the website about her own experience. They are inspired to learn about her relatively late mastery of the French tongue that many of them find difficult even when they began studying it in elementary school or in preschool. When they turn to the website, they are struck by the terms the author employs to describe what the apprenticeship of this second language was like for her:

> It was a brutal experience. I wasn't very young. I was twenty-five when I arrived in France. When you are twenty-five and you learn to say the most elementary things like "My name is Chahdortt. I'm twenty-five and you?," the first few weeks are very joyful. It's fun because there is something childlike about it, but then it becomes depressing. You feel ill-at-ease. You feel unable, totally incapable because of this break with the past. It's a very violent experience. I learned my first expressions at the Alliance Française. I took the plunge and fought a bit with the language. I ripped the words from the dictionary one by one. It was very much like what I described in *How Can One Be French?*. But it is fictionalized. Nothing happened exactly that way, but the history of the language that runs throughout this book is based on reality, only it lasted several years, not several pages.

While it is common for non-native speakers to describe the difficulty of learning French, it is unusual for them to do so with such words as "brutal" and "violent," and to adopt such dramatic expressions as "*débattre avec la langue*" ("fight with the language") and "*arracher les mots du dictionnaire*" ("rip words from the dictionary"). Students respond with surprise to the intensity of this account of linguistic apprenticeship and they say it stands out in contrast with their own rather mild experience of studying French. In Djavann's case, students find it especially useful to juxtapose this oral commentary on learning the language to the fictionalized rendering of the experience in her book, for the latter provides additional sensitivity to the many challenges this foreign woman faced upon her arrival in France and her sudden immersion in the French culture and language, and this contextualization is very useful to students when it is placed alongside the intense commentary found in the interview. They are, of course, deeply aware of the background the writer and her main protagonist share as a woman from a Muslim country who feels out of place in the French capital city for a variety of reasons that are not just linguistic.

If Djavann recalls her experience with learning French as "violent," it is fascinating to note elsewhere in the interview that she affirms the act of writing in French as precisely related to the violence that often surrounds her, and that is also present within her. She remembers that Samuel Beckett, another writer of French whose native tongue was not French, responded to the omnipresent question "Why do you write?" with the answer: "It's all I'm good at." She claims that she could respond in the very same way, but goes on to say that those who ask may not really want to know why authors choose to write, for the answer can be brutal: "I write to contain, to focus a life force that is extremely violent. I write in order to not assassinate, to not master. This response would shock people." This confession has precisely the impact on students that Djavann predicts in her comments; they are struck by the intensity of her deeply personal proclamation that she takes up the pen in order to avoid taking up arms. While they speculate that this is a metaphorical use of the verb "*assassiner*," the seriousness and the sincerity with which Djavann utters these words in the filmed interview give them pause, and they aren't certain how to interpret her statement. What they are left with, after deliberations, is the assurance that writing provides a necessary form of expression that is helpful and healing for those who, like Djavann, have suffered in their native lands and have also experienced difficulty in their adopted country. When the writing itself is described in such stark terms, students begin to view the reading experience in a whole new light, understanding that for many who put words to paper, it is not an anecdotal activity but rather an exercise that involves tremendous thought and intellect, as well as one's self, and that deserves attentive analysis.

Literature as a Response to Human Experience: Genre

A few of the students who come to the French-language classroom have already come across the work of a theorist like Julia Kristeva in their courses in gender studies or literary theory. But those who are familiar with her name are often unaware that she left her native Bulgaria to come to France when she was in her mid-20s, like Djavann. While Kristeva had the advantage of already speaking French fluently when she arrived in Paris as a student thanks to her early education in a French school in her homeland, she nonetheless had some lacunae when it came to this foreign tongue, as she explains with clarity and concision in the interview:

> So, at the end of my analysis, I became a mother, and the linguistic apprenticeship I went through with my son, reconciled me in a way with the French of infancy, since I had learned the French language at the Dominican school beginning at the age of five or six. My parents had placed me in the French kindergarten, but it was nonetheless a second language and I didn't have those first five years. I tried to relearn through a child how to speak French. I tell myself that, at any rate, saying that through motherhood and accompanying my son through the early years, I acquired a more childish French, more sensorial, more day-to-day, more impregnated with perceptions and dreams, more childlike. This allowed me, I believe, to switch languages in my career. I began to write novels, like *The Samurai*, and even my essays became more "literary." It is a more abstract language, a knot between psychoanalysis, maternity, and style. This shows a veritable rebirth. We have several opportunities in our life to "change our skin," but it's more than the skin, it's the fibers themselves that change.

These comments inspire classroom discussions on genre, and the ways certain writers focus only on a particular genre in their work, while others move from one genre to another in their writing, and still others inventively straddle genres or even create new ones. Students find it intriguing to reflect on their own relationship to writing and contemplate the genres in which they perform best as well as those to which they are most compellingly drawn. After studying the opening chapter of *Strangers to Ourselves* by Julia Kristeva for an example of a more traditional academic analysis, we then examine her hybrid essay "Stabat mater" that places a scholarly study next to a poetic reflection, after which we explore a selection from *Murder in Byzantium*, one of her novels that incorporates music into the work of fiction. This exposure to different styles prepares students for a series of writing assignments that ask them to move in similar fashion from literary analysis to mixtures of genres of their own design, in French.

Literature as a Response to Human Experience: Activism

In *Le Selfie*, my advanced course on autobiographical literature, students read Fatou Diome's collection of short stories titled *La Préférence nationale* (The National Preference). The in-class discussions on the first story in the book, "The Beggar and the Schoolgirl," lead to comments on the tremendous ingenuity of the young protagonist who comes up with a plan to help a leprous beggar make a living, all while protecting her own hard-earned money—and herself—from the man with whom she rents a room while attending middle school. We examine the structure of the story together, observing that the order of the title, with its emphasis on the other woman coming first, parallels the order of the narrative in general, as the first-person narrator recounts this episode without presenting herself as its central character, or touting her own crucial role in the positive outcome of the events. When we address the apparent humility of the author during our conversation, we find ourselves wanting to learn more. Of course, as readers of autobiographical texts are wont to do, we wonder how faithful the text is to the lived reality of the writer. But we also desire to discover how the author perceives of her own actions, and what her larger philosophy is, when it comes to helping others and making a difference in her native Senegal. At this point, it is very effective to turn to the portion of the filmed interview, featured on the website, in which Diome responds to a question about this short story. She fills in some of the blanks, providing her own perspective on what happened during this moment in her childhood, and makes some statements about the mentality that led her to help this person in this particular way:

> "The Beggar and the Schoolgirl" is a true story … This woman was begging. She had leprosy. She held out a hand and people gave her ridiculous things. Some rice or millet. Or a little bit of dried fish. Whom does that save? … Since I had pocket money as a junior high student who had worked, I gave her the money and she bought a bag of peanuts. It's as simple as that. The wood was there, the salt was there, and the water was there. So she made peanuts and sold them in front of the school … Sometimes something so small can change somebody's life.

University students are impressed that such a young protagonist possesses such pertinent insights and the courage to act on them in order to provide a suffering woman with a steady income. In the class discussion following this portion of the interview, some of them bring up their own experiences with homeless individuals and address their attempts to make a difference in the lives of those who inhabit the street. They express admiration for the solution the writer found in her childhood for the adult problems that she encountered.

Elsewhere in the interview, Diome illustrates a similar approach to helping those in need when she pronounces the slogan of the association she founded in her native Senegal after she met with success as a writer in France: "*Aidons-les à ne plus avoir besoin de nous*" ("Let's help them to no longer need us"). This articulation of the crucial importance of making a lasting impact rather than occasionally meeting a punctual need touches those who hear it.

Diome's commitment to helping others to no longer live in lack and to restoring their dignity is explained in the filmed interview in a way that resonates with students who have social concerns and want to adopt measures to improve living conditions both within their communities and in other locations.

Juxtapositions: Diversity and Proximity

What the *Francophone Metronomes* website reveals is that women from many backgrounds have known, like Chahdortt Djavann, the sentiment of otherness and exclusion in France. Even those who have risen to prominence as "French feminist theorists" have expressed on many occasions their own struggles with both misogyny and ethnocentrism in France, in various forms, and have been made to feel like foreigners in their adopted homeland. Such iterations come together in significant ways in the Highlights section of the website, a page comprising two films in which the writers' viewpoints and personal experiences are juxtaposed in ways that bring out convincing points of comparison as well as noteworthy divergences. It is in these moments that their voices mix and intermingle in meaningful fashion, often in harmony but also in dissidence. The highlights make it easy to appreciate the individual, idiosyncratic rhythms of each writer's contributions. The resonances of these voices, their facial expressions and oral inflections, take on special strength here as these worldwide women writers address the following wide-ranging topics: Paris; publications and categorizations; Francophones and Francophonies; French tongues; multilingualism; accents; body and image; musicality; names; itineraries; women and feminism; identities; immigrations; writing and literature. Much of the footage featured in the highlights is not available in the individual interviews on the website. For the final paper in a graduate course on Francophone literatures, I invite students to focus on one of these chapters as an integral part of their research.

What the website permits, on different levels and in various contexts, is a great deal of student agency; I have found that it creates space for students to explore and make choices about the issues that interest them most, and participate in the design of their learning experience. The various backgrounds of the women who have come to writing in French speak to a lot of students who themselves may be of Japanese or Korean descent, or who may hail from Africa or Eastern Europe. New forms of intersectional identities become possible through the study of these different voices and their contributions to a worldwide understanding of Francophone writing today. These women have all crossed borders to reach France and their compositions in French reveal familiarity with other cultures and forms of expression. Many of them have overcome tremendous challenges, and they serve as sensational examples in the classroom, as they have championed written work in French as a way to send uplifting yet clearheaded messages about hardship and hope, working to counteract many of the contentious questions that may characterize their places of birth, but that are not limited to those locations: France is fraught with tough questions today and it has not proven to be utterly open to certain individuals and to specific changes that it might have chosen to accept more proactively. But the combined work of contemporary women writers from around the world contains great potential. Making these voices readily and easily accessible on the web, bringing them together to show how their singularities contribute to a larger movement pointing toward openness and acceptance, and opening up to the promise that multiple talents can lead to creative reconfigurations of categories. This optimism is what underlies *Francophone Metronomes*, a positive outlook that emerges when Julia Kristeva remembers the French capital city where she first set foot in the mid-1960s, a time of intellectual effervescence that shaped her as a scholar and a person, and that inspired her thought:

> So, this was the Paris that welcomed me and without this opening [*cette ouverture*], I think that all that I have done since could not have taken place. I know that when I go to the United States now, I am considered to be someone who represents this cosmopolitan openness of the city of Paris, if not of all France, and that I hope will be France herself one day.

These weighty words suggest how the writing of worldwide women in French represents a powerful possibility for Paris and for all of France, as well as for French-language pedagogical settings that seek to communicate an embrace of diversity and open exchange that these wide-ranging works and their talented authors embody.

Note

1 This and all translations are mine.

References

Diome, Fatou. "La Mendiante et l'écolière" ["The Beggar and the Schoolgirl"], in *La Préférence nationale* [The National Preference]. Présence Africaine, 2001, 11–35.

Djavann, Chahdortt. *Comment peut-on être français?* [*How Can One Be French?*]. J'ai Lu, 2007; Flammarion, 2006.

Kristeva, Julia. *Étrangers à nous-mêmes*. Fayard, 1988. *Strangers to Ourselves*, trans. Leon S. Roudiez. Columbia University Press, 1994.

Kristeva, Julia. *Meurtre à Byzance*. Paris: Fayard, 2004. *Murder in Byzantium*, trans. C. Don Delogu. Columbia University Press, 2008.

Kristeva, Julia. "Stabat Mater." in *Histoires d'amour*. Denoël, 1983. *Tales of Love*, trans. Leon S. Roudiez. Columbia University Press, 1987, 225–247.

Rice, Alison. "Francophone Metronomes: Worldwide Women's Writing." http://francophonemetronomes.com/

4

"REPRESENTING THE SELF"

Contemporary French Lit Meets the Twenty-First-Century Student

Dawn M. Cornelio

"The incredible edible egg!" "Got milk?" While slogans are familiar to many North Americans (perhaps you even started humming the egg jingle), the humanities at large, foreign-language learning in general, and writing in French by women (or men for that matter) don't have an advertising agency like eggs and milk do to promote them with snappy slogans. Announcements of the neurological and behavioral benefits of reading fiction seem to only circulate between professionals as Facebook "shares," and while our "competition" has the cool buzz-word acronym *STEM* (science, technology, engineering, math), the newly revised *STEAM* (science, technology, engineering, *arts*, math) has been described as so much hot air. What we do have, however, is our knowledge and our passion, with which we recruit students and life-long learners one at a time, on a very personal level. Certainly, the "crisis" in arts and humanities has been going on for as long as I can remember, as they have been criticized and belittled for being optional, frivolous, and more or less irrelevant when a new graduate is on the job market. Elementary schools, high schools, colleges, and universities all push for their students to attain "literacy," but we seem to forget that arts and humanities are the pathway to this very destination. Some students are happy to be non-conformists, disregard their parents' concerns and their peers' disdain, and plunge into their arts education with joy and intellectual curiosity. Others need to be drawn in with distribution requirements, tantalizing course descriptions, colorful posters of our own design placed in strategic locations across our campuses, or our reputations as exceptional educators. Whatever gets them through the door, it is then up to us to explicitly, overtly, and determinedly show them all they can learn through the courses we've designed.

In southwestern Ontario, where I teach and do research, since French is one of Canada's official languages, it doesn't struggle as a discipline as it may in the US, though there is a trend for students to major in more "practical" fields and minor in French or another humanities subject. Nonetheless, while the majority of our classes are literature-based, our students are often more interested in the language than the literature of French-speaking places. Without the kind of advertising agency mentioned above, we continue to fail to adequately show our students—and our societies—how reading in multiple languages leads to many kinds of fluency in addition to grammatical fluency. At least partly for these reasons, in 2016, French studies at the University of Guelph rolled out new undergraduate courses ranging from the second to the fourth year. The result of more than two years of reflection, research (including student input), and reorganization, these new courses were designed not only to better reflect faculty interest and expertise but also to be more overtly relevant and attractive to students. Furthermore, they were designed with the university's five overarching learning outcomes in mind: critical and creative thinking, literacy, global understanding, communicating, and professional and ethical behavior ("Learning Outcomes"). This chapter will present an analysis—along with some ideas for future modifications—of the first offering of one of these courses, a third-year literature class entitled "Representing the Self." By including comments from an end-of-semester survey and an example of student production, this contribution attempts to provide the perspective of both the instructor and the students who took the course at that time.

The Undergraduate Calendar's description indicates that in "Representing the Self" students will examine a variety of texts told by a real or fictional "I" and explore such literary concerns as believable or unbelievable narrators, biography, autobiography, and the construction of the self, ultimately mobilizing their learning about the construction of the self in the creation of their own first-person narrative in French. While designed to be taught in a variety of ways according to any given instructor's interest and expertise, this offering focused on autofiction, the creation of self-image, the perception of public image, textual "believability," and the authors' use of rhetoric and style to achieve their desired effects. The works on the syllabus confronted students with contemporary, "real-world" issues, specifically mental health, family relationships, societal norms and pressures, and public and private selves, as these issues are some of the pervasive characteristics of autofictional literature. Throughout the semester, the readings, lectures, activities, discussions, and assignments led students to new ways of understanding not only mediated selves, but also so-called "taboo" subjects (i.e., eating disorders, suicide, sexual relationships). Additionally, given the nature of autofiction, this course prompted critical thinking in asking students to consider various narrators' believability and the nature of truth in memory, along with the creation of selectively narrated "selves" on social media, and the way we mediate our constructed identities.

The Reading List: Pros and Cons of Student Choice

The reading list was designed partly around the idea that it would be beneficial for students to read two novels[1] by the same author, since, in autofiction, the same life events are often examined from different perspectives and at different times. Therefore, Delphine de Vigan's *Jours sans faim* (*Days without Hunger*) and *Rien ne s'oppose à la nuit* (*Nothing Holds Back the Night*), Christine Angot's *Incest* and *Un Amour impossible* (*An Impossible Love*), and Frédéric Beigbeder's[2] *14€99* and *Un Roman français* (*A French Novel*)—presented in this order—became the novels on the reading list. As most students at Guelph are not native French speakers, and their language abilities can be quite heterogeneous, it seemed that asking them to read six rather intricate novels while discovering such a complex concept as autofiction would be burdensome for them. Nonetheless, it also seemed that having the class read only four novels by two authors over our 12-week semester would give them too narrow a view of autofiction as a literary genre. For this reason, each student was required to read both works by two of the authors on the reading list, and a scholarly article on the third.[3] Presenting this choice to students establishes a sense of independence and control over their work since the act of choosing immediately makes students active partners in their learning, something the University of Guelph stresses through its focus on "learner-centredness."[4] Indeed, in "Engagement through Partnerships: Students as Partners in Learning and Teaching in Higher Education," Healey et al. conclude that "[e]ngaging students in partnership means seeing students as *participants* in their own learning and is the most common way that students act as partners. Active learning is the key to meaningful student learning" (36, my emphasis). In addition to the benefit of encouraging student engagement through such an active choice, allowing students to select the works they'd read allowed them to eliminate direct contact with a work whose content they did not feel prepared to read, such as *Incest* or *Days without Hunger*, whose main character has anorexia. Overall, as students mentioned in the end-of-semester survey, choosing the readings "increased my enthusiasm because they were my own choice," "enhanced [my] participation and out-of-class reflection," "helped with feeling overwhelmed and allowed me to focus on personal interest," and "avoid triggers—I'm glad not to have read *Incest*." The survey results suggest strategy of choice did achieve its goal of increasing agency[5] among learners by offering a chance for empowerment, participation, and partnership in the course.

While the strategy of choice was overwhelmingly positive, there was one negative outcome that will need to be addressed for future offerings of the course: few students read the last author, Beigbeder. Since attendance typically decreases in the last three weeks of the semester, this made any in-class discussion activities difficult since few students read this author's novels. For some students, their choice of readings, made after five class meetings, was based simply on time-management factors, as they had come to expect to be busier later in the semester due to its onslaught of final projects, the side effects of procrastination, and the loom of final exams. For others, their choice was based thoughtfully on research it was suggested they do on the authors and works early in the semester. For some it was determined by what their friends chose, or the professor's perceived opinion, according to the survey. Again, in an effort to engage students by making them partners in learning, by showing interest in their ideas and opinions, they were asked in the survey what they would do to have more learners opt for the final novel. Some suggested reducing the number of authors studied to four with all students reading all novels; however, not only would this make the course too narrow, it would remove that agency of choice, without necessarily influencing how many students kept up with the reading and attended the last classes of the semester, as factors external to the class would remain unchanged. For similar reasons, the suggestions of limiting the number of students per author or having students pick their authors on a first-come-first-served basis or at random are not efficient ways of addressing the issue. There are, however, at least three suggestions that students made that will be implemented in the next offering of the course.

First is the suggestion of reorganizing the due dates to wrap up the last author in the penultimate week of classes, rather than in the last week. The two benefits of this would be giving students who choose this author more time to complete both their author essay and final project, as the inevitable proximity of the due dates deterred some students from choosing him. This would also allow more time to discuss the final creative writing project, and is feasible with some reworking of the calendar. Moreover, the benefits of freeing time to work on—and hopefully improve—the final project and of allowing more manageable due dates for students reading the last author are clear. The second of the implementable suggestions is to assign shorter or less complex novels that also meet all the goals of the class. This would certainly be possible with, for example, a change to two novels by Annie Ernaux such as *A Woman's Story* and *I Remain in Darkness*, in place of any of the current authors. Finally, supplementing the required critical article on the "unread" author with a selection of excerpts by her or him would have the advantage of having a greater number of students reading a greater number of pages by each author, and allow for a greater number of prepared students to attend class and make meaningful contributions to discussions and activities, whether graded or not.

Assessment: Group, Objective, Individual, and Creative Assignments

Keeping in mind a university directive to offer learners frequent opportunities for feedback, the course included ten graded assignments, nine of which were required for each learner. Each student completed five out of six in-class group activities (combined for 25 per cent of the final grade), one short essay for each of the authors they read (15 per cent each), a rough draft of their final project (15 per cent), and the final project (30 per cent). The group activities and mini-essays required understanding and analysis of the novels along with a synthesizing of theory on autofiction, and were therefore relatively traditional assignments in which students analyzed literature according to critical theory. The final project and its rough draft gave the students the opportunity to exercise their creativity and write their own autofictions.[6] Because of the time constraints under which they were written, the in-class activities were graded primarily on the basis of ideas, with little weight accorded to grammar. However, for all the remaining assignments the quality of the ideas and of their grammatical expression were both taken into account. For the first of their short essays, learners had the opportunity to revise and resubmit according to the corrections received and thereby increase their grade by up to 10 per cent, as long as they achieved at least 60 per cent on the first version. While they have the option to do the same in many classes, they remain appreciative of it and find that it is "very helpful and makes [them] aware of learning" (survey). The goal of making students *active learners*, with emphasis on both halves of the term, is directly served by the task of revising their work, as the students are active in correcting their language inaccuracies and in improving their organization and expression of their ideas by following suggestions given in comments on their first submission. Through these activities, students are given the opportunity to develop mastery in a number of transferable skills, including, but not limited to, grammatical accuracy, critical reasoning, and effective communication of complex ideas. As one student commented on the assessment methods used in this course, they were not only an "interesting and educational way to teach," but also "relieve[d] the pressure of midterm, [because] evaluations allowed us to show what we'd learned" (survey).

Biweekly in-class group activities instead of reading quizzes were used not only for assessment, but also to foster greater comprehension through the continuous exchange of ideas and perspectives. Two students out of 27 who completed the course and the 20 who completed the survey were dissatisfied with the group assignments.[7] In one case, the learner thought she was consistently the strongest member of the group and that her grades were negatively impacted by the others, and in the other the questions were described too "obscure" to be answered in the time allotted. Nevertheless, in the survey, a greater number of students of all achievement levels commented that the activities were the class's most beneficial aspect, allowing them to learn from each other, and affording the opportunity to become better acquainted. Although their research involved using responses to clicker questions to determine student understanding in very large science classes, Smith et al.'s data show that "[m]ost instructors report that the percentage of correct answers, as well as students' confidence in their answers, almost always increases after peer discussion" (122). Just as their students reported "discussion is productive when people do not know the answers because you explore all the options and eliminate the ones you know can't be correct" (124), one student in the "self" class observed, for example, the group activities were "a great way to share ideas and understand concepts with others, two brains are better than one" (survey). In line with the class goals, these assignments encouraged active learning and fostered a sense of agency among students—allowing them not only to collaborate to self-determine their best answers, but also to choose which questions to answer, or even to try to answer their own questions through discussion.[8] An additional benefit of group work is the (perceived) decrease in anxiety as it helps learners realize that it is acceptable to have difficulty understanding a new concept, and it demonstrates that they are not the only ones who don't know all the answers when they walk into the classroom. Two students reported that the discussions were useful as their ideas were never discredited, and that their opinions and interpretations were always valued by classmates and the instructor, which enhanced their own engagement.

The remaining pieces of assessment were linked to the final project: the students' short autofiction, which presented an opportunity for them to reflect on their own representations of self. While they navigate an age where social media dominates the daily routine, and are already somewhat acquainted with the concept of construction of the self, as many have multiple profiles or filters to determine who sees what, increased self-reflection is needed. Likewise, the choice of a creative-critical task is easily associated with autofiction as it is such a self-reflective genre, and adding the creative aspect to the assignment offers the opportunity to capitalize on the fact that "students often treat creative assignments quite personally, treating their writing as if it's an expression of their true selves," as Austen argues (141). Throughout the semester, students examined in class several author-moderated websites and Facebook, Twitter, and Instagram pages to compare the images the authors seemed to try to create for themselves, along with video clips of interviews where broadcasters may attempt to subvert the author's chosen image[9] and stimulate learners thinking about the creation of selves. In order to get them thinking about the autofiction they would write at the end of the semester, at about the halfway point they were required to imagine the main character of their autofiction, and demonstrate as much as possible of her or his personality and life through a simulated Wikipedia page or Facebook/Instagram/Twitter account, or those who preferred graphic expression had the option of designing a tattoo or Google Doodle encapsulating the individual, with an accompanying short explanation of about 250–350 words. The final project was composed of two parts, an autofiction of 3000–3500 words, and a reflective text of 400–500 words detailing the link between the theories of autofiction and the student's own writing. Fifty-five per cent of the final project grade was based on language, with the remaining divided between originality (15 per cent), coherence and development of ideas (15 per cent), and the relation between autofiction and theory (15 per cent).

It is not unusual for students to have to write creatively both in language-based and in literature classes in their foreign language, yet it may be somewhat more uncommon for their final and most heavily weighted assignment to favor creativity over objectivity. Nonetheless, arguments in favor of creative writing to enhance reading comprehension and textual awareness are not hard to find, especially among professors of English. For example, in "Fiction Writing in Literature Classes," Gebhart identifies a number of values of fiction writing in literature courses, including the improvement of careful, detailed reading; internalization of what is studied; formation of explicit and organic connections between technical terms and the concrete reality of works of fiction (noting that when concrete connections are made, there is a greater chance of knowledge being retained); heightened appreciation of literature; improvement of their expository writing through work on rhetorical style in their own writing; and increased sensitivity to the problem of evoking the desired response in readers (151–2). Furthermore, Austen echoes Gebhart and elaborates five somewhat similar benefits of incorporating creative writing in a literature class, notably "(1) dispelling the awe of literature and creating active learners; (2) developing critical readers; (3) furthering student understanding of literary criticism; (4) inspiring deeper commitment to excellence; and (5) motivating class bonding and dismantling the classroom hierarchy" (139). Finally, in "Creative Writing and Critical Response in the University Literature Class," Wilson stresses the mutual and reciprocal benefits that connect creative writing and literary analysis: "Creative writing is seen ... as a means to better critical reading, but ... the relation is reciprocal and critically informed reading can be the context for genuinely talented creative work" (441). Many of these teacher-scholar points can be seen in particular in the autofiction of one student who took "Representing the Self." In his own final project, "Jusqu'ici tout va bien," he wrote:

> Bon, ça suffit. Dans la manière la plus directe, RM est Rachel Moon—cela est comment elle est inscrite dans mon cellulaire. JM est Jocelyn Moon. CM est Chloe Moon. Finalement, RM est encore Rachel Moon. Dites, monsieur grand auteur—l'auteur qui est l'héro de sa propre histoire qui dit ce n'est pas sa propre histoire, ce qui nous rend confus—étiez-vous, ou enfin parce que c'est moi qui parle à moi-même, étais-je ensemble avec des filles de la même famille—les sœurs? Ben oui, cela c'est moi; un véritable salaud ... Surtout pas! Lecteur imaginaire de mes pensées, j'étais en train de regarder l'extrait sur mon avant-bras, celui du Dernier Verre!
>
> *(Bell 9–10)*[10]

In this short excerpt, we can see very overt references to the autofictional novels and the theory that the student read throughout the semester. The use of initials or false names to mask real people in the author's life (for the present publication the names have been further changed from the original submission at the student's request, since they were the names of people in his life); the repetition of phrases or information ("RM est [encore] Rachel Moon"); the address to the self with a combination of the first and second grammatical persons; and the address to the reader are some of the more overt inclusions. In addition, however, there is a subtler nod to Christine Angot, with the final item, "le Dernier Verre," the last drink, since in *Incest*, Angot insists that the last drink does not repeat an alcoholic's first drink, but that the first drink repeats the last. Just as Angot referenced Deleuze's assertion that Monet's first water lilies repeats all the others, Bell references Angot and applies the analogy to two sisters the narrator has been involved with romantically. Elsewhere, he imitated Angot and Delaume's technique of intertextuality and inserted Philippe Forest's definition of autofiction into his creative work, thereafter using it to discuss the identity of his text's protagonist. As one of his classmates pointed out at the end of the class survey, this assignment represented "a great way to digest material instead of memorizing and forgetting" (survey).

Looking Back, Moving Forward

Wanting to make students more aware of why I read not only for my profession but also for pleasure, I began "Representing the Self" with some graphics that visually demonstrated what reading has to offer, in terms of both understanding and insight: for example, an image showing two individuals: the one standing on a pile of books is able to see over the wall obstructing the view of the other, and a GIF showing an individual literally stepping into a book, which turns the scene he is in from a blank page to one with a more engaging landscape. Looking back on the design of this course it seems that all aspects of it—from those initial images to the student's final autofictional and critical writing—collaborated in paving the way for the students to reach the goals the course intended including that of making the study of French and Francophone literature relevant, meaningful, *and* useful to twenty-first-century students. In the next offering, along with the changes outlined here, I will be even more explicit in sharing the tangible and intangible skills students are acquiring in this course in particular and in literature courses in general, in the hope that one day, they will band together to be the voice of the French and Francophone studies advertising agency whose greatest achievement will be the successful articulation of the benefits of studying the arts and humanities.

Notes

1 For simplicity's sake, all these texts will be referred to as novels, though there may be arguments for and against this label.
2 While this volume focuses on teaching French and Francophone women, the course described has no mandate to focus on women's writing, therefore a male author is included. This allows for greater inclusivity of all genders of students and can promote the discussion of possible gender differences in literature.
3 These were Natalie Edwards's "Autofiction in the Dock: The Case of Christine Angot," Elise Hugueny-Leger's "Broadcasting the Self: Autofiction, Television, and Representations of Authorship in Contemporary French Literature," and Ralph Schoolcraft's "Pour prendre au sérieux Frédéric Beigbeder."
4 The term was inaugurated with the June 1995 Strategic Plan and has been a core value and goal of the university ever since (www.uoguelph.ca/info/strategic/recommend1.shtml, accessed August 28, 2017).
5 For a detailed discussion of agency and engagement, see Reeve and Tseng's "Agency as a Fourth Aspect of Students' Engagement during Learning Activities" (2011).
6 Since autofiction often involves very personal, traumatic themes, and because it would be inappropriate to invade students' personal lives, they had the option of inventing both the fictional and autobiographical aspects of their autofictions.
7 Two negative responses do not warrant the elimination of group assignments, although in the future, the composition of the groups will vary.
8 For example, "Choose a sentence you have trouble understanding, and try to explain it together. As you explain it, notice the syntax, the vocabulaire, and the writer's autofictional project."
9 For example, a comparison of the selves presented in Angot's novels, in the biography published on christineangot.com (last accessed August 28, 2017), and during her appearance on *Tout le monde en parle* for the publication of *L'Inceste*, which aired on November 13, 1999 (last accessed on August 28, 2017 on www.dailymotion.com/video/xf8opa).
10 Ok, that's enough. To be as direct as possible, RM is Rachel Moon—that's how she shows up on my cell. JM is Jocelyn Moon. CM is Chloe Moon. Again, RM is Rachel Moon. Tell me, Mr. Bigshot Writer—the author who is the hero of his own story that says it's not his own story, which confuses us—were you, or rather since I'm the one who's talking to myself—was I with girls from the same family—sisters? Yup, that's me; a real bastard … Definitely not! Imaginary reader in my mind, I was looking at the excerpt on my forearm, the one about the Last Drink! (my translation).

References

"2017–2018 Undergraduate Calendar." University of Guelph. www.uoguelph.ca/registrar/calendars/undergraduate/current/c12/c12fren.shtml. Accessed August 23, 2017.
Austen, Veronica J. "The Value of Creative Writing Assignments in English Literature Courses." *New Writing* 2. 2: 138–150. dx.doi.org.subzero.lib.uoguelph.ca/10.1080/14790720508668953. Accessed 23 August, 2017.
Bell, Jordan. "Jusqu'ici tout va bien." University of Guelph, "Representing the Self" (FREN 3130), final project, submitted December 13, 2016.
Edwards, Natalie. "Autofiction in the Dock: The Case of Christine Angot," in *Protean Selves: First Person Voices in Twenty-First-Century French and Francophone Narratives*, ed. Adrienne Angelo and Erika Fülöp. Cambridge Scholars Publishing, 2014, 69–81.
FREN*3130 anonymous end-of-semester survey. Administered by student assistant to 20 learners on December 2, 2016.
Gebhart, Richard C. "Fiction Writing in Literature Classes." *Rhetoric Review*, 7. 1(1988): 150–155. www.jstor.org/stable465540. Accessed August 23, 2017.
Healey, Mick, Abbi Flint, and Kathy Harrington. "Engagement through Partnerships: Students as Partners in Learning and Teaching in Higher Education." Higher Education Academy, 2014. www.

heacademy.ac.uk/system/files/resources/engagement_through_partnership.pdf. Accessed July 5, 2018.

Hugueny-Leger, Elise. "Broadcasting the Self: Autofiction, Television, and Representations of Authorship in Contemporary French Literature," in *Life Writing* 14. 1(2017): 5–18. DOI: 10.1080/14484528.2016.1219215. Accessed July 4, 2018.

"Learning Outcomes." University of Guelph. www.uoguelph.ca/vpacademic/avpa/outcomes/. Accessed August 23, 2017.

Reeve, Johnmarshall and Ching-Mei Tseng. "Agency as a Fourth Aspect of Students' Engagement during Learning Activities." *Contemporary Educational Psychology* 36. 4(2011): 257–267. DOI: 10.1016/j.cedpsych.2011.05.002. Accessed August 23, 2017.

Schoolcraft, Ralph. "Pour prendre au sérieux Frédéric Beigbeder," in *Frédéric Beigbeder et ses doubles*. Rodolpi, 2008.

Smith, M.K., W.B. Wood, W.K. Adams, C. Wieman, J.K. Knight, N. Guild, and T.T. Su. "Why Peer Discussion Improves Student Performance on In-Class Concept Questions." *Science* 323(2009): 122–123. https://doi.org/10.1016/j.ydbio.2009.05.104. Accessed August 23, 2017.

Wilson, Peter. "Creative and Critical Response in the University Literature Class." *Innovations in Education and Teaching International* 48. 4(2011): 439–446. DOI: 10.1080/14703297.2011.617091. Accessed August 23, 2017.

PART II

New Beginnings, New Horizons: Women Writers in Beginning and Intermediate French Classes

5

TEACHING FRENCH AND FRANCOPHONE WOMEN AUTHORS ONLINE

Sage Goellner

"There has never been a great age of science and technology without a corresponding flourishing in the arts and humanities," writes scholar of technology Cathy N. Davidson (707). As an educator in the University of Wisconsin-Madison's Division of Continuing Studies and a scholar of French literature, I envisioned using this "flourishing of technology," namely, the internet, as a vibrant resource for developing and teaching an online course on French and Francophone women authors.

The majority of my career has been in a department dedicated to serving non-traditional students whose access to university courses is increasingly through online modes of instruction. In this essay, I describe an online course on French women's literature I developed and taught, and specifically present its promises and challenges, based on the experience of its creation, instruction, and the students' perceptions of the course. The greatest value of this online literature course was the guest lectures by several faculty experts, an experience that would not have been as readily available in a traditional classroom, whereas the greatest challenge of the course was the workload it entailed. My experiences creating and teaching this online class may prove of interest to other instructors, providing them with useful tools and examples to emulate similar online courses in French and Francophone women's literature.

Changing Perceptions

Online learning can generate both excitement and fear; it is safe to say not all faculty are eager to embrace this approach to teaching. A leading recent survey by Elaine Allen and Jeff Seaman about online higher education found a relatively low perception (30 per cent) of value and legitimacy about online education, even as the number of faculty involved in online instruction is increasing (26). Thus, even though increasing numbers of instructors are engaging in online instruction, they believe it an inferior educational experience to that of the traditional brick-and-mortar classroom. In addition, whereas many faculty use technologies on a regular basis in face-to-face courses (including but not limited to course-management systems, webpages, online discussion, blogs, Wikis), fewer have taught fully online courses, although that number is steadily increasing and shows no sign of stopping. These technological tools are commonly integrated into a course of study to complement classroom contact and standard methods of sharing insights. However, most of us face a steep learning curve to become acclimated to fully online education because technologies are ever changing, requiring a constant need to learn new techniques and technologies.

My experience with how online education supports French language, culture, and literature has continued to evolve in the new millennium. For faculty in more traditional settings, teaching online "entails a willingness to reconsider the most cherished assumptions and structures of their discipline" (Davidson 715). Most people have not experienced online education yet or have done so only in one role; I have experienced distance education for over a decade and from two different positions: professor and program director. Each role afforded me insights and contributed to a unique perspective on what makes online learning successful. I have directed a variety of distance-learning courses, including correspondence courses, email classes, and fully online courses. A main outreach arm of the university, my department serves lifelong learners seeking personal development through the study of art, music, history, and languages, and offers learning experiences in a variety of modalities: face-to-face classes, workshops, online courses, and educational travel study tours. Activities that are now routine to me may still be foreign to others because I regularly teach and develop online courses in French. Working in online learning environments has become an integral part of my professional life.

In my experience in both face-to-face and online courses, participants and instructors become collaborators in the advancement of learning and community; the online environment is no different, as I have discovered through my experiences. The offering of online courses is increasingly key to increased access to education and higher enrollments (Lancashire 16). Parents with small children, individuals with physical disabilities, and those whose work schedules conflict with courses held on campus may elect to take courses online. As Devoney Looser argued in her essay for *The Chronicle of Higher Education*, "Why I Teach Online," digital pedagogy is increasingly a "matter of social justice and a feminist practice" (1). She writes, "Many of my online students—the majority of them hard-working women with very complicated lives ... The degrees that many of our online students are earning today would have gone unearned a generation ago" (3). Online students can exercise a greater degree of control over their learning as they balance their lives of work and study. In addition, it can allow students to shape their own learning by communicating their ideas together, even when they are not physically or temporally in the same place. In particular, as was the case with the course I developed, technology can enhance pedagogy by offering an unprecedented diversity of perspectives to learners. Finally, online courses encourage experimentation in teaching and learning and, as in a traditional classroom, an interest in developing their own learning.

Idea for the Course

As I began working in my position at the University of Wisconsin, the inspiration for offering my course, "French and Francophone Women Writers Online," was not long in coming. In 2007, the university's alumni association had offered an online outreach course on Russian history using archival lectures from Russian historian Michael Petrovich (1922–89). The creation of a similar course on a topic in my research area, French and Francophone women authors, was thus within reach. Whereas the Russian history course had a single source for its lectures, I developed a co-taught course comprised of guest lectures, including archival presentations by noted French literature scholar Elaine Marks (1930–2001) as well as by colleagues around the country. While researching Elaine Marks's published works, I stumbled upon an audio recording she had done for a cassette curriculum in women's studies published by Everett Edwards in 1976.[1] This curriculum is part of a larger series, a veritable treasure trove of lectures on authors ranging from Anne Bradstreet to Richard Wright, all available on WorldCat and via interlibrary loan. The curriculum also included a lecture on Madame de Staël, and with the discovery of these two recordings, I found the beginnings of this course. For two other units, I used a documentary on George Sand and an interview with Hélène Cixous, which were available at that time for streaming from the Films Media Group.[2] My colleagues graciously agreed to record lectures for the remaining units.

My goal was to create a feminocentric course that demonstrated how women's experiences spanned the boundaries of time and space, conveyed a message of female empowerment, and subverted historical stereotypes. I created the course with the core idea that it would be stronger with contributions from multiple women scholars; this approach to pedagogy adopted a core principle of feminism: that it must be polyvocal, in order to acknowledge multiple perspectives. Instead of a single lecturer, the course would be enriched by a multiplicity of voices. For each "lecture," then, I used either of archival material that I had digitized, guest lectures from colleagues, and these films. This approach to teaching through the invitation of guest experts can be used in a variety of courses and offers a benefit more difficult to achieve in a traditional face-to-face classroom.

Course Development

Before developing the course I knew I would need resources, so I applied for and received a small grant to pay for course development and honoraria for the guest lecturers, obtained the services of one of our department's instructional designers, and set to the task. It took me the better part of a summer to put this labor of love together.[3] The amount of work that this course required cannot be adequately underscored. If, as Ian Lancashire warns, "[a]n instructor should think twice before accepting an offer to teach online," they should think even harder before developing an online class (5). In addition to the audio lectures, I gathered images of the authors, their homes, contemporaries, and other visual contextual markers, and made slideshows to accompany each of the guest lectures. Although the overall project was time consuming, students definitely appreciated the effort in this media enhancement of the course. One student wrote, "I thoroughly enjoyed listening to the lectures. I was able to pick up nuances in meaning which may have escaped me during the reading. For example, 'remembering' as putting the body parts back together vs. 'remembering' as used in [the Assia Djebar lecture]." Another reported, "I found it such a pleasure to tune in each week and listen to all of the lecturers. It helped me learn pronunciations of our authors' names and some of the French concepts that were presented in French."

Description of the Course and the Students

The course took place in a 100 per cent online format using Desire2Learn (D2L) over nine weeks, with a different 60-minute "lecture" each week. Students were not required to be "in class" at a specific time; instead, I posted the new material, readings, and set of discussion prompts each week. Each of the nine units included my prerecorded introduction of the author, which I had done earlier, including a brief overview of the week's author, the socio-historical context, and presentation of the lecture and readings. The participants listened to my introductions, the audio lectures, and each week responded to prompts via the discussion board. The majority of the online assignments were designed to prepare the students for their readings before they delved into the primary texts as well as the post-reading discussion to encourage learners to apply and transfer their newly gained knowledge to the authors and contexts. As expected, the majority of the students considered the weekly online conversations the most helpful assignment for synthesizing the material.

For example, in the unit on Marceline Desbordes-Valmore, the students listened to my introduction, the lecture by Deborah Jenson, "Marceline Desbordes-Valmore," read sections of the novella *Sarah*, and replied to my discussion prompts for that week, which follow:

1. How is slavery represented in the novella?
2. Which characters are silenced and why?
3. Comment on the representations of mixed identities in the novella.

One student replied with the following comment:

> [Desbordes-Valmore's] experiences in the Caribbean required her to think deeply into definitions of slave and free. I believe she saw slaves as being without voice. In *Sarah*, children (Edwin and Sarah) were also without voice … Desbordes-Valmore uses the voiceless and the named in *Sarah* to demonstrate the humanity of people who are without voice and the way in which this role can switch so easily based on who is defining whom.

This thoughtful response was typical of the students' work in the course. There were eight adult students in the course in the fall of 2008, all of whom had already earned their bachelor's degree. All women, they came from a variety of professional backgrounds: an economist, a guidance counselor, a corporate librarian, an insurance agent, an artist, a computer programmer, and a study-abroad advisor. They were from Arizona, Arkansas, Illinois, Florida, Minnesota, and Wisconsin. Two were retirees, and the rest were working adults. All had enrolled in the class out of intrinsic interest in the subject; one was interested in honing her literary-analysis skills and one had just returned from an alumni association trip to France. Two participants had been English majors in college; one had taken a women's studies class while pursuing her undergraduate degree; another was an active member of a book club; and one participant was "very concerned about women's issues, and right now especially with the overt sexism in politics and the media." In a very special turn, one student had her first child during the course session; the flexibility of the course allowed her to study while on her maternity leave.

Discussion Threads

The essential work of the course was reading the authors' works, viewing the narrated slideshow while listening to the expert's lecture, and responding to written discussion prompts via the D2L discussion board. The efficacy of online threaded discussions has been demonstrated in several studies: instructional benefits include energetic interactions between students and instructors, active and collaborative learning, increased engagement, and increased ability to deal with controversial topics (Kirk and Orr, Andresen). In particular, responding to literature online is greatly beneficial for quieter students who may not feel comfortable participating without more forethought. The discussion board allowed students to reflect more deeply on the content rather than rely on spur-of-the-moment responses. As one student wrote, "I read these materials over a week ago and my feelings as I read my notes over to respond have not changed." Another commented, "I really enjoyed the readings ... I've been mulling over them all week."

Students demonstrated their understanding of assigned readings and in the video/audio components. These course features stimulated their critical thinking and expression skills, allowing them to extend their discussions of the works to broader contexts, and even within their own personal lives. As Beeghly's study reported, participants engaged with each other just as much as with me, the course facilitator. She writes, "discussing a book online over a period of time enhanced both [students'] individual understanding and the quality of their group's discussion"; this was the case in this course (16). As one participant in the course put it, "I thought a lot about the responses to questions, and reading others' comments was useful to me."

In addition, my experience teaching the course was consonant with Dringus's findings that there was "an energy level in an online learning environment, an energy that is the collective effort expended by a group" (cited in Kirk and Orr 8). While students were engaging deeply with the text, they were also creating collaborative and personal affiliations through the threaded discussions. What would extend this engagement even further, perhaps, in future iterations of the course, would be the inclusion of available guest lecturers in the threaded discussions online; as Eveleth and Baker-Eveleth have shown, this "activity is well liked and ... impact[s] students' acceptance and understanding of the material" (420).

Conclusion

Resistance to online teaching does not come as a surprise, because there is not yet an effective and comprehensive training manual for online education. Rather, we most often learn by doing. Even though online courses have been in existence since the 1990s (and distance learning at least a century before that), educators are still learning how to create and instruct effective online courses with each iteration. Each online course comes with its successes, failures, sticky wickets, and breakthroughs. As Davidson argues, "there are always glitches and bugs and viruses and transitional eras" (714). But as each year brings with it a new set of technological innovations that we can weave into our pedagogy, there is still much to be accomplished in contributing to online pedagogy. Looser puts it concisely, "Online teaching—like any kind of pedagogy—can be done well or poorly."

I want to conclude with a final thought. Just as the pioneers of women and gender studies made significant shifts in literature curricula for on-the-ground classes, we now have the ability to offer a richer and more diverse online curriculum to more learners using online pedagogy. In the case of the course I described above, its unique contribution was the polyvocal feminocentric group of special lectures from nationally known experts on French women's literature. The current increase of online courses must include those that shed light on marginalized groups, in this case, women authors. Teaching French and Francophone women writers online can help engage a wider audience of traditional and non-traditional students with rich literary and cultural legacies. A student's closing sentiment speaks to the course's potential to positively influence students' understanding of the field. She wrote, "This has been a beautiful course. I have learned so much ... I feel I have gained a timeline for French feminist writing in the most soul-searching and yet fully embodied way."

Notes

1 Thanks to the flexibilities offered by the 2002 TEACH Act, applicable to digital online courses, and the Fair Use provisions of copyright law, I was able to use these copyrighted works on the password-protected and time-limited Desire2Learn course site.

2 At the time of writing, the film on George Sand is currently available from the Films Media Group, www.films.com, but the interview with Hélène Cixous is no longer available in streaming format. The DVD is listed in the References.
3 The most work-intensive activities included assembling the texts in translation, recording introductions, facilitating the guest lecturers' recordings, getting transcriptions for all the audio so that the course would be accessible, and working closely with the instructional designer on the look and feel of the course.

Appendix: Course Units, Readings, and Lectures

Unit 1: Heloise, Abelard, and Romantic Love

- Reading: the first letter of Heloise to Abelard, in *Abelard and Heloise: The Letters and Other Writings*. Trans. William Levitan.
- Lecture by Professor Emerita Jane T. Schulenburg, an expert on medieval women (original interview from "Medieval Women," "University of the Air," 1995).
- Additional resource: BBC Radio 4, *In Our Time*, "Abelard and Heloise."

Unit 2: In Defense of Women: Christine de Pisan

- Reading: pages 5–20 of *The Book of the City of Ladies* by Christine de Pizan. Trans. Rosalind Brown-Grant.
- Lecture by Professor Emerita Jane T. Schulenburg (original interview from "Medieval Women," "University of the Air," 1995).

Unit 3: Madame de Staël on Women Writers

- Reading: Staël, "On Women Writers." In *Madame de Staël on Politics, Literature, and National Character*.
- Lecture by Professor Susan Tenenbaum, specialist of political philosophy (lecture digitized from the audiocassette recording entitled "Madame de Staël" by Susan Tenenbaum).

Unit 4: Marceline Desbordes-Valmore and Colonialism

- Reading: Desbordes-Valmore. *Sarah*. Trans. Deborah Jenson and Doris Kadish.
- Lecture by Professor Deborah Jenson, specialist in nineteenth-century French and Caribbean literature and culture (recorded lecture, 2007).

Unit 5: Matters of the Heart: George Sand

- Reading: excerpts from *The Country Waif*. Trans. Eirene Collins.
- Film: "George Sand: The Story of Her Life," 2004.

Unit 6: Colette: A Force of Nature

- Reading: "My Sister with the Long Hair," "The Spahi's Cloak," "My Mother and the Forbidden Fruit," "The Seamstress." In Colette, *Claudine's House*. Trans. Andrew Brown.
- Lecture by Professor Emerita Elaine Marks (1930–2001), scholar of feminist theory and Jewish studies (lecture digitized from the audiocassette recording entitled "Colette" by Elaine Marks).

Unit 7: **Becoming a Woman/A Woman Unbecoming: Simone de Beauvoir**

- Reading: "Introduction." In Beauvoir, *The Second Sex*. Trans. H.M. Parshley.
- Lecture by Professor Emerita Elaine Marks (original recording from "A Sound Portrait of Simone de Beauvoir," 1981).
- Additional resource: interview with Beauvoir from Studs Terkel, *Voices of Our Time*.

Unit 8: **Hélène Cixous and "l'Ecriture feminine"**

- Reading: "The Laugh of the Medusa." Trans. Keith and Paula Cohen.
- Excerpt from Cixous, *Reveries of the Wild Woman: Primal Scenes*. Trans. Beverley Bie Brahic.
- Lecture by Professor Elizabeth Berglund Hall, specialist in women's writing and autobiography (recorded lecture, 2007).
- Additional resource: DVD interview with Cixous, "Writing Not Yet Thought: Hélène Cixous in Conversation with Adrian Heathfield."

Unit 9: **Exile: Assia Djebar**

- Reading: Assia Djebar, "There Is No Exile." In Djebar, *Women of Algiers in Their Apartment*. Trans. Marjolijn de Jager.
- Lecture by Professor Emerita Judith Sarnecki, scholar of twentieth-century French literature and gender studies (recorded lecture, 2007).

References

Allen, Elaine and Seaman, Jeff. "Online Report Card: Tracking Online Education in the United States." Babson Research Group, 2016.

Andresen, M. A. "Asynchronous Discussion Forums: Success Factors, Outcomes, Assessments, and Limitations." *Educational Technology and Society* 12. 1(2009): 249–257.

Beauvoir, Simone de. "Introduction," to *The Second Sex*, trans. H.M. Parshley, in *New French Feminisms*, ed. Elaine Marks and Isabelle de Courtivron. University of Massachusetts Press, 1980.

Beeghly, Dena G. "It's about Time: Using Electronic Literature Discussion Groups with Adult Learners." *Journal of Adolescent and Adult Literacy* 49. 1(2005): 12–21.

Hall, ElizabethBerglund. "Hélène Cixous and l'écriture féminine." Liberal Arts and Applied Studies, University of Wisconsin-Madison, April 12, 2007. Guest lecture.

Cixous, Hélène. *Reveries of the Wild Woman: Primal Scenes*, trans. Beverley Bie Brahic. Northwestern University Press, 2006.

Cixous, Hélène and Jonathan Rée. "Hélène Cixous." Princeton, NJ: Films for the Humanities and Sciences, 2004.

Cixous, Hélène and Jonathan Rée. "The Laugh of the Medusa," trans. Keith and Paula Cohen, in *New French Feminisms*, ed. Elaine Marks and Isabelle de Courtivron. University of Massachusetts Press, 1980.

Colette. "My Sister with the Long Hair," "My Mother and the Forbidden Fruit," and "The Seamstress." In *Claudine's House*, trans. Andrew Brown. Hesperus Press, 2006.

Davidson, Cathy N. "Humanities 2.0: Promise, Perils, Predictions." *PMLA* 123. 3(2008): 707–717.

Desbordes-Valmore, Marceline. *Sarah*, trans. Deborah Jenson and Doris Kadish. MLA, 2008.

Djebar, Assia. "There Is No Exile," in *Women of Algiers in Their Apartment*, trans. Marjolijn de Jager. University Press of Virginia, 1992.

Eveleth, Daniel M. and Lori J. Baker-Eveleth. "Student Dialogue with Online Guest Speakers." *Decision Sciences Journal of Innovative Education* 7. 2(2009): 417–421.

"George Sand: The Story of Her Life." Films for the Humanities and Science, 2006.

"Heloise to Abelard," in *Abelard and Heloise: The Letters and Other Writings*, trans. William Levitan. Hackett Publishing, 2007.

Jenson, Deborah. "Marceline Desbordes-Valmore." Liberal Arts and Applied Studies, University of Wisconsin-Madison, April 12, 2007. Guest lecture.

Kirk, James J. and Orr, Robert L. "A Primer on the Effective Use of Threaded Discussion Forums." ERIC Document Reproduction Service No. ED47273, 2003.

Lancashire, Ian, ed. *Teaching Literature and Language Online*. Modern Languages Association, 2009.

Looser, Devony. "Why I Teach Online." *Chronicle of Higher Education*, March 20, 2017.

Marks, Elaine. "Colette." Audiocasette, Everett-Edwards, 1976

Pisan, Christinede. *The Book of the City of Ladies*, trans. Rosalind Brown-Grant. Penguin, 1999.

Sand, George. *The Country Waif*, trans. Eirene Collins. University of Nebraska Press, 1977.

Sarnecki, Judith. "Writing Violence, Affirming Life, Assia Djebar, Algerian Writer in Exile." Liberal Arts and Applied Studies, University of Wisconsin-Madison, April 12, 2007. Guest lecture.

Schulenburg, Jane T., Emily Auerbach, and Norman Gilliland. "Medieval Women." Audiocassette, University of the Air, Wisconsin Public Radio, 1995.

Staël, Madamede. "On Women Writers," in *Madame de Staël on Politics, Literature, and National Character*, ed. Monroe Berger. Doubleday, 1964.

Tenenbaum, Susan. "Madame de Staël." Audiocassette, Everett-Edwards, 1976.

Terkel, Studs. *Voices of Our Time*. Highbridge Company, 1950.

6

INTEGRATING WOMEN'S VOICES AND CONTEMPORARY CULTURAL MATERIALS THROUGH E-JOURNALING

Elizabeth Berglund Hall

This chapter explores the use of interactive e-journals as a tool to expand the breadth and scope of the language classroom and as a means to include diverse French and Francophone women's voices and new media forms of artistic expression by women. The interactive e-journal utilizes a hybrid classroom to promote explorations of modern women in the Francophone world through contemporary media, to enhance students' cultural competence through interactions with and analyses of cultural differences through new technologies, and to develop independent, self-motivated learners and global citizens. The interactive e-journal is an excellent way to engage students successfully in the study of language beyond grammar, in a way that appeals to their interests in social media and larger questions of globalization, gender, diversity, and their "place" in the world. In this chapter, I will give specific examples of the innovative e-journaling activities that I have developed in a third-semester French course (Intermediate French I) at the University of Virginia, with the intention that these activities may be adapted and used at various levels of the French curriculum.

Approaching Culture

In August 2014, the American Council on the Teaching of Foreign Languages (ACTFL) published a "Global Competence Position Statement," affirming the language classroom as a key location for the development of global competence, which entails the exploration of diverse perspectives. The statement describes global competence in the following passage:

> This competence is developed and demonstrated by investigating the world, recognizing and weighing perspectives, acquiring and applying disciplinary and interdisciplinary knowledge, communicating ideas, and taking action. Global competence is fundamental to the experience of learning languages whether in classrooms, through virtual connections, or via everyday experiences.

In addition to emphasizing the development of students as responsible global citizens, higher education today places importance on the internationalization of the curriculum. The foreign-language classroom is evidently of central value as a locus to foster intercultural competence and to develop global citizenry. While, as language instructors, we are thoroughly aware of the importance of the language classroom within the goals of a liberal arts education, the integration of culture into language classrooms remains challenging and often neglected.

The challenge of integrating culture into the language curriculum may be due to various factors such as over-reliance on the textbook, continued use of traditional testing methods, persistent division of the undergraduate curriculum and faculty into language and literature/culture courses, or instructors' hesitation to teach a culture that they may not have experienced personally or learned about in a formal classroom setting themselves. In their article, "Mindsets and Tools for Developing Foreign Language Curriculum Featuring Thoughtful Culture-as-Content," Jason Martel and Nicole Pettitt discuss the difficulties of integrating culture and make the following suggestion: "[F]oreign language teachers, both new and veteran, could benefit from additional resources not only for cultivating sophisticated understandings of culture and intercultural communicative competence, but also for integrating these constructs into their curriculum development in ways that foster *both* culture-as-content *and* language learning" (171).

Focusing on the instructors as the change agent in the classroom, Martel and Pettitt begin their article with a discussion of mindsets that they believe are "vital for designing a curriculum that features thoughtful cultural content" (172). The mindsets that they highlight include the necessity of understanding intercultural communicative competence, approaching the language through content and organizing by theme rather than topic, dealing with controversial topics, and using the textbook as a "point of departure for improvement and expansion" (175). The instructor's mindset is thus critical to transforming the curriculum in a way that includes a meaningful integration of cultural content.

While I use different tools in my e-journaling project to develop intercultural competence through the inclusion of Francophone women's perspectives in the language curriculum, I share Martel and Pettitt's view of the outlook necessary for the incorporation into the classroom of cultural questions such as diversity and women's voices. Adding to what they have set forth on the importance of the conviction of the instructor to a meaningful integration of cultural content, I would emphasize that the attitude of the student is equally important. The student also must participate in transforming the curriculum as an engaged and active contributor in the process of learning. Building on Martel and Pettitt's description of mindsets and tools for integrating culture and also keeping in mind ACTFL's Performance Descriptors for Cultural Awareness as guides for developing students' cultural awareness, I will outline my method for moving beyond the classroom to introduce women's voices into the hybrid curriculum through the use of authentic cultural materials and to engage students with their peers and the larger global community through the use of e-journals.

Engaging Students through E-journaling

Informal writing serves as an important formative task for students learning to use linguistic structures and to communicate in a foreign language. At the University of Virginia, as at many other institutions of higher education, language programs are utilizing the e-portfolio as a tool that allows the instructor, the department, and the student to track the student's progress as well as to collect, showcase, and reflect on student work. One of the functions of the e-portfolio is to collect both formal and informal writing and speaking samples, and to demonstrate the student's interaction with cultural practices, products, and perspectives. Informal writing in the form of an e-journal serves multiple functions as I set it up for my classes: it allows students to work through linguistic structures in a low-stakes assignment, to interact with cultural artifacts and encounter new media and different viewpoints, to engage with other classmates and their opinions on cultural artifacts, and to reflect on their progress in both linguistic skills and cultural awareness through the course of the semester. In addition, the e-journal serves as a "writing-to-learn" strategy in the Writing across the Curriculum movement.

In my third-semester French-language class (Intermediate French I), which uses Champeny's *Imaginez: Le Français sans frontières* (3rd edition), students are required to write a series of e-journal entries through the semester, as well as to comment on other students' journal entries. These entries and comments are all posted to their e-portfolio, and are viewable by the instructor and the other members of the class, extending the class community outside of the classroom. The journals have been housed on e-portfolios created on WordPress and on Digication in various past semesters. Both of these programs have key features for the e-journal. They allow for blog-type sequential text entries, accompanied by links to the sources and/or images of the topic, and they also include comment boxes on the page, which permit students to comment on classmates' journal entries. For each e-journal entry, students must interact with a cultural product that relates to the unit's themes, write a paragraph that both summarizes what they read or heard, and also gives their reaction to the artifact. The prompt for this activity is relatively open-ended and serves as a prompt for all entries through the semester. The goal is to give students the freedom to choose their own topics and to allow them to explore language and discover cultural artifacts independently.

> e-Journal prompt: During the course of the semester, you will choose (at minimum) six cultural artifacts as the topics of your e-journal entries. Your artifact must be associated with the themes of the unit currently being studied in class.* In your e-journal entry, you will write a summary or description of the artifact and your reaction (with justification). Write a paragraph of at least eight sentences. Do not forget to give the source of your journal entry (web address, image, embedded audio or video). As you prepare each e-journal entry, you will also add to your personal dictionary three or four new words that you have discovered during this activity.
>
> * Your instructor will give you a list of suggestions for each unit, but you are encouraged to do your own research according to your own interests.

In order to expand the cultural products with which they interact through the semester, students have a "menu" of types of texts from which they choose, including the following: 1) literature 2) film, 3) audio (podcast), 4) press article, 5) video (news clip), 6) song, 7) advertisement, 8) art object, or 9) interview (by the student) with a Francophone. The following is a sample menu given out in class. Students are asked to mark off the tasks as they complete them.

- Read a French or Francophone poem or short story.
- Study a French or Francophone piece of art or cultural object.
- Listen to a French or Francophone podcast or radio program.
- Watch a French or Francophone film.
- Interview a French speaker.
- Read an article from a French or Francophone newspaper.
- Listen to a French or Francophone song.

- Watch a French or Francophone newscast.
- Examine a French or Francophone print or video advertisement.

Through the course of the semester, students choose a variety of types of cultural documents in the menu of options. Since they are asked to write a minimum of six e-journals, they do not necessarily complete all the tasks on the menu; however, even within the six-entry minimum, their choices will demonstrate the examination of a breadth of cultural products as well as interaction with cultural perspectives from a range of Francophone countries and on a variety of topics. The goal of the activity is to expand outward from the classroom and to challenge students to research and find cultural documents that interest them.

Integrating Women's Voices

Although students are invited to do their own research for each unit topic, I also give them a list of suggestions, as indicated in the prompt. It is through this list of suggestions that an instructor can find ways to personalize the content that she is teaching. In my class, I emphasize French and Francophone women's voices in the list of suggestions in order to supplement and further develop women's voices introduced into the curriculum at this level. The hybrid nature of the e-journal topics permits me to present students with a variety of artifacts that display women's artistic expression in the Francophone world, including, for example, new social media, accounts of entrepreneurs and start-up companies, artists' public artwork, and stories of social activists on campuses and elsewhere.

In one particular unit, the linguistic focus is past tenses, the theme is technology and the media, and the cultural topic is Québec. My list of suggested e-journal topics draws on and supplements what we study together as a class. For example, the class reads a short bio of Marcelle Ferron, a Québecois artist. Ferron (1924–2001) was an important artist associated with the *Automatiste* movement in Québec, and is best known for her non-figural stained glass, which can be seen in several Montréal metro stations and public buildings throughout Québec. Following up on the short text that we read together in class, I give students a link to her stained-glass windows at the Champ-de-Mars metro station in Montréal[1] as the art object option on their menu of suggestions. For their e-journal, students follow the link to her artwork and briefly research her life and art, finding more information about her online. They then summarize what they have learned and give their reaction to the artwork in the e-journal entry.

Another menu item suggestion that builds on the same theme is the song "All Right" by Québecois musician Marie-Pierre Arthur, who is mentioned in the cultural text for the unit in the context of several other popular musical groups in Québec. I post links to a few of her videos, many of which also have the lyrics available, and students can watch, listen, read, and react. For this same unit that includes themes of technology and the media as well as the cultural theme of Québec, I suggest the short story "Yellow and White" ("*Jaune et blanc*"), by Monique Proulx, from her collection *Aurora Montréalis* (*Les Aurores Montréales*). "Yellow and White" recounts the story of a young immigrant Chinese woman who faces the difficult cultural adjustment to life in Montréal and an overwhelming feeling of *dépaysement* (disorientation/culture shock) as she stands in the aisles of a big box store. The story is written in the form of a letter to her grandmother still living in rural China. "Yellow and White" challenges students to consider the themes of the unit (the influence of technology and the media) in a more abstract, global way through the lens of immigration and the changing industrialized world. For this same unit on technology and media, but relating thematically to the vocabulary which includes television and cinema terms, I also suggest the poem "La Vedette" ("The Movie Star"), which narrates the interior monologue of an actress as she walks the runway, by Belgian-Israeli poet Esther Granek, whose poetry is accessible and appealing to students at this level.

The news-related cultural texts rotate each semester, as I try to find current articles, videos, and podcasts that expand on a particular unit's themes and also introduce students to women's voices from various regions of France and Francophone culture. Students of this generation are interested in technology and social media, so for the same unit mentioned above, I suggest an article from the newspaper *Le Figaro* by Elisa Braun on SMS-form epistolary novels for the new "Snapchat generation."[2] The author of the article discusses what she means by the "Snapchat generation" and its interest in consuming literature in a different way than previous generations. She refers to *Dangerous Liaisons* as a comparable way to tell a story via messages (albeit long letters as opposed to short text messages). The article reviews apps such as Hooked and Wattpad, and discusses the history of "chat fiction." Students often have different reactions to Braun's article; some are interested in the new technology itself, while others engage with the description of their generation and the notion of fiction. For e-journal topic suggestions for other units, I suggest an animated video from FranceInfo's "Draw My News" series by artist/journalist Linh-Lan Dao,[3] in which one watches a two- or three minute fast-motion video of the artist's hand drawing images on a whiteboard that explain or illustrate news of the previous week. Like the article about "chat fictions," this news video pushes the boundaries of conventional genres and allows students to engage with language and French media in new and exciting forms.

Some of the suggestions that I give for the e-journal also consider women as active members of society and social influencers, such as entrepreneurs, athletes, and social organizers. In one podcast, students listen to a Radio Canada interview about the expanding use of videos on social media with Winy Bernard, president of a marketing company, interviewed by Marjorie April for her radio show "Y a pas deux matins pareils"[4] ("No two mornings are the same"). In other examples, I suggest an episode of the podcast "Esprit d'initiative" ("The Spirit of Initiative"), which introduces two women entrepreneurs who travel selling bulk organic foods from a van,[5] and a video news clip about AfriMarket, a business co-founded by a woman that allows Africans in France to send products (food, medication, tech items), rather than money, to their families in Africa.[6] In some units, the topic is polemical; for instance, for a unit on diversity and social movements, I give students the option of analyzing a controversial ad for the Rio Olympic Games criticized for its homogenous depiction of the athletes as white males.[7] Students watch the advertisement and read an article in *L'Équipe* about the controversy, then react in their e-journal.

Each of these cultural documents integrates and expands on various aspects of what students have studied in the classroom, and require that they engage on many levels to understand, synthesize, and react to the cultural artifact under consideration. By moving out of the classroom into the virtual interactive space of the e-journal, we as instructors may transform the curriculum and guide students in their own cultural exploration, while at the same time exposing them to diverse perspectives so that they may make deeper cultural connections. The menu of choices for the e-journal also allows the instructor to exploit the many resources available on the internet, as a means to bring women's voices and artistic expressions into the virtual classroom. As a result, students may become interested in new media forms and social issues in the larger Francophone world, and they may then go outside of the classroom to explore more cultural practices, perspectives, and products that they can find independently.

Learning Outcomes of E-journaling

For the e-journal assignment, all three modes of communication are in play: presentational, interpretive, and interpersonal. The e-journal entry focuses on presentational and interpretive modes of communication, and students generally rely more heavily on the presentational (summarizing what they read or heard). Considering the ACTFL performance descriptors, students at this level usually show intermediate range of presentational communication in the target language in this activity, in that their journal entry "[u]ses some culturally appropriate vocabulary, expressions, and gestures [and r]eflects some knowledge of cultural differences related to written and spoken communication" (ACTFL, 2012, 19). To reinforce the culturally appropriate vocabulary that they encounter in the reading, listening, or viewing of these cultural documents, students keep a personal dictionary that complements the work of their journal, and for each journal entry, they add three or four words to the dictionary (see e-journal prompt above). The dictionary is also housed in the e-portfolio, and can be easily accessed throughout the semester by the student, who will thus incorporate these words into her working vocabulary.

A second part of the e-journal assignment is the interactive comments that students leave on their classmates' e-journals. For this aspect of the e-journal assignment, the web program chosen needs to have the possibility to include comment boxes in the e-journal pages. For the comments, students are required to read a classmate's journal entry and to write a short commentary that demonstrates both an understanding and a reaction to the journal. The comments are posted and are available for viewing by the instructor and the entire class. This engages interpretive and interpersonal modes of communication, and students often find this to be one of the most interesting and exciting aspects of the assignment since it allows them to see other students' work and to receive comments on their own work. Occasionally, the required comment turns into a conversation. With the suggested topics leading many students to choose the same texts, films, articles, or podcasts as others in the class, this necessarily creates a shared experience and a focus for conversation in the classroom, on the e-journal, and between classes. Furthermore, because I choose many women's voices as suggested menu options, this collaboration furthers the discussion of global women's issues and women's roles in Francophone cultures in the curriculum, as well as giving students basic familiarity with a variety of Francophone women authors and artists through the semester and the tools to make independent discoveries beyond the coursework.

Finally, in order to promote student interactions with cultural texts and documents on a deeper and more significant level, I ask students to write one or two reflections based on their e-journal at the mid-point and at the end of the semester. This assignment is designed to push them to enhance their interpretive skills, moving from the intermediate range, in which they still rely mainly on their own cultural knowledge, to the advanced range, in which they interact with the cultural product with knowledge of the target culture's practices and products. The first reflection aims at comparison, asking students to reflect on what they learned in one journal entry and to compare the topic to something from their own culture. A second reflection, at the end of the semester, asks students to choose and reflect again on one artifact from their entire e-portfolio and to explain, through reflection on that artifact, their progress in the course in terms of linguistic skills and cultural awareness, and to discuss their future goals in French and as a global citizen. These two reflection assignments are also posted as markers of their progress through the semester.

While the introduction of women's voices into the curriculum through e-journaling is a simple way to develop students' cultural awareness and breadth of knowledge, it is also an effective teaching tool that engages students, guides them toward their own exploration of language and culture as well as to deeper understandings of the practices, products, and perspectives of both their own and other cultures. Using language in context both in interacting with the cultural artifacts through reading and listening as well as writing and interacting about the cultural product reinforces linguistic functions, expands vocabulary, and integrates culture into the virtual language classroom as a supplement and support for the work done in the physical classroom. The amount that a student might gain from these activities is dependent on her motivation, but the role of the instructor is to challenge and drive the student to greater linguistic and cultural proficiency, and hopefully thereby to make the student more motivated to explore these topics on her own. This is a straightforward way to facilitate learning, to move learning outside of the classroom, to draw on the instructor's expertise and interests, and to introduce students to women's voices in French and Francophone culture. Students move from shared texts discussed within the classroom to individual work on the transmission of women's voices through new media in the Francophone world, back again to a collaborative effort of sharing and interaction between classmates, and finally to independent exploration beyond the classroom with women's voices through cultural products that abound in the form of podcasts, articles, interviews, videos, films, and artwork. By motivating learners to interact and expand the classroom into the hybrid space of e-journals and by bringing women's stories, women's issues, and questions of diversity into the e-journal activity, students begin to engage with global inquiries and to move their study of language as text toward a study of language as context for a discussion of global issues and women's voices.

Notes

1 www.metrodemontreal.com/orange/champdemars/index-f.html
2 www.lefigaro.fr/secteur/high-tech/2016/12/26/32001-20161226ARTFIG00004-les-chat-fictions-la-litterature-epistolaire-adaptee-a-la-generation-snapchat.php
3 www.youtube.com/channel/UCpcd7UA71-eBeJnWftXx9HA
4 http://ici.radio-canada.ca/emissions/ya_pas_deux_matins_pareils/2015-2016/chronique.asp?idChronique=434810
5 www.franceinter.fr/emissions/l-esprit-d-initiative/l-esprit-d-initiative-31-aout-2016
6 dai.ly/x4p210q
7 www.lequipe.fr/Medias/Actualites/France-3-fait-polemique-avec-son-clip-de-promotion-des-jo/703813

References

American Council on the Teaching of Foreign Languages. "Performance Descriptors for Language Learners." Alexandria, VA: American Council on the Teaching of Foreign Languages, 2012.
American Council on the Teaching of Foreign Languages. "Global Competence Position Statement." August 25, 2014. www.actfl.org/news/position-statements/global-competence-position-statement.
Champeny, Séverine. *Imaginez: Le Français sans frontières: cours de Français intermédiaire* (3rd edition). Vista, 2016.
Martel, Jason, and Nicole Pettitt. "Mindsets and Tools for Developing Foreign Language Curriculum Featuring Thoughtful Culture-As-Content." *French Review* 90. 2(2016): 171–183.

E-journal Resources

Afrique, Jeune. "Afrimarket: champion des courses en ligne—video Dailymotion." *Dailymotion*, August 17, 2016. dai.ly/x4p210q
"Draw My News." *YouTube*. www.youtube.com/channel/UCpcd7UA71-eBeJnWftXx9HA
"L'Épicerie mobile de produits bio en vrac." *France Inter*, August 31, 2016. www.franceinter.fr/emissions/l-esprit-d-initiative/l-esprit-d-initiative-31-aout-2016

FigaroTech. "Les 'Chat-fictions', la littérature épistolaire adaptée à la génération Snapchat." *Le Figaro*, December 26, 2016. www.lefigaro.fr/secteur/high-tech/2016/12/26/32001-20161226ARTFIG00004-les-chat-fictions-la-litterature-epistolaire-adaptee-a-la-generation-snapchat.php

Granek, Esther. *Ballades et réflexions à ma façon*. Editions Saint-Germain-des-Prés, 1978.

Métro Champ-De-Mars. www.metrodemontreal.com/orange/champdemars/index-f.html

Nokovitch, Sacha. "France 3 fait polémique avec son clip de promotion des JO." *L'Équipe*, July 6, 2016. www.lequipe.fr/Medias/Actualites/France-3-fait-polemique-avec-son-clip-de-promotion-des-jo/703813

Proulx, Monique. "Jaune et Blanc." *Les Aurores Montréales: nouvelles*. Boréal, 2012, 53–57.

Radio-Canada. "Le marketing avec Winy Bernard expansion marquée de la vidéo sur les médias sociaux/Y a pas deux matins pareils." *Radio Canada*. ici.radio-canada.ca/emissions/ya_pas_deux_matins_pareils/2015–2016/chronique.asp?idChronique=434810

7

LINKING BEGINNER AND ADVANCED LANGUAGE LEARNERS THROUGH IMAGES OF WOMEN

Joyce Johnston

François Ozon's 2002 film *8 Women* has been examined by scholars and by mainstream media for its use of camp, queer visual pleasures (Waldron), pastiche (Angelo), and whether it decries feminine subjugation to patriarchy (Pengrum) or simply bolsters stereotypes of femininity (Cairns). The cast of iconic actresses clad in splendid, eye-catching fashion, I have found, evokes a variety of reactions among students: some are fascinated, some repulsed, and some simply do not know what to make of it. Ozon creates a film reminiscent of George Cukor's *The Women* (1939), though it is based on Robert Thomas's 1960s play *8 Femmes*. As he himself has proclaimed, Ozon is not afraid of theatrical style (Lally 3) and plays up the fame of his cast while breaking the fourth wall as the final moments of the film display the actresses lined at the edge of the stage as if ready to take a bow. Everything about the film is over the top. As Roger Ebert explains:

> Here it is at last, the first Agatha Christie musical. Eight women are isolated in a snowbound cottage, there is a corpse with a knife in his back, all of the women are potential suspects, plus six song and dance numbers. The cast is a roll call of French legends.

The women in question are all connected to each other and to the corpse, Marcel, who was husband to Gaby (Catherine Deneuve), father to Suzon (Virginie Ledoyen) and Catherine (Ludivine Sagnier), and brother to Pierrette (Fanny Ardant). Gaby's sister Augustine (Isabelle Huppert) was secretly in love with him, while he has been having an affair with the maid, Louise (Emmanuelle Béart). Gaby's mother, Mamy (Danielle Darrieux), and maid Chanel (Firmine Richard), who is in love with Pierrette, round out the cast of suspects. Throughout the film, each of the screen icons sings an equally iconic French pop song which reveals her inner sentiments.[1] Ozon has stressed that the actresses are made vulnerable by their songs because they do not control this craft as well as they control their acting (Pengrum 81), a fact which has prompted my students to ask why on earth these actresses would all be asked to sing when they don't all do so very well. From these problematic facets often spring the best class discussions in film, culture, or film and literature classes. However, the film also works quite well in the first-semester French-language class allowing students a taste of what they will examine in advanced coursework should they opt to continue along in their French studies. Many instructors shy away from asking students to analyze gender in film in the first semester based upon "the assumption that because introductory-level students have limited linguistic abilities, they cannot engage in activities requiring critical thinking, reflection, or interpretation, nor can they explore social, historical, or cultural perspectives using the FL" (Allen and Paesani 124). I will argue that a critical discussion in a beginner-level class is possible and that gendered themes which surface in Ozon's *8 Women* render it a wonderful text to facilitate analytical discourse even at a beginner level. As one of two full-time French professors at my university, I routinely teach an advanced class and two or three beginner classes during the same semester. I began experimenting how to integrate what I was teaching at one level with the other and I found *8 Women*'s versatility appealing. Using this single cinematic text as the basis of lessons at the same time in both an advanced and an introductory class allowed me to foster a link between the beginner and advanced language learners while emphasizing critical analysis in both classes.

Preliminary Considerations: The Gap in Contemporary Language Teaching

My aim in linking beginner and advanced learners through an examination of a film centered on the representation of societal expectations for women and cinematic clichés embedded in *8 Women* was to address the all-too-common gap between basic (first- and second-year) language classes and advanced coursework. I am by no means the first to underscore the problematic nature of this gap whereby we focus on the mastery of linguistic forms and communication of basic personal information in beginner-level classes often to the exclusion of developing language skills for analytical purposes. Advanced coursework is where students explore loftier topics and employ their critical thinking skills while using the language. Indeed, my challenge has been to make meaningful, content-based, critical discussions doable and engaging for beginner students. Doing so is crucial at my rural, regional university where, due to the small number of high school French programs in our region, the overwhelming majority of our French majors and minors start off in a first-semester class. I cannot realistically expect students to spontaneously discuss social issues and politics a mere two years after beginning their French studies if they are never prompted to examine them prior to undertaking junior-level coursework.

Moreover, while I certainly enjoy getting to learn about my students' family members, pets, classes, and social interests, common points of discussion in a communicative, beginner course, students become too comfortable with this overpersonalized discourse if I do not push them to think beyond their own individual worlds. Cheryl Krueger describes the danger in such an approach: "it is tempting to overpersonalize speaking and writing activities in the lower-level courses ... how will students in language courses learn to express themselves engagingly, if they repetitively narrate and describe details of their lives, with little concern for how this material might anesthetize their audience?" (Krueger 19). Krueger continues, stating that, "personalizing activities too often or too extensively will lead students to become insensitive to their interlocutors and readers, and perhaps by extension to become only mildly engaged listeners and readers themselves" (Krueger 19–20), and correctly asserts that if students only speak about themselves, they tend to repeat their "favorite" phrases as opposed to challenging themselves to take risks with new structures or vocabulary. While textbooks often incorporate modified authentic texts or images to give students the opportunity to go beyond personal narrative in their language production, the inclusion of these tends to be watered down, culturally and socially neutral, and minimally engaging to students. Marianna Ryshina-Pankova has analyzed such textbook images and concludes that the presentation of ostensibly cultural images tends not to "encourage critical engagement with the themes or values under consideration" (171) elements which are inherent to a true understanding of the image in question. It is therefore up to the instructor to seek out written, audio, or visual texts which allow our students to employ even limited language tools to engage in higher-order thinking.

While the lessons I created on *8 Women* were not intentionally based on a multiliteracies approach, they could easily be incorporated into a classroom which centered on this pedagogy. My approach uses the visual text, *8 Women*, as a basis to examine images of women and as an introduction to film analysis. In so doing, beginner students become critical viewers, realizing that texts, including film, are not neutral. Before delving into how I facilitate beginner learners' discussion of *8 Women*, I will first describe possibilities for the second, perhaps more accessible side of the project: that of engaging advanced learners in a discussion of women's roles represented in film and literature.

Textual Possibilities for the Advanced Literature Class

Ozon's film worked well in my beginner literature classes. Clichés of womanhood leap off of the screen in such evident, self-aware fashion that students easily take notice. Thus, the film serves as a nice springboard for the course itself which follows the theme of gender. As is the case with many introductory literature survey classes, the instructor's goal is to introduce many genres, many literary periods, and many styles while helping students further develop their linguistic competencies. This common approach to the survey class exposes students to a variety of literatures, however, the result is often disjointed, a course in which texts are selected solely as language samples appropriate for the level. The theme of images of women in texts by women and men authors is a flexible one which allows for tweaking over the years without fully reinventing a course. During the first day of class I ask students what sort of women characters they are used to seeing in films and books in general. Discussion generally solicits responses such as *femme fatale*, the "good girl," the vamp, the spinster, the mother or mother figure, the strong woman making it in a "man's world," just to name a few. I generally ask students at the advanced level to consider the following in viewing the film: What cinematic female types are presented? Are we to take these types seriously or is there another purpose to Ozon's presentation of them? How does the fact that the film places some of the most recognizable French actresses in clichéd roles affect how we interpret the filmmaker's intent? While I rarely have students who are familiar with the Hollywood melodrama, many of them mention the 1985 film *Clue* which spoofs whodunnits and boasts similarly clichéd performances.

After opening with Ozon's overt presentation of these clichés I am able to move into a literary analysis of texts which present women whose lives disintegrate when they find they are unable to live up to societal expectations. Two texts by women which my students have enjoyed include Sophie Cottin's epistolary novel *Claire d'Albe* (1799) and Simone de Beauvoir's short story "Monologue" (1967), a rant by a (mad)woman. These disparate texts from different time periods share one common theme: women suffer and are condemned as a result of how they are perceived within the patriarchal society of their day. Hence, Ozon's caricatures of the vamp, the virgin, the humble servant, and a range of *femmes fatales* integrate smoothly into other views of women.

The eponymous heroine of *Claire d'Albe* presents a clear case for why unrealistic expectations women encounter, expectations which allow for no self-fulfillment, bring forth disastrous consequences. Through the letters which make up the novel, we learn the story of Claire who, upon her father's death, is married off at age 16 to his best friend, the upstanding and kind M. d'Albe. We later meet Frédéric, the handsome 19-year-old relative M. d'Albe has invited to live at his estate so that he can serve as mentor to the sensitive, but intelligent youth. M. d'Albe intends for Claire to serve as a mother figure to Frédéric, a ridiculous and naïve assumption which ignores the fact that the two are quite destined to fall in love, a detail students pick up on quickly. The remainder of the novel chronicles Claire and Frédéric battling their true feelings for one another, Claire doing so with the goal of staying true to her image as perfect, devoted wife and mother. When the two lovers consummate their passion—literally on the grave of Claire's father—Claire's guilt is so overwhelming that she dies shortly after.

Key discussion questions for students as they explore this novel involve the status of women and marriage shortly after the French Revolution when the novel takes place. Essential to understanding the novel itself is projecting to the students that marriage and love, at the time, did not go hand in hand. In Cottin's novel, marriage can only lead to the annihilation of the wife given unrealistic societal expectations which force women to ignore their own passions in favor of submission to her husband. We discuss if the story had a lesson for women (or men) of Cottin's day. Two centuries later, Ozon too underscores that women remain trapped in and by marriage through the character of Mamy who reveals to her daughter, Augustine, that in her day divorce was not an option (Pengrum 82). Hence, although she is presented as a murderess (she has killed her husband to escape her marriage) and alcoholic, the director offers an explanation if not a justification for her acts. Gaby, however, demonstrates that more recent generations have somewhat more liberty than their predecessors. As Pengrum explains:

> (Gaby's) preparations to quit her husband for her lover suggest a degree of freedom unavailable to her own mother, and yet equally indicate the perpetuation of female dependence on men, making it clear why not only the legal but the economic liberation of women has long been a priority of liberal feminisms.
>
> *(83)*

The character of Suzon from *8 Women* serves as an interesting counterpoint to Claire in that both are expected to embody the idealized woman of their day, yet both fall short when they prove to be morally flawed. Suzon, who early on assumes the position of detective upon return home from school, seems the most level-headed of all the women in the household. However, it is later revealed that she is pregnant with Marcel's child, a man she assumes (incorrectly) to be her father. Her credibility seems instantly impinged.

My students have often used the term "crazy" to describe both film and characters. Indeed, the deliberately hysterical exchanges among the characters support this interpretation. The film nonetheless serves as an accessible segue into exploring women and sanity. Paired with Simone de Beauvoir's "Monologue," it can be a perfect introductory text for students new to discussing this topic in a second language. The text presents the first-person rant of Muriel, a woman whose daughter has committed suicide and whose first and second husband have both abandoned her. Muriel's monologue presents key characters (Albert, her first husband; Tristan, her second husband; Sylvie, her deceased daughter she had with Albert) providing neither context nor background. The style is deliberately confusing and forces the reader to reconstruct who is who. For this reading our first day examining "Monologue" is devoted to sorting out who the characters are. Day 2 allows us to focus on deeper considerations including Muriel's narcissism, her feelings of being trapped in a society which judges her constantly on her looks, her mothering, and her ability to seem the perfect wife. The most disturbing—and perhaps the one which elicits the most intense class discussion—is de Beauvoir's presentation of Muriel's inability to accept what is obvious to all others: that her overbearing mothering led to Sylvie's suicide. In her attempt to initiate Sylvie into "womanhood" which, for her, means living a morally perfect life she essentially smothers her daughter whose suicide note underscores that she cannot exist in such a world. Muriel thus serves as the strong arm of the patriarchy, stifling Sylvie much as in the case of Claire d'Albe. Students react to Muriel's rants with both laughter and shock. As a follow-up activity, students are asked to write their own monologue modeled on de Beauvoir's. They have produced humorous pastiches (a student during finals week lashing out at unreasonable professors and their assignments) as well as haunting narratives (one student wrote from the perspective of a jilted lover plotting revenge). The advanced students' connections to the film and texts taught alongside it, I have observed, have enhanced their interactions with beginner students tackling the same content.

Coming Full Circle: Connecting Advanced and Beginner Learners

Clearly, advanced students are capable of far more complex expression than their beginner counterparts, but at some point they too were in the beginners' shoes. I use this often recent memory to my advantage as I teach *8 Women* in first-semester French. At the beginner level, students' discourse remains mostly descriptive. In first-semester French courses students typically learn colors, clothing, physical description, personality traits, emotions, and gender of adjectives. Particularly in the case of colors, instructors across the board develop imaginative games or have students describe the colors of what they are wearing, etc. However, the tendency is stay on a surface rather than analytical level when treating these vocabulary sets. And while college students enjoy the occasional silly game like color bingo, such activities tend to infantilize them and fail to enhance their critical thinking skills. Herein lies what has been my greatest challenge in teaching first-semester students: how do I offer students the opportunity to engage in critical thinking when they have little proficiency in the language at hand? Some instructors opt to include in-depth, critical essays in English, and indeed for state assessment purposes this action is necessary. However, I contend that when students discover that they can analyze gender and cinema while using their French, we spark their interest on a higher level.

Thus, I find that studying the film *8 Women* in a first-semester French class offers students the opportunity to do just this. My approach melds use of the vocabulary typical in a first-semester class with overarching concepts from the film and for discussing images of women. As an example, in any beginner course students learn the basic colors. When viewing Ozon's film, one cannot help but be struck by the vibrant colors and by the fact that each actress has a designated shade which refers to either her true character or the image she intends to portray to others. For example, Virginie Ledoyen's character Suzon wears a prim pink 1950s skirt and sweater buttoned to the neck. While she seems to be the perfect, innocent daughter, she is actually pregnant by a man whom she thinks is her father. The vampy Fanny Ardant wears a tight-fitting red ensemble with hints of black, while prude aunt Augustine (Isabelle Hupert) wears a frumpy brown outfit up until her transformation into a siren who dons a slinky aqua, mermaid-like dress. Prior to viewing the film, I conduct an in-class activity which asks students to associate ideas to basic colors. On one side of the whiteboard or chalkboard I make a list of colors. To the right I write the words *émotions/associations*. For example, regarding the color red, students often call out the following French terms: *passion, danger, furieux, sexy*. A worksheet I give them to use when viewing the film contains a table which lists all eight women characters to the left. French column headings ask for words related to *physical description, personality*, and *associated color*. I then ask students questions regarding why characters wear the colors they do and what this represents. Students quickly recognize visual cognates *représente, ironique*, and even *évoque* which is a term that allows them to express sophisticated thoughts within a simple sentence.[2] For each character I ask students, "What is her secret?" as each character indeed has a secret ranging from gambling to murder, lesbianism to financial wrong-doing. Inevitably, a student comments that in the film "il n'y a pas d'hommes" (there are no men) which, although a simple phrase, brings forth an essential facet of the movie.

One can also preview the film for students and prepare them for what they are about to see by showing them the opening scene in class. Immediately following the opening credits, the majority of the cast enters one at a time in the following order: Suzon, Mamy, Chanel, Gaby, Louise, Augustine, Catherine. The instructor should show this scene from the moment Suzon walks into the house up until the Catherine's song and dance number without sound, assigning small groups each a character to analyze. She can ask students to brainstorm any aspect related to the character, but obvious prompts would involve the colors they wear, age, whether they seem rich or poor, confident or submissive, and their emotional state. The actresses play their roles in melodramatic, exaggerated fashion which gives students a variety of obvious elements to describe. After students present their character, the instructor can ask them for predictions about what they were saying or what they might do in the film. At this point, the instructor can either play the scene with subtitles or can leave the students to view the film on their own as homework to return for a class discussion at a later time.

After students have seen the film outside of class, I put them in groups during class and ask them to consider the following categories: women as types, color symbolism, and transformation.[3] This is an ambitious task as I ask students to move from basic description characteristic of the level to analysis despite limited vocabulary. To alleviate their frustration and to add variety to the class, I enlist my advanced students who have also studied the film to help the beginners. Part of my advanced students' grade was an assignment based on coming to a beginner class to serve as group leaders for discussions topics I mentioned above. I devoted one class period with the advanced group to what to expect when working with beginners, how to avoid English, how to help the beginners express complex thoughts with access to a limited linguistic tool box, what leading questions to ask, etc. I asked them to remember how they felt in French class just a couple of years prior. When they came to class they sat with groups of students. The advanced student helped the beginners brainstorm terms related to color symbolism, stereotypes of women, and transformation, topics assigned to the groups of four–five. After about ten minutes of group work, the advanced students left the groups and each group presented their ideas on their topic to the rest of the class. Quieter students seemed at ease asking their peers for help.

Manipulatively, I always "accidentally" end this class session a few minutes early. This results in beginners chatting with the advanced students after class and hearing what it is like to study at a higher level. My advanced students end up "selling" our program, giving study tips and validating the beginners' experiences. At times the advanced students learned new insight into the film from the beginners and, often, the students continue to discuss the film after class—in English, yes, but I am indeed pleased at the connections. Notably, on the beginners' final exam students had to write an essay about the film on a topic related to the discussion. I found they were able to discuss feminine stereotypes, fetish, and color symbolism in paragraphs that went beyond "décrivez votre famille" or "décrivez votre maison" as one finds on the typical French I exam. Thus, when writing the final test for the course, students focus on analysis and move away from simple personal narrative.

Our educational institutions are as diverse a group as we are: some of us teach in large departments where teaching assistants handle first-year courses while others of us routinely teach all levels of French. Whatever our situation, we all must be concerned with enrollment, recruitment, and retention at all levels. I have presented but one idea for using a single cultural text at different levels and for fostering interaction and peer teaching. Admittedly, beginner students' advanced peers often serve as more effective recruiters than faculty. Through creating these connections I hope to continue to foster a sense of community within the French program.

Notes

1 The actresses perform popular songs "Toi jamais" by Michal Mallory, "Mon Amour, mon ami" by Eddy Marnay, popularized by Marie Laforêt, and Dalida's hit "Pour ne pas vivre seule," to name a few. One could ask students to research popular music artists or songs as an offshoot activity.
2 It is helpful to offer students a list of vocabulary including of *sembler, tuer, amoureuse, enceinte, une liaison, servante, lesbienne, bisexuelle,* and other terms which, while rather simple, allow them to interpret the film with greater depth.
3 Because the French terms for these are cognates, one can easily avoid using English in this activity.

References

Allen, Heather Willis and Kate Paesani. "Exploring the Feasibility of a Pedagogy of Multiliteracies in Introductory Foreign Language Courses." *L2 Journal* 2(2010): 119–142. https://escholarship.org/uc/item/9rd471cs

Angelo, Adrienne. "'C'est une joie et une souffrance': Mimetic Speech and Generic Pastiche in François Ozon's 8 Femmes," in *Patois and Linguistic Pastiche in Modern Literature*. Cambridge, 2007, 119–129.

Beauvoir, Simone de. "Monologue," in *La Femme rompue*. Gallimard, 1987.

Cairns, Laura. *Saphism on Screen: Lesbian Desire in French and Francophone Cinema*. Edinburgh University Press, 2006.

Cottin, Sophie. *Claire d'Albe*. MLA, 2002.

Ebert, Roger. "8 Women Movie Review and Summary." September 27, 2002. www.rogerebert.com/reviews/8-women-2002

Krueger, Cheryl. "Form Content, and Critical Distance: The Role of 'Creative Personalization' in Language Content Courses." *Foreign Language Annals* 34. 1(2001): 18–25.

Lally, Kevin. "Femmes Fatales: François Ozon Directs Legendary French Divas in 8 Women Ensemble." *Film Journal International*, October 27, 2004.

Pengrum, Mark. "Virgins, Vixens, Vamps and Victims" François Ozon's 8 *Femmes* and the Sexual (Sub) texts of French Popular Culture." *Australian Journal of French Studies* 42. 1(2005): 76–93.

Ryshina-Pankova, Marianna. "Understanding 'Green Germany' through Images and Film: A Critical Literacy Approach." *Dei Unterrichtspraxis/Teaching German* 46. 12(2014): 163–184.

Waldron, Darren. "'Une Mine d'or inépuisable': The Queer Pleasures of Francois Ozon's 8 *Femmes*/8 Women (2002)." *Studies in French Cinema* 10. 1(2010): 69–87.

8

BUILDING BRIDGES FROM LANGUAGE TO CIVILIZATION THROUGH GISÈLE PINEAU'S *UN PAPILLON DANS LA CITÉ*

Natalie Edwards and Christopher Hogarth

This chapter discusses a French civilization course that uses the work of a Francophone woman writer to explore, nuance, and further students' understanding of French society. The course is intermediate level; students have completed one year of intensive beginners' language training before moving onto this course. French civilization, or a version of this title, is a standard offering in many French curricula in the United States and is normally conceived as a content course that presents students with an overview of important elements of French history and of contemporary society. Students study cultural materials relating to France and the Francophone world and thus build both their linguistic and cultural competence. Some instructors use literary texts, such as short stories or excerpts, to supplement the non-literary course material. In our course, by contrast, we use a literary text as the central organization of the course readings: Gisèle Pineau's *Un papillon dans la cité*. The specific innovation of this course is that the literary text is the focal point that provides the thematic and sequential basis of the course. We taught this course for several years in a small liberal arts college in New York City and have since adapted it to different courses in Australia. In this article, we first present the theoretical underpinnings that determine the shape of the course. We then discuss the course itself and how we manipulate the literary text in order to foster a series of specific learning outcomes.

Theoretical Underpinnings

We both began teaching French civilization according to a traditional approach; we focused upon the historical context of twentieth- and twenty-first-century France, aiming to provide an overview of political, cultural, and social institutions. Our course was divided into modules such as "The Five Republics," "Political Institutions," and "The Family in France." We worked from textbooks that presented authentic, non-literary material in the target language and our assessment focused on students demonstrating their understanding of these discreet modules. We soon realized that compartmentalizing French and Francophone culture into a series of artificially separated units was a jarring way of approaching our material. We concluded that we were presenting culture in the same way as a language textbook presented grammar: as a series of building blocks that contribute successively to a set of functional skills and knowledge. While it is sensible to move from a module on the present tense to one on the perfect tense and on to another on the imperfect, it seems far less so to move from a module on the family to another on religion to another on regional France. Instead, we developed an approach that is based upon fluidity, emphasizing connections between aspects of culture and society and upon the links between France and the Francophone world. We first revised our learning outcomes of the course. These were based upon students demonstrating an understanding of the major historical developments and the most important social institutions. We revised them to encourage students to demonstrate an awareness of *positions* and *perspectives*. That is to say that we cannot give an overview of French and Francophone cultures within a semester but we can give students the tools to understand how different individuals and groups are positioned and what kinds of perspectives this may lead them to develop. Our course is grounded in four interlinking theoretical positions that together form the basis of the structure, materials, outcomes, and evaluation.

The first theoretical position is linguistic. One of our principal aims in the course is to challenge and support students in the transition from beginner to intermediate level in this crucial stage in the language curriculum. When students arrive in our course, they have had one year of intensive study of the French language. They are therefore able to read and understand basic material but struggle to respond in speech and writing to more complex tasks. This is a notoriously difficult stage in language learning since students are required to broaden their linguistic and cultural competence and to perform a wider range of cognitive and analytical tasks. Moreover, students in an intermediate course have varied levels of linguistic skills and cultural and intercultural understanding and they have different motivations for studying language and culture. Applied linguist Beatrice Dupuy notes that first-year language courses are aimed at developing social language proficiency, which consists of basic interpersonal communication skills (BICS), and that this is the main reason for the gap—she in fact calls it a "chasm"—between beginner and intermediate stages (206). Our awareness of the multiple difficulties in this stage of language learning led us to experiment with a single literary text that would provide focus and continuity through the semester. Students are required to read other non-fiction materials of increasing difficulty but the literary text at the core of the course brings them back to something that they can read and understand, and something to which they can come back, throughout the semester. The literary text that runs through the whole course functions like an island of safety to which students can return amid the more challenging material.

The second theoretical position that we use to inform our approach in this course concerns the transition between language and literature courses. In many university departments in the U.S., U.K., and Australia, a dichotomy has developed between "language courses" and "literature courses" and—even more disturbingly to us—between the teaching staff who are responsible for the two strands. We both hold Ph.D.s in literary studies but consider ourselves modern linguists whose teaching stems from our commitment to exploring, understanding, and analyzing literature and culture. We aim in all of our courses to bridge language and culture in a way that melds the two and refutes any false dichotomy between them. We have both taught all levels, from first-year French to the senior capstone course, in French, comparative literature, and literary studies. We demonstrate a commitment to language and literature across all of these levels and believe that a separation between language and culture is a forced, unnatural division. This notion is emphasized by scholars in the field of intercultural communication, who highlight the need to foster awareness of the language–culture nexus, as opposed to teaching language and culture as separate and discreet entities. Anthony J. Liddicoat and Angela Scarino, for example, state that "as the processes of globalization, increased mobility, and technological development have come to shape ways of living and communicating, there has been a growing recognition of the fundamental importance of integrating intercultural capabilities into language teaching and learning" (1). Moreover, we take issue with the practice of labeling literature courses as "content courses" since we believe that all of our courses are content courses regardless of the proportion of literary to linguistic content. In this course, therefore, we have developed a curriculum that is based upon the simultaneous study of language, culture, and literature and approaches all three as a necessary part of the mosaic of French and Francophone societies. Our lessons are not divided into a "grammar lesson," a "vocabulary lesson," or a "literature lesson," for example, but instead incorporate a variety of materials that we present as intersecting. Positioning the literary text at the center of the course enables us to exploit it to foster learning objectives that are linguistic, cultural, and literary; our lessons consist of structured and unstructured oral and written exercises that push students to learn about the language and culture at the same time, rather than by introducing a false dichotomy between them.

Third, we consider ourselves to be practitioners of a teaching–research nexus in which our teaching informs our research and vice versa. As scholars of gender theory and women's writing, we have a strong commitment to gender equity and we approach our teaching from a social justice perspective. We continually strive to render our courses as inclusive as possible, in terms of our course material, our choice of classroom activities, and our modes of assessment. Inspired by scholars such as Maurianne Adams, Lee Anne Bell, and Pat Griffin, an awareness of oppression and social justice is crucial to our pedagogical practice, and we aim to find ways both to challenge oppression and to promote social justice through our teaching. Particularly in a discipline such as French literature that has a traditional canon that is predominantly male, this can be challenging. Brian Nelson in the recent *Cambridge Introduction to French Literature* devotes 29 chapters to individual writers in the French tradition, from Villon to Beckett (supplemented by a thirtieth chapter entitled "French Literature into the Twenty-First Century"). Only one chapter is dedicated to a woman writer: Madame de Lafayette. By contrast, we aim to work in a position of resistance to exclusion and invisibility through the core materials of our courses. We teach writers and texts that present to students an array of subject positions: writers such as Julian Green, Hervé Guibert, and Fatou Diome and texts such as *Journal du Voleur, Thérèse et Isabelle*, and *Ourika*, for example. In the course in question here, we chose a first-person narrative by a woman writer whose narrator is black and from a Francophone region. The fact that Gisèle Pineau's text is partially autobiographical furthers the work that we can do in this course as we empower the students to read a first-person account of racial, socio-economic, linguistic, and gendered prejudice.

The fourth theoretical underpinning is of a geographical and socio-cultural nature. As Nelson's volume also demonstrates, "French literature" has traditionally been considered as a monolithic entity that unites a specific language, history, people, and space. Traditional survey courses of French literature span centuries of well-known, influential writers such as Rabelais, Balzac, Stendhal, Apollinaire, and Colette. As scholars of migrant, diasporic, and African literature, we also aim to incorporate into our courses not just Francophone authors but authors who demonstrate the interconnectedness of France and the Francophone world. The "global turn" in French studies has contributed to a renewed understanding of French culture as the product of mobility and movement: a productive contamination that suggests that "French literature" is a highly restricted term. Christine McDonald and Susan Suleiman contend in *French Global* that the history of French literature is not unitary or monolithic but is instead the product of myriad cultural influences over centuries. Mireille Rosello also suggests that France's position at the Mediterranean crossroads has given rise to a series of "performative encounters" that render French culture a myriad, plural construction. The term "national literature" may be a comfortable moniker that denotes a familiarity and a boundary that can be known or mastered, but in reality it may be a misnomer. In this vein, we attempt in our courses to emphasize the movement between France and its former colonies and between France and the rest of the world. By studying *Un papillon dans la cité*, students gain insights into an example of the interconnectedness of France and the Francophone world. The text centers upon a migrant subject written by an author from the diaspora. The plot moves from Guadeloupe to France and the first-person narrator emphasizes her cultural, linguistic, and historical plurality.

The Course

From the first day, we inform students that the literary text comes first and is the spine of the course. This approach is quite different to their previous language courses, which are structured around a textbook. On the first day of class we read the first pages of the text together, speculate upon the meaning of the book's title and discuss the identity of the narrator. Pineau's text is narrated by a child and tells the tale of her journey from Guadeloupe to Paris. Félicie is ten years old at the beginning of the story and lives in a hut with her grandmother in rural Guadeloupe. The text recounts her journey to a *cité* on the outskirts of Paris, where her mother lives with her partner and their young child. We follow Félicie's development through approximately three years, as she goes to school and on to *collège* in this impoverished, multiracial, and multilingual environment. The fact that it is narrated by a child who gives her perspective in first-person narrative renders the vocabulary and grammar relatively simple. Students find it challenging to read an entire novel after one year of study of the language but the fact that we devote a whole semester to it and support them through a variety of other materials makes it a manageable task.

The book contains five chapters and we divide the course into five thematic units that link the chapters to the course objectives. We begin each unit by studying the literary text, then examine non-literary materials in the following week. In Unit 1, "French beyond France," students begin by reading the first chapter of *Un papillon dans la cité*, which is set in Guadeloupe. We focus class discussions on the experiences of an individual living in a colonized nation, pointing to the fact that the official capital of Guadeloupe is Paris, that citizens of Guadeloupe have French citizenship, and that residents vote in French presidential elections. We pay particular attention to the representation of language, since the text includes Creole. Following the study of this chapter, we assign a non-literary passage from the textbook *La France contemporaine* that presents the countries of the Francophone world. We teach about the ROM (*Régions d'outre-mer*) and the colonial legacy, discussing France's colonial *mission civilisatrice*. We study a speech given by Jules Ferry, available on the website of the *Assemblée Nationale*, in defense of this, which also paves the way for later discussions of the laws on *laïcité* with which Ferry's name is associated. Our American students were surprised to learn that a French territory still exists in the Americas – Guyana – and our Australian students are always enthralled by the proximity of Wallis et Futuna, Tahiti, and New Caledonia, which are only two hours by plane from Sydney. The literary text is thus the motor that drives the course content and allows students to engage with the core concepts of the course in a different way to that offered by traditional, non-literary material.

Following "France beyond France," our second topic is "Immigration in France." Chapter 2 of *Un papillon dans la cité* recounts Félicie's journey from Guadeloupe to Paris at the behest of her mother. In class, we focus upon the discrepancies between Félicie's expectations of France and the reality of her experience. Her knowledge of France has come from magazines and textbooks so she is unprepared for the impoverished *cité* and the multiracial community in which she finds herself. We highlight the many nationalities mentioned in the text and discuss how the text represents cultural assimilation. Following study of the text, we use supplementary, non-literary materials to provide other perspectives of the experiences of immigrants in France. We show clips from films such as *De l'autre côté de la Périph* and *The Intouchables* to offer contemporary representations of social differences in urban contexts. In addition, students listen to rap songs by Francophone immigrants like Corneille and Abd Al Malik recounting their experiences in metropolitan France and Canada (such as "Seul au monde" and "Parce qu'on vient de loin" by the former and "Les autres" and "Soldat de plomb" by the latter). The songs expose students to the varying registers of French used in the *banlieue*, including the common *verlan* (Pig Latin, contained in Malik's song *Allogène (j'suis un stremon)*, for example). To accompany these popular materials, we include an academic resource about the history of immigration which was developed by the French Museum of the History of Immigration (www.histoire-immigration.fr). The site contains a 40-minute film tracing immigration to France from 1676 onwards and includes a series of thematic dossiers on working patterns of immigrants in France, participation of foreigners in wars for France, and integration and xenophobia (the site is progressively adding materials as it aims to become an online encyclopedia of the history of immigration). Students are instructed to read one of the multimedia portraits of individual immigrants in France on a weekly basis and to listen to podcasts from the site's "Univercité" about specific issues linked to migration, such as "Migration and French Music" and "Psychological Life of Refugees." We inevitably discuss the rise in popularity of the French *Front National* from its founding by Jean-Marie Le Pen, to its current formation under Marine Le Pen. The evolution of the party's inflammatory anti-immigration policies is of particular interest to students of history and politics and we examine excerpts from speeches by each Le Pen, as well as those from opposition movements such as *SOS racisme*.

We use *Un papillon dans la cité* as a link to the next topic of the course, which is religion in France. The text portrays a successful relationship between the Catholic Félicie and her Muslim classmate Mohamed Ben Doussan. Mohamed lives in the *cité* in an identical apartment to Félicie's but its interior is very different. The text provides lengthy descriptions of the two apartments, contrasting Félicie's quiet, understated space with the abundant cultural and religious symbols in the home of the North African family. Mohamad's grandmother—an important parallel to Félicie's grandmother in Guadeloupe—introduces her to couscous and loukoum and to the stories of the Muslim family's ancestors. We examine representations of Christianity and Islam in France. We move from the literary text to a selection of newspaper articles. We first discuss an article about "l'affaire du voile" from *Confluences Méditerranée* and use this as a vehicle to discuss the separation of Church and State in France. We then examine the official French government site www.diplomatie.fr, which lists and responds to "10 Misconceptions about Islam and Muslims in France." Since our aim is to explore various French portrayals of interfaith relationships, we also watch clips of the film *Monsieur Ibrahim*, which portrays the relationship between a Jewish child and a Muslim neighbor. We supplement this viewing with extracts from Eric-Emmanuel Schmitt's novella *Monsieur Ibrahim et les fleurs du Coran*, asking students to compare the language associated with religion in this and Pineau's text (specifically the celebration of Christmas, pp. 46–52). Finally, we look at the place of religion as set out in 1905 *loi Ferry* as well as the 1789 *Déclaration des droits de l'homme et du citoyen* (article 10) and in the first article of the 1958 Constitution of the French Fifth Republic.

The literary text again provides the bridge to the next part of the course, which studies political and social institutions. Félicie goes to a *collège* in the *cité*, despite the fact that her primary school teacher advised her mother to send Félicie to another school due to her academic potential. Alongside the representation of education in France, this part of the text also represents the social welfare system in France, referring to the precarious situation of the migrant families, their professional opportunities, and their health and social provision. We discuss these representations in class, focusing upon Félicie's perspective of the impact of social institutions upon individuals. We then study an excerpt from a textbook on social welfare law in France. We highlight social provision such as unemployment benefit, the extent of which is often surprising to American students. We also examine websites that demonstrate important aspects of family law in France. We discuss French government initiatives to increase the birth rate, for example, such as monthly allocations paid to families who have more than one child and the former policy of awarding medals to mothers who had large numbers of children. We present the major political parties in France and ask students to research these parties' positions on social issues by examining their official websites. We then ask them to play the roles of different party representatives in mock debates over immigration, religion, and France's colonial past.

The final chapter of *Un Papillon dans la cité* leads to an examination of gender equity in France, the final topic of the course. The text recounts the experiences of a young female in largely female households. There are very few male characters in this text since Pineau is clearly concerned with presenting the impact of migration upon women in particular. We discuss the series of female characters, asking the students to compare and contrast the situation of each one, including the French school teacher, the two grandmothers, the Guyanese childminder who has 11 infants in her charge, and Félicie's mother: a seamstress in a "sweat shop" factory who instructs Félicie to tell her school friends that her mother works "dans l'habillement" (67). Following the study of the literary text, we examine an excerpt from a textbook that shows the major developments in *la condition de la femme* in France, from Olympe de Gouges's "Déclaration des droits de la femme et de la citoyenne" to the present day. In particular, we discuss the evolution of the body that is now called "le ministère de l'égalité entre les femmes et les hommes" (literally, the Ministry for Equality between Women and Men). The beginnings of the body as a state secretariat under Valéry Giscard d'Estaing and its varying fortunes as a ministry created by François Mitterrand also allows us to introduce students to influential French political figures. More importantly, however, we take the opportunity to introduce students to French laws pertaining to women and to the fundamentals of French feminist thought. We circulate a document entitled "Les femmes et la République en France," which we have adapted from the website of the *Association Thucydide* and which provides an outline of the history of women's rights in France and ends with a list of ten key dates in women's working rights. The list is especially interesting to South Australian students, who rarely hesitate to point out that women in their state received the right to vote in 1894, 8 years before the federal Australian parliament granted women's suffrage, and more than 50 years before their counterparts in stereotypically liberal France. We finally consider the evolution of the female author in Francophone literature, pointing to the relative rarity of black Francophone female writers even today. Thus we underline the accomplishment of Pineau in becoming a successful author of international acclaim and compare her trajectory to that of other contemporary black female writers living in France, such as Calixthe Beyala and Fatou Diome.

The assessment materials that we have developed in this course are fourfold. First, we use regular in-class reading tests to ensure comprehension of the texts. Second, we have developed a series of structured oral and written activities that are assigned regularly throughout the semester. In one such assessment, students work in pairs to prepare and present to the class a conversation between Félicie and her grandmother ten years after the events recounted in the text. As an example of a written assessment, students individually write a series of diary entries that Félicie could have written as a diary. Third, we assign group presentations on social/cultural phenomena that require students to carry out their own research. Crucially, we have moved from asking students to research a specific topic or question to asking the students to generate their own topic based upon their interpretation of the text. For example, some students have been inspired to research the idea of social classes in France, others have researched the various Creole languages in the world, life in the *banlieue*, the military involvement of former colonies in French wars, and patterns of migration from Africa to Europe. The final assessment is a longer written assignment in which students are required to analyze the representation of one of the five course topics in *Un papillon dans la cité*. They are obliged to consult at least five sources, all of which must be in French. This is a difficult task but we have spent the semester modeling how to use websites, newspapers, and academic resources to shed light upon a literary text, so students are generally well prepared for the challenge.

Students' reactions to the course have been very positive. Students find it challenging to read a whole novel in French after just one year of language study. Nevertheless, they are often surprised to realize at the end of the semester that they have achieved something of which they did not initially feel capable. They are able to follow the story of Félicie and understand the nuances of her situation as a migrant in a French *cité*. Moreover, since this is a first-person text that is partially autobiographical, they are able to understand the impact of forces such as migration, colonialism, and poverty on one individual. Nancy K. Miller observes that many texts of life writing entail a process of identification and de-identification between the reader and the narrator, which in this case leads to a sensitive and nuanced appreciation of aspects of contemporary French culture (11). Furthermore, the course appeals to a wide variety of students' interests since it melds literary and non-literary texts and focuses on an array of aspects of French culture.

Overall, then, positioning a woman writer at the center of a course on French civilization enables us to develop an alternative approach to the study of French culture. Rather than presenting French culture as a series of compartmentalized, discreet units as directed by a textbook, this course uses a literary text with a first-person narrator to enable students to see the connections between cultural practices. *Un papillon dans la cité* demonstrates how individuals may be positioned within cultures and how they may develop perspectives as a result of this. We insist that this is one character's experience and should not be taken to represent the whole of France. Nevertheless, this literary text provides a fresh perspective that students at this level can understand and use as a springboard to examining French and Francophone cultures autonomously. Our main goal in our approach to French civilization is to demonstrate that France is not a monolithic, monoethnic, monolingual, or monoracial entity and *Un papillon dans la cité* is an invaluable tool in doing so.

References

"L'affaire du voile: repères." *Confluences Méditerranée* 59. 4(2006): 31. www.cairn.info/revue-confluences-mediterranee-2006-4-page-31.htm. Accessed May 25, 2018.

L'Assemblée nationalie. "Jules Ferry: Les fondements de la politique coloniale (28 juillet 1885)." www2.assemblee-nationale.fr/decouvrir-l-assemblee/histoire/grands-moments-d-eloquence/jules-ferry-28-juillet-1885

L'Association Thucydide. "Les femmes et la République en France." www.thucydide.com/realisations/comprendre/femmes/femmes7.htm. Accessed May 25, 2018.

De l'autre côté de la Périph'. Film. Dir. David Charhon. M6 Films, 2012.
Dupuy, Beatrice C. "Content-Based Instruction: Can It Help Ease the Transition from Beginning to Advanced Foreign Language Classes?" *Foreign Language Annals* 33. 2(2000): 205–223.
The Intouchables. Film. Dir. Olivier Nakache and Éric Toledano. Gaumont, 2011.
Liddicoat, Anthony J. and Angela Scarino, eds. *Intercultural Language Teaching and Learning*. Wiley-Blackwell, 2013.
McDonald, Christie and Susan Rubin Suleiman, eds. *French Global: A New Approach to Literary History*. Columbia University Press, 2011.
Miller, Nancy K. *But Enough about Me: Why We Read Other People's Lives*. Columbia University Press, 2002.
Nelson, Brian. *The Cambridge Introduction to French Literature*. Cambridge University Press, 2015.
Pineau, Gisèle. *Un papillon dans la cité*. Sepia, 1992.
Rosello, Mireille. *France and the Maghreb: Performative Encounters*. University Press of Florida, 2005.
Schmitt, Eric-Emmanuel. *Monsieur Ibrahim et les fleurs du Coran*. Magnard, 2006.

PART III

Colonial and Postcolonial French Women Writers: Teaching Diversity on Shifting Ground

9

PEOPLES, AUTHORS, PROTAGONISTS

Teaching Francophone Women Authors through Gender Identity Themes

Laurence M. Porter

Of what are women capable? On this subject, our beliefs are social constructs, and popular expectations limit the training that women receive; in turn, such discrimination limits their prospects for leadership and advancement. My own eyes were opened one day in the weight room of the Michigan Athletic Club, when I saw an average-sized woman leg-press 950 pounds. In mid-May 2017, the first group of women graduated from the 14-week U.S. Infantry training boot camp, having matched the physical standards required of the men. In politics, on May 17, 2017, the newly elected President of France, Emmanuel Macron, appointed a cabinet of ministers that immediately achieved four major goals: shrinking government (from 37 ministerial posts to 22); eliminating most professional politicians (only two holdovers remained); attaining *parité* (11 of the 22 were women); and avoiding gender stereotyping (women ministers were placed in charge of several conventionally "masculine" domains such as the economy, defense, and sports (the new minister of which had won an Olympic gold medal in fencing).

What does this have to do with literature, and what does literature have to do with the real world? Good literature inspires us with visions of better worlds, warns us against possible worse ones, and enriches our imagination with realistic depictions of existing worlds we have not yet encountered. Excluding the special case of Haiti, after World War II and especially after 1954, the former French colonies over four continents gained either independence or the right to representation in the French government. Soon, many excellent Francophone women writers emerged (in Canada, they arguably equal or excel male writers both in quantity and quality): the crux of most of their writings is a searching examination and re-evaluation of traditional gender-based identity themes—of life possibilities for the formerly silent majority of the population: women. Both by criticizing the patriarchy from the outside (items 1–2), and by creating new and more just fictional worlds of their own (items 3–5), contemporary Francophone women authors have contested traditional male political and social views of appropriate gender roles.

1. Through a fictional biography that creates a realistic portrait of a well-meaning but ineffectual male national leader, the woman writer vicariously associates herself with a leadership role, while demonstrating superior insight that would have avoided her—unlike the male protagonist—becoming ensnared by a corrupt political system (West Africa: Aminata Sow Fall, *L'Ex-père de la nation*).

2. Through a philosophical perspective, the woman writer deconstructs the patriarchal myths dominant in society by exposing their absurdities and internal contradictions (Québec: Louky Bersianik, *L'Eugélionne*—not treated in this chapter, but appropriate for an honors or graduate class).
3. Imagining a world where a woman escapes subjugation to males, and is freed for travel and adventure (Maghreb and France: Leila Sebbar, *Les Carnets de Shérazade*).
4. Depicting a realistic fictional world in which women altruists of superior strength of character manage to preserve society despite male selfishness and irresponsibility (Québec: Arlette Cousture, *Les Filles de Caleb*).
5. Imaging a mythic world in which a heroic female leader—implicitly compared to the Old Testament Moses—leads a people out of exile, through a wilderness to their rightful homeland (Maritime Provinces of Canada: Antonine Maillet, *Pélagie La Charette*).

Each example in this list is taken from a different area of the postcolonial Francophone world, not so much in order to "cover everything," but rather to dissociate the issues of gender and postcolonial identity construction from a specific location, and to introduce students to the wide varieties of postcolonial feminist writing.

Syllabus Week 1: General Background

Francophone women authors have had to struggle against three interwoven, mutually reinforcing traditions that have long denied them due recognition and autonomy.

Military Domination

Introduction to the rise and fall of the French Empire and the history of colonization, which created a *cultural substrate* (the original inhabitants) and *superstrate* (the new rulers), into which a few members of the substrate may be *assimilated*. One can discuss distinctions among *territories, languages* (versus *patois* and dialects), *religions, cultures,* and *races*. The concept of race is particularly arbitrary. Eventually, organized groups of the substrate may secure greater autonomy (Canadian Maritime Provinces and Québec Province) or even national independence (Haiti, countries in West and North Africa). Because literature usually seeks coherence by focusing on one strand of salient historical events at a time, because it creates themes (suggestions concerning the meaning of life) by selecting and simplifying, students can gain a clearer sense of its messages by studying the complex historical backgrounds of realistic fictions such as those read in this course. I recommend assigning each student a five-minute oral presentation covering the places and periods treated in our required readings, and explaining the significance of the selections of topics by each author from among the possibilities offered by history.

Cultural Domination

The realities of the marketplace put great pressure on authors in underdeveloped countries to publish in the former colonizer's language, and to emigrate to their country. Aminata Sow Fall has remained in Africa, and Cousture and Maillet have stayed in prosperous Canada, but Sebbar has moved to France, and Condé to the U.S. In Africa or the Caribbean, lower literacy rates and poverty (book purchasing is a luxury) make it difficult at best for authors to earn a living. Publishing abroad, in the colonizer's or former colonizer's language, ensures a much greater market for a book. In the Caribbean, for example, only about 10 per cent of the native population are first-language speakers of French, whereas 90 per cent primarily use Creoles. In Senegal, French is currently the official language. But there, Wolof is the language most widely used (understood by 90 per cent), although rarely read in other countries.

A strong sense of social responsibility, and *nostalgia* for their country of origin, frequently leads expatriate authors to incorporate stories translated from oral tradition into their novels and plays, to preserve a body of historical understanding and wisdom that otherwise risks being lost in a world of print and electronic culture. Many also try to preserve a limited memory of the language of their cultural origins. Some, like Condé, Cousture, and Maillet, go further, sprinkling their characters' conversations with words, expressions, *proverbs, fables*, and children's stories from the substrate's original languages or dialects, often providing notes or a glossary to translate them. Condé's autobiography explains that her parents knew Creole but never used it in front of her: she had to rediscover it for herself. Such cultural self-suppression is frequent among immigrant or colonized families, who want to help their children assimilate to the dominant new culture.

Gender Domination

Issues regarding women's rights and social status can be raised briefly in an opening overview, together with the women authors' views regarding their social roles. They dramatize the heroism of women's everyday lives as mothers and/or members of helping professions (Cousture); as political actors (Maillet, Sow Fall); as critics of their adopted countries (Sebbar, via the protagonist) or home countries (Condé, via the narrator). Condé and Sow Fall demonstrate their gender-transcending creative capabilities by treating history from the point of view of men; others, like Cousture, may practice a form of *l'écriture féminine*, depicting women's often neglected experiences of puberty, sexual desire, menstruation, childbirth, breastfeeding, and motherhood in direct narration—thus greatly enriching literature—while also dramatizing a strong woman character's psychic need to secure relative autonomy within a *phallocratic* society. Cousture also uses *represented discourse (style indirect libre)* masterfully to penetrate male consciousness.

Some Possibilities for Discussion

(1) From the viewpoint of American students, the characters described are foreigners. Ask the class how the cultures depicted in the readings differ from our cultures, and how the roles that the main characters play *within the story* differ from the roles our students are enacting in their own lives. (2) Beyond creating an engaging work of art, what are the author's intentions in communicating her message (the *themes* of the text) to her audience? (It helps to make a sharp distinction between a *subject* or *topic*—the raw material, like dough—and a *theme*: the moral or pragmatic evaluation of events, like the baked loaf.) (3) How do the texts raise gender issues? (4) How are the issues of imposed and perceived ethnic inferiority presented when the authors are depicting colonized subjects, exiles, or immigrants, the last often suspect even when legal residents? (Examples: Germans in the United States during World War I; the Japanese civilians imprisoned in U.S. camps during World War II.) Invite students to give examples of these four discussion points from literature that they already know.

Syllabus, Weeks 2–5: From Acadian to "Cajun" and Return, 1755–80

Antonine Maillet's heroine *Pélagie-la-Charrette*, from the maritime provinces of eastern Canada, was one of the French settlers forcibly deported from their fertile farms by *le Grand Dérangement* in 1755. After the English defeated France in the battle of the Plains of Abraham, just west of Québec city, Canada as a whole was ceded to the British Empire. The British then erased Acadian history and culture from the conquered Atlantic territories as much as possible: they were renamed as the provinces of Newfoundland and Nova Scotia, while the Acadian dialect, and French in general, acquired no official nationwide status until 1969. Often, only spoken English was allowed in schools—an experience that Maillet herself had to endure. Her Pélagie, a Moses figure, works tirelessly for 25 years to bring her exiled people back within sight of their Promised Land, and then dies from exhaustion. Some major topics are *exile* and *return, woman as leader*, cooperation with a co-equal male hero, and *oral tradition* as a storehouse of indigenous culture and resolve. Ask students to comment on examples from within the text, such as the stories of the White Whale (white animals are manifestations of the supernatural in many folk traditions) or the Frozen Words. In this text, Pélagie postpones her love quest indefinitely so that she can lead her people home: she has to cross territory where most of the inhabitants are indifferent or hostile, adding a social obstacle to the economic and physical ones. The *tag-names* reflect the respective heroines' character: quasi-religious devotion in Evangeline; the sea (Greek *pelagos*) in Pélagie, corresponding to her destiny of eternal wandering. Maillet's novel adds extra layers of *substrate*: native Americans pre-existed with French settlers, as both allies and foes; as aliens, the Acadian exiles were suspect to both the rebellious American settlers and the British loyalists (defeated in the States, triumphant in Canada).

Syllabus, Week 6: Condé's Drama of Black Revolution, 1789–1802

Maryse Condé's characters are slaves and descendants of slaves shipped from West Africa to the Caribbean islands of Guadeloupe and Haiti (then called Santo Domingo) to work in the sugar cane fields. Her play *An tan révolisyon* ("In the Time of Revolution") takes place mainly in the author's birthplace, today the French overseas *département* of Guadeloupe. Zéphyr, the spirit of history, narrates from the stage, somewhat like Shakespeare's Puck in *The Tempest* or the narrator in Thornton Wilder's *Our Town*. In the first act, the slaves in Guadeloupe rejoice at the news that the revolutionary government of France has abolished slavery overseas, on the premise that all men are equal. The French Republic begins. But in 1802, the inspirational French leader Toussaint Louverture is tricked into trusting the French. Extradited to France, he dies in prison. Napoleon reinstitutes slavery. Louverture's co-revolutionary Dessalines avoids capture and remains in Haiti as a dictator, but on Guadeloupe, the rebel leader Louis Delgrès and 300 of his men are besieged in a fortress, where they finally blow up the ammunition dump, along with themselves and many French attackers. The island remains under French rule. (Haiti, in contrast, became the first free Black Republic in 1804.) Condé advocates for the freedom and equality of all French subjects, whether women or men, of African or European origin. In her play, she is the *griot* (oral historian) for the entire Caribbean region. With her dramatized Creole-language version of the abolition and restoration of slavery in the French colonies of the Caribbean, Condé has reached out to members of her culture who cannot read, or do not know French well. The multiple plot lines balance historical triumph with defeat; Black Liberation remains a work in progress. Like Antonine Maillet, Maryse Condé has become a particularly wide-ranging historian and custodian of her oral tradition and language of origin. Both have contributed greatly to school programs and children's literature.

Syllabus, Weeks 7–9: Quebec from Church to Factory, 1892–1918

Arlette Cousture's *Les Filles de Caleb*, in three volumes, is a *roman-fleuve* encompassing four generations from about 1890 to 1950. In the first and second generations, women play traditional roles as homemakers, nurses, grade school teachers, or nuns. In the second, Emilie, a strong-willed, brilliant young woman, teaches, starting at age 16. The development of her independent character offers rich resources for discussion. As a child, she courageously defies her father to ensure fair treatment of her younger sisters. As a teacher, she disciplines a male student bully much bigger and stronger than she. Then love undermines her life without lessening her independence. Instead of a well-to-do but affected superintendent of her school district, she marries a strong, handsome, but unstable former student who will frequently abandon her to work in the woods that he loves. Lacking contraceptives, she has a child every year. Eventually, her husband succumbs to alcoholism. After she agrees to move to a noxious industrial town where he can find a more lucrative job, he becomes sober but addicted to gambling, and must separate from his family to flee his creditors. Volume I ends here; in subsequent volumes, Emilie takes complete charge of her family, and moves back to the country to teach under primitive conditions. Volumes II and III trace the urbanization of Québec, the declining influence of the Catholic Church, and the improving careers in medicine gradually opening for Émilie's daughter and granddaughter. The trilogy ends in 1960, but does not touch upon the postwar provincial independence movement and the *révolution tranquille*.

Syllabus, Weeks 10 and 11: The Perils of Independence, West Africa after 1960

Aminata Sow Fall's *L'Ex-Père de la nation* focuses on a fictive, newly elected president of a nameless, recently independent country in Sub-Saharan Africa. Mentions of desert terrain to the north, swampy forests to the south, and the imprisoned president's final confinement in a room overlooking the sea, strongly suggest Senegal. The ruinous loans imposed on the newly independent country by its former French overlords (compare Haiti) perpetuate the abuses of colonization, although in a non-violent form. The well-meaning president is weak; most of his ministers—all male—are greedy and profoundly corrupt, uncaring for their wretchedly poor people. By depicting the unscrupulous white businessmen and politicians only as remote, abstract forces, Sow Fall focuses responsibility for malfeasance on the wealthy African Blacks. The inner story of polygamy transforms both the president's wives into active agents, in contrast to Mariama Ba's *Une si longue lettre*, where the female letter writer is a passive sufferer, and the second wife does not appear in the foreground. Plot outcomes often involve a clear but unspoken moral. Here the president's second wife is evil—emphasized by her incarceration at the end—but the first one demonstrates a principled integrity and commitment to the marriage relationship. She has refused any further sexual contact with her unfaithful, imprisoned former husband, but assumes the maternal role of bringing him breakfast and visiting him in prison every day. As for the main narrative, a diary written by the male protagonist, we cannot tell whether it represents a confession that will lead to his contrition and moral regeneration, but for the African reader, it is a cautionary tale.

Syllabus, Weeks 12 and 13: Caught between Africa and France, Mainly Paris in the 1970s

Lelia Sebbar's *Shérazade, 17 ans, brune, frisée, les yeux verts* is the first volume of a trilogy focusing on the second generation of immigrants from Algeria to their former colonists' home country, France. They are suspended between two cultures during the 1970s. As frequently happens, the first generation wants their children to assimilate, and does not teach them the parents' original language. Aside from Shérazade's social status as a second-generation immigrant, among all the protagonists of our five texts she is closest to many of our probable students because of her age, residence in a first-world country, and separation from her family. One might ask those members of the class who are first- or second-generation immigrants to raise their hands—but only if they are entirely comfortable doing so. In any event, consider asking the class to discuss Shérazade as a namesake of the protagonist of *The Arabian Nights*, who also wins and maintains her independence. Point out that the full title of Sebbar's novel is a missing-person announcement, an appeal from the family for her to come home. Ask how she responds to it. Shérazade expresses no rancor against her family, and sends news to show she's all right, but without revealing her address.

Like other second-generation immigrants, she feels nostalgia for the unknown land of their origin. Like them, she asserts her independence from France by becoming an accomplice to criminal activity (although she is not tempted by terrorism). To maintain freedom from her family, she lives by her wits. Although at times a companion or an accomplice, in any relationship Shérazade always withdraws from serious commitment, and preserves her autonomy. Modern Western clothing styles fascinate her, however, as they do the rest of her generation. This is an opportune moment to ask the class to discuss what they themselves find really trendy and fashionable, and how their tastes compare to Shérazade's. Then one can deepen the discussion by exploring the metaphorical meanings of clothing as related to personal identity, social status, and self-definition.

Reading only the first volume of the Shérazade trilogy may at first frustrate the reader, because the first ten chapters are disconnected character sketches without narrative continuity: the heroine moves from squat to squat (she couch-surfs) and from one friendship to another. But she is just beginning to explore her own cultural heritage (ask students where, how, and why the text illustrates this). To introduce the novel, one can stage the discussion by asking students to discuss their own "identity themes" (or their refusal to think of themselves in that way). Then ask them: "What would you be doing now if you—like Shérazade—were not in college? If you wanted to be completely independent of your family? If you didn't know what you wanted to do with your life?" To conclude, the instructor can explain (or ask students who want to do extra reading for a term paper to explain) how, in the final volume of Sebbar's trilogy, the heroine explores her North African heritage, while successfully eluding the man who loves her, and who wants to direct a film celebrating her. What is her appeal? Part of it is her ability to surprise us. She does not follow a predictable narrative arc.

A teenage second-generation immigrant who has lost contact with her native country, Algeria, Shérazade has half-forgotten her parent's native language, Arabic. She has drifted away from their religion, Islam; and has stopped visiting her family, although they live nearby. She appears to be heading for Algeria as Volume I ends, but even by the end of the second volume of her trilogy, she has not left France. Throughout, she stays free of entangling relationships. A modern female parasite and *pícaro*, she works when it amuses her, and turns the tables on those who would exploit her. She serves as a satiric, outside observer like

Montesquieu's Persian traveler in *Les Lettres persanes*, Satan in Mark Twain's *Letters from the Earth*, or Salinger's Holden Caufield in *Catcher in the Rye*—physically *in* her new society, but not *of* it. As a woman, does she face more pressure to conform than a man would?

Syllabus, Week 14: Overview of Feminist Authorial Strategies

Women's lives matter—not just for themselves, but for the preservation of their cultures, and of humanity in general. Chronicles and memoirs, generally a masculine domain, tell of victors who impose their culture on others. In contrast, as a form of scholarship, historiography tends to tell the story of a geographical region, while characterizing the successive waves of uniting and fighting groups that occupied that land. But women's imaginative literature tends to emphasize the importance of the family as the core of a community. To reinforce this idea, it may span several generations. Antoinette Maillet's Pélagie leads three generations of Acadian exiles back from deportation in South Carolina to their homeland in Nova Scotia: bearers of tradition, resistance, and promise. The many other rival groups competing at the time for New England and the future Maritime Provinces (as many as 18) are depicted mainly as blocking characters. Likewise, Arlette Cousture's *roman-fleuve* (one spanning several generations) dramatizes a brave grandmother, mother, and daughter who carve out lives of valuable teaching and nursing despite oppression from the Catholic Church and the British overlords. Maryse Condé, embodying authorial omniscience in the allegorical figure of the Spirit of History, Zephyr, judges human folly, greed, cruelty, and betrayal from a great height—detachment makes the spectacle bearable. Leila Sebbar's cynical, precocious protagonist seeks a culture to which she can honorably commit herself. In contrast, Aminata Sow Fall approaches gender issues from the opposite, negative side: masculinist critique via the first-person viewpoint of a weak, flawed president, who ruins his own family by indulging in polygamy, and his country by lazily basking in the insincere praise of corrupt male advisers. In contrast, his loyal first wife models insight and integrity. The main message is a general condemnation of African politics and continuing Western neglect and exploitation.

Conclusion

The best foundation for a successful course is student involvement. The course described in this chapter encourages students to feel a connection with the material they study. Their comments, questions, and interest in the texts enlightens both student and instructor and creates a sense of community. While the course questions complex relations of identity, community, and belonging, its success is due in part to the sense of community through the exploration of gender identity themes through the teaching of texts of Francophone women.

References

Required Reading

Condé, Maryse. *An tan révolisyon*. L'Amandier, 2015. 17–81. 1789, 1794, 1802. Guadeloupe and Santo Domingo, Haiti.

Cousture, Arlette. *Les Filles de Caleb: Le chant du coq*, Volume 1 of 3. Libre Expression, 2003 [1985], 17–453. 1892–1918. Quebec Province, Canada.

Maillet, Antonine. *Pélagie-la-Charrette*. Prix Goncourt, 1979. Leméac, 1979. Grasset, 2002 [1991]. 1755–80, epilogue 1880. Acadia (Maritime Provinces), Canada, to South Carolina and return.

Sebbar, Leïla. *Shérazade, 17 ans, brune, frisée, les yeux verts.* Stock, 1982. 1970s. Paris, with references to Algeria.

Sow Fall, Aminata. *L'ex-père de la nation.* L'Harmattan, 1987, 7–189. 1960s–70s (unspecified nine-year period). A West African democracy.

Optional Reading and the Web

Azodo, Ada Uzoamaka, ed. *Emerging Perspectives on Aminata Sow Fall: The Real and the Imaginary in Her Novels.* Africa World Press, 2007, interview with Sow Fall, 271–302.

Brière, Eloise A. "Antonine Maillet and the Construction of Acadian Identity," in Green et al., 3–21.

Crecilius, Kathryn J. "L'Histoire et son double dans Pélagie-la-Charrette." *Studies in Canadian Literature* 6.2(1981): 212–220.

Demers, Frédéric. "La Ville, la campagne, l'anglais, Les Filles de Caleb et la mémoire historique: notes sur quelques liens difficiles à démêler." *Francophonie d'Amérique* 21(Spring2006): 67–81.

Films de Femmes: www.filmsdefemmes.com

Gaensbauer, Deborah B. "Protean Truths: History as Performance in Maryse Condé's An tan révolisyon." *French Review* 76. 6(May2003): 1139–1150.

Giltrow, Janet and David Stouck. "Survivors of the Night: The Language and Politics of Epics in Antonine Maillet's Pélagie-la-Charrette." *University of Toronto Quarterly* 71. 3(Summer2002): 735–754.

Green, Mary Jean, Karen Gould, Micheline Rice-Maximin, Keith L. Walker, and Jack A. Yeager, eds. *Postcolonial Subjects: Francophone Women Writers.* University of Minnesota Press, 1996.

International Movie Database: www.imdb.com

Lionnet, Françoise. "Introduction: Logiques métisses: Cultural Appropriation and Postcolonial Representation," 1–21 and "Narrative Journeys: The Reconstruction of Histories in Leila Sebbar's Les Carnets de Shérazade," 167–186 in *Postcolonial Representations: Women, Literature, Identity.* Cornell University Press, 1995.

Makward, Christiane. "L'Ironie comme stratégie dramatique dans La Tragédie du Roi Christophe d'Aimé Césaire and An tan révolisyon de Maryse Condé." *Francophonia* 31(Autumn2011), 109–123.

Meese, Elisabeth. *(EX)TENSIONS: Refiguring Feminist Criticism.* University of Illinois Press, 1990.

Miller, Mary-Kay. "Aminata Sow Fall's L'Ex-père de la nation: Subversive Subtexts and the Return of the Maternal," in Green et al., 98–111.

Mohanty, Chandra Talpade. "Under Western Eyes: Feminist Scholarship and Colonial Discourse." *Feminist Review* 30(Autumn1988).

Schwartz, Lucy M. "Revaluing Traditional Patrimony," in *Emerging Perspectives on Aminata Sow Fall: The Real and the Imaginary in Her Novels*, ed. Ada Uzoamaka Azodo. Africa World Press, 2007, 43–64.

Sebbar, Leila and Nancy Huston. *Lettres parisiennes.* Barrault, 1986.

Thério, Adrien. "Caleb et ses filles." *Lettres québécoises* 44(Spring1989): 11–15.

Waterson, Carolyn. "The Mythical Dimension of Pélagie-la-Charrette," in *Francophone Literatures of the New World*, ed. James Gilroy. Denver, CO: Department of Foreign Languages and Literatures, 1982.

Weidmann Koop, Marie-Christine and Catherine R. Montfort, eds. "French and Francophone Women, 16th–21st Centuries: Essays on Literature, Culture, and Society with Bibliographical and Media Resources." *Women in French Studies* special issue: 2002.

10

INCORPORATING OCEANIAN WOMEN WRITERS INTO THE FRANCOPHONE LITERATURE CLASSROOM

Julia L. Frengs

The French-speaking region of Oceania (French Polynesia, Kanaky-New Caledonia, Wallis and Futuna, and Vanuatu) is not a widely studied region in North American universities. Even less frequently examined are the literatures emanating from this region. While providing an in-depth historical and cultural background of the region is not possible within the scope of this chapter, what I intend here is to offer instructors unfamiliar with Oceania possible approaches to examining Oceanian women's works that introduce students to a region of the "Francosphere" whose literature is burgeoning.[1] These works not only enable students to problematize the notions of canonical literature and "francophonie," but they also help them to consider the "woman question" from outside of Western parameters. Women writers from Oceania tend to engage in conversations concerning the marginalization of women from both inside and outside of indigenous communities, domestic and sexual abuse, and other sensitive, "taboo" topics such as abortion. For writers attempting to valorize their native cultures, denouncing patriarchal practices from within their own communities can be especially fraught. How do we teach students to engage with these texts in ways that allow women authors to successfully communicate their multiple, nuanced messages? How do we ensure that students do not leave the classroom with stereotypical, exoticized views of the indigenous societies of the Pacific, especially with regard to the treatment of women and women's place in these societies? How do we avoid setting up binarized, simplified beliefs pitting the "colonizer" against the "colonized" and men against women when we teach these underexamined texts?

When we choose to include a text (in an introductory course to Francophone literature, for example) we are necessarily forced to "exclude" another, often a text that one is expected to include. I intentionally place Oceanian women's texts alongside both what has come to be considered "canonical Francophone" literature (Aimé Césaire's *Cahier d'un retour au pays natal*, for example) and Oceanian works by male writers. Students are thus able to see that the women's works we read are not simply "responses" to the canon, and that they are equally valuable and revelatory in scholarly examination. As previously mentioned, some of the concerns I have when choosing materials for inclusion in my courses are inadvertently reinforcing polarized stereotypes about marginalized groups and tokenizing women's literature. Yet what I have found particularly advantageous and enlightening about teaching Oceanian women's literature is that it encourages students to confront questions of alterity, of culture, of gender roles, and of tradition in ways that differ from the "canon." It shows students that getting uncomfortable and reflecting on this discomfort can lead to a practice of empathetic reading, listening, and critical engagement with the world outside of the West, and presses them to reconsider some of their own cultural assumptions.

In what follows, I propose suggestions for primary readings, secondary reading materials, theoretical approaches, and in-class activities to facilitate the inclusion of Oceanian women's literature in the Francophone literature and culture classroom. I have chosen to focus on three women authors I have included in an upper-level course on Francophone literatures and cultures and in courses focused exclusively on the Oceanian region. I begin by proposing strategies for teaching Chantal T. Spitz's first novel, published in 1991, *L'Ile des rêves écrasés* (*Island of Shattered Dreams*), which is a novel that questions the notions of francophonie as well as the canon, while simultaneously provoking reflection on feminist engagement. I subsequently discuss the inclusion of Ari'irau Richard-Vivi's daring *Matamimi, ou La vie nous attend* in a graduate seminar taught in the Spring of 2017. Finally, I address my use of Déwé Gorodé's provocative works in the undergraduate and graduate classrooms.

I have taught Spitz's *L'Ile des rêves écrasés* in several courses at Quest University Canada and at the University of Nebraska-Lincoln, both in English and in French. It is the ideal text to introduce students to French Polynesian works, as it is considered the first (indigenous) French Polynesian novel. Beautifully written and easily accessible for undergraduate students, I consider it essential for graduate students as well. The novel begins with the Tahitian origin story written in reo mā'ohi (the Tahitian language), which precedes an abridged version of the Judeo-Christian Genesis. Following the two origin stories, a prologue recounts the arrival of Europeans to Tahiti, lamenting assimilationist mentalities and the loss of cultural knowledge that results from colonization. The principal narrative follows a linear structure in a type of family saga: love stories of three generations are paralleled with the history of French Polynesia from the years between the two world wars to the construction of the nuclear experimentation plant (the Centre d'Expérimentation du Pacifique) in the 1960s. The novel thus exposes students to the primary preoccupations of French Polynesian writers, and lends itself well to multiple theoretical approaches, particularly to post (or anti)colonial readings, to ecocriticism, and to feminist or womanist approaches. The inclusion of the Mā'ohi origin story in reo mā'ohi without a translation in either the French or the English versions of the novel facilitates discussions on translation, glossing, and language choice commonly seen in postcolonial literatures.[2] When beginning study on this novel, I refer students to the discussion of subversive language choices in chapter 2 of *The Empire Writes Back*, as the decision not to gloss the oral creation story in Spitz's work results in giving the indigenous language primacy over the dominant French language. Students read Spitz's short essay, "L'Ecrire colonisé," in which she audaciously describes the French language as: "unique pourvoyeuse des valeurs occidentales donc universelles qui nous aspire nous digère nous rejette pantelants clos dans une fascination mortifère un naufrage invisible" (lone supplier of occidental, hence universal, values that sucks us in, chews us up, spits us out and leaves us panting for breath in a toxic fascination, an invisible shipwreck, 68). Spitz thus joins in the chorus of voices from the French-speaking world who have critiqued the notion of francophonie as playing a role in the institutionalized marginalization of non-European French speakers.

Spitz's equally critical condemnations of nuclear testing in the Pacific enable students to examine the text through an ecocritical lens, and while considering this angle, I like to introduce an ecofeminist reading.[3] In *L'Ile des rêves écrasés*, the author refers to the feminine names of the testing sites. As Dina El-Dessouky remarks in an article considering Spitz's novel as an example of postcolonial ecological literature, the naming of the nuclear testing sites (Brigitte and Hortensia) was an effort to make nuclear testing appear more benign. She argues that the assignment of female code names to the islands comprising Moruroa "suggests France's vision of the atoll as a series of barren, female striking zones at the disposal of French nuclear violence. That the names are also European suggests France's desire to erase records of any indigenous language, history, or presence" (261). El-Dessouky cites Val Plumwood's *Feminism and the Mastery of Nature*, one of the foundational texts of the ecofeminist movement, wherein Plumwood demonstrates that feminism and environmentalism theoretically merge based on similar experiences of domination. Plumwood points out that, like the vocabulary that has contributed to the domination of women, the definition of "nature" has often been associated with the ideas of passivity, "as the 'environment' or invisible background conditions against which the 'foreground' achievements of reason or culture (provided typically by the white, western, male expert or entrepreneur) take place" (4). The naming of the islands is thus an insidious form of manipulation, which Spitz is not shy to condemn. Students quite easily pick up on Spitz's environmental and feminist assertions in the second half of *Island of Shattered Dreams*, when the only female engineer working in an all-male environment realizes that "while the principle of equality seems to be established in her country, this is only a theoretical acceptance" (93) and is accused of having a "typical female sentimentality" (94).[4]

Students also remark that while Spitz includes both male and female protagonists, the only characters who write are women. The fact that the female engineer is a French woman who maintains a diary further complicates the notion of the inclusion of women's voices in the novel – both indigenous women and European women are permitted to say "I." Students observe that Spitz risks perpetuating stereotypes in her descriptions of beautiful Tahitian women (and, for that matter, strong, handsome Tahitian men). Furthermore, students often view Spitz's portrayals of the colonizers versus the colonized as excessively binarized. It is essential to point out that Spitz lays blame on the Mā'ohi community as much as she does on European colonizers. This novel is thus an excellent choice for the Francophone literature and culture classroom whose goals might include questioning the canon, confronting stereotypes, and demonstrating how Francophone women writers discuss "women's issues" in multifaceted and oftentimes seemingly contradictory ways.

Of a younger generation of French Polynesian writers, Ari'irau Richard-Vivi provides a different perspective on Tahitian identity than one finds in Spitz's works. The author, who prefers to be referred to simply as Ari'irau, is the daughter of a Frenchman and a half-Tahitian woman. She grew up between France and Tahiti and obtained her doctorate in French literature at New York University, and has since settled permanently in Tahiti. Due to her upbringing "between" France and the islands, she is sensitive to the various racial and political tensions that impact daily life in French Polynesia. Her two novels *Je reviendrai à Tahiti* (2005) and *Matamimi, ou La Vie nous attend* (2006) both treat the rarely broached, "taboo" topic of abortion. Simultaneously, however, like Spitz's work, Ari'irau's texts are political commentaries on the status of French Polynesia.[5] In my graduate seminar taught at the University of Nebraska-Lincoln, students read Ari'irau's second novel, *Matamimi, ou La Vie nous attend*, which is essentially an extended apostrophe to the narrator's imaginary daughter, Matamimi.[6] The reader does not discover until the final few chapters that the daughter does not exist – in fact, that she never existed – because, as we read in the chapter entitled "Exit la fiction," the narrator underwent an abortion in a clinic in Kansas. Ari'irau's eponymous narrator interweaves memories of her own childhood, historical events such as nuclear testing and independence protests, and Tahitian oral stories into a novel that is, like the character of Matamimi, fiction. This blending of fiction with real-life events adds complexity to a text whose subject matter is already quite delicate. Students were troubled by the message they felt the novel conveyed concerning women's choice, as the author/narrator expresses regret for having undergone an abortion. They were also unsettled by the mixing of such a personal topic with political content, as they felt this rendered the text an attempt at political persuasion. On the final day of reading *Matamimi*, one student asked his peers how the mixing of the political and the personal affects the reader's experience: does the political commentary detract from the moving and personal experience of the principal narrative?[7] Students had trouble dissociating the author's political stances on the Polynesian independence movement from her personal experiences with regard to her body. The mantra the narrator repeats throughout the novel, "Your body is your country, your country is your body," further complicates this debate, as Ari'irau seems to be advocating not only political but also corporeal independence, all while expressing regret for the choice she made to abort her child. In this way, it is almost as if the author enables the reader to participate in her experience. The tensions in the conflicting emotions as a woman facing this choice are palpable; the ambiguous political/personal message mirrors the uncomfortable and painful process of coming to a decision and of living with that decision. As she notes on the last page of the novel, however, writing provides for her a sort of catharsis: "Écrire, c'est ma survie. Parce que si je n'avais pas fait renaître ma fille sur du papier, je me serais détruite de l'intérieur" ("Writing, it's how I survive. Because if I hadn't made my daughter come alive on paper, I would have destroyed myself from the inside out," 128). This ending led to a brilliant conversation concerning the motivations behind an author's writing and the ethical responsibilities of an author concerning her readership.

Since I am addressing my incorporation of Ari'irau's novel in a graduate-level course focused exclusively on Pacific Ocean literature, I would like to permit myself a slight digression from my focus on Oceanian women's literature to briefly discuss the arrangement of this course. As I found in my Pacific Ocean literature courses taught in English at Quest University Canada (2015 and 2016), determining how much context to provide students before approaching contemporary Oceanian works was a challenge, since they have so little historical knowledge of the region. Because many of the contemporary works we read respond explicitly or implicitly to eighteenth-, nineteenth-, and twentieth-century depictions of the exotic or indigenous "Other" and to European representations of encounter, I wanted to ensure my students had exposure to these works. We therefore spent the first three weeks of class reading excerpts from Louis Antoine de Bougainville's *Voyage autour du monde*, Denis Diderot's *Supplément au Voyage de Bougainville*, Pierre Loti's *Le Mariage de Loti*, and Georges Baudoux's *Pastorale Calédonienne*. These texts, accompanied by critical and theoretical readings, served to contextualize the remainder of the course and helped students to understand just how deeply entrenched the exoticized images of the Tahitian vahine (woman) or the dangerous, "cannibal" Kanak (aboriginal New Caledonian) people have become in the Western imaginary.[8] Notably, these texts were all written by European men. I found it important to point out that there were also women writing at the end of the nineteenth and the beginning of the twentieth century in New Caledonia (*communarde* Louise Michel, for example, spent time with the Kanak people when she was deported to the island, and wrote *Légendes et chants de gestes canaques*, 1885). It is equally important to mention, however, that women's literature from this period is much more difficult to access, and that while there were exceptions in both works written by women and by men, women were not immune to the tendency to exoticize or dehumanize indigenous populations. Spitz, Ari'irau, and Gorodé's texts all respond to the eighteenth- and nineteenth-century works I included at the beginning of the semester. Students saw that Oceanian women writers must not only contend with exoticized notions of Pacific peoples in general, but that they must also contest stereotyped images of Oceanian women that have been perpetuated throughout centuries of European literature.

Like Spitz and Ari'irau's works, Déwé Gorodé's writing addresses these stereotyped images, but she also goes beyond a "response" to these depictions to critique patriarchal practices from within indigenous Oceanian communities. As students notice with the two authors from French Polynesia, the Kanak author refuses to paint an idyllic image of Oceanian peoples. Rather, Gorodé seeks a balance between celebrating Kanak customs and traditions and critiquing the elements of those traditions that marginalize women. Gorodé is the first Kanak novelist, a Kanak independence activist, and has been involved in every government of Kanaky-New Caledonia since 1999. Her oeuvre is influenced by her political activism, especially her 2012 novel *Tâdo, tâdo, wéé! ou "No More Baby"* which is the novel I chose to include in my graduate-level course. The novel is a panorama of Kanak-New Caledonian history spanning from the end of World War II to the rise of the Arab Spring, recounted principally from the perspectives of a series of female characters, eponymously named Tâdo. When beginning this novel, I had students read a translated English version of the Kanak oral story, "Tâdo et Crabe," to provide context, as throughout the novel, the crab appears in multiple forms.[9] In the oral story, a crab repeatedly visits a little boy, Tâdo, whose parents are away working. The crab steals and eats the boy's food, tickling him to distract him (an act which can be read as a metaphor for sexual predation). Tâdo finally tricks the crab, luring him into a pot to cook him and eat him for dinner. Students immediately ascertain that the Tâdos of Gorodé's novel are female, and that the crab becomes a referent for anything malevolent, and particularly for anything that harms the female body and subjugates women. Gorodé associates the figure of the crab with (female) sterility, cancer, and more explicitly, as a character remarks, "le harcèlement sexuel au quotidien" ("daily sexual harassment," Gorodé 293). The author thus subverts and rewrites the traditional Kanak oral story to provoke reflection on women's condition in Kanaky-New Caledonia.

Gorodé's 350-page *Tâdo, tâdo, wéé!* is an autofictional account of women's involvement in Kanak politics (it may be argued that the Tâdo of the principal narrative is an avatar of Gorodé, who similarly ascended the political ranks during the 1970s and 1980s, eventually becoming vice president of the New Caledonian government and minister of "la condition féminine"). While she critiques male domination and sexual predation, however, she is careful to include male characters who ally themselves with women. She also complicates the struggle for women's rights within Kanak society when confronted with tradition: women frequently do "women's work," preparing food and cleaning, while men satisfy traditional male roles and make decisions for the clans. The author's nuanced portrayal of the gendered separation of work alongside women's ascent within Kanak politics lends itself to a thought-provoking discussion on the confrontation between tradition and "modern" or Western conceptualizations of women's roles.

While Gorodé's *Tâdo, tâdo, wéé!* provides a fascinating overview of Kanak history, political struggles, and women's role in both, it was my students' least favorite novel of our course due to its reliance on the reader's prior knowledge and awareness of Kanak-New Caledonian history (as well as world history). In a second iteration of this course, then, I recommend reading Gorodé's first novel, *L'épave* (2005).[10] *L'épave* is shorter and more plot-driven than *Tâdo, tâdo, wéé*, so the reader's background knowledge, while important for understanding cultural aspects of the novel, is not essential to the understanding of the plot. It is much more challenging stylistically, however, and the content is onerous and trauma-laden. As supplementary material, I recommend students read Raylene Ramsay's article, "Indigenous Women Writers in the Pacific: Déwé Gorodé, Sia Figiel, Patricia Grace: Writing Violence as Counter

Violence and the Role of Local Context," which provides background on the realities of sexual violence and domestic abuse in Oceania. I included *L'épave*, translated by Ramsay as *The Wreck*, in my (undergraduate) course on Pacific Ocean literature at Quest University Canada. Generally, most students enjoyed the novel and appreciated its sophisticated style, despite its traumatic content.

L'épave is not simply Gorodé's first novel – it is the first Kanak novel, a fact I highlight before students begin reading, as it is significant that the first Kanak novel is an audacious denouncement of rampant sexual abuse in a society that has suffered under French colonialism and neocolonialism. As one of the first literary voices of the Kanak community, Gorodé is faced with the desire to celebrate Kanak values and traditions, along with the burden of denouncing predatory sexual practices that are unfortunately all too common in New Caledonia, both in Kanak clans and in the more Europeanized capital city of Nouméa. The novel's difficult, hybrid structure reflects the dilemma in which the author finds herself. In the novel, a young man meets a woman during a political rally promoting Kanak independence; they quickly fall for each other and escape to make love near a ship wrecked on the beach. The plot becomes extremely complicated, as the young woman, Léna, has flashbacks of repressed memories from her childhood, in which both she and her mother were raped by a community elder near an old wrecked canoe. The storyline switches between the perspectives of Léna, her mother, her aunt, the young man Tom, with whom Léna becomes involved, and Lila, an outspoken storyteller murdered for daring to denounce the men who raped her and the patriarchal society that perpetuates rampant rape and sexual abuse. The fluctuating narrative perspectives, resistance to linear chronology, and the hybrid blend of genres (the novel contains not only poetry but music, rap, verses from the Bible and the Koran, and extensive dialogue) render the text extremely complex.[11]

In my course at Quest, students led discussion activities in which I asked them to prepare questions to provoke interesting debate and include a creative activity they felt would help their classmates better understand the novels and the questions the novels elicit. Student discussion leaders gave groups of their peers passages from the first half of the novel, asking questions about the significance of the stylistic choices, the subversive quality of the passages, the symbolic use of language, and who was speaking in these passages. These questions provoked a discussion on the aesthetics of violence: how can such a disturbing theme, a disturbing text, be beautiful? If it is not stylistically beautiful, does it have the same effect on the reader? The second set of discussion leaders asked their colleagues to brainstorm about how many times a wreck appeared in the novel, both literally and metaphorically, and to think about how this metaphor works. Ultimately, they determined that the recurring image of the wreck invokes the idea of cyclical oppression. The discussion of cyclical oppression was what I hoped students would retain from *L'épave*: that these ostensibly gratuitous scenes of sex and of rape were not in fact gratuitous, and that the cyclical, spiral-like structure of the novel in which domestic violence is ceaselessly repeated, rewritten, or reiterated is an indication of deeper Caledonian societal problems related to Kanak traditional practices as well as to colonial trauma.

The reading materials I have suggested here elicit the types of question that, while often uncomfortable, are relevant to our students' lived experiences: sex, race, gender, domestic abuse, and the decisions a woman makes involving her body are all subjects of contemporary debate in North America. Exposing students to different ways of conceptualizing these epistemological issues is a valuable way to contribute to and nuance conversations in the Francophone literature and culture classroom. In my experience, placing Spitz's *L'Ile des rêves écrasés* alongside more "canonical" texts enables students to see how writers from "outside" the canon insert their voices into the current debates concerning francophonie, while Ari'irau and Gorodé's provocative works facilitate intersectional conversations regarding women's bodies and choices.[12] All three writers' oftentimes ambiguous stances provoke stimulating discussions and provide opportunities for instructors to rethink how we frame these crucial conversations in the contemporary Francophone literature classroom.

Notes

1. For access to works beyond those I suggest here and on my course syllabi included on the accompanying website, please visit the website for the publishing house Au Vent des îles, located in Papeete, Tahiti (www.auventdesiles.pf/). Many of the texts are available via ebook. The website Pacific Book-In (https://pacific-bookin.com/) also has a large collection of Caledonian and Oceanian books and music.
2. I like to discuss the importance of respecting diacritical marks when using indigenous vocabulary in students' written work. Inserting a macron, a common diacritical mark in Polynesian languages, requires changing settings on one's computer. There is thus a temptation to ignore diacritical marks due to this inconvenience. Bringing up this issue in class sparks interesting debates on the continued colonial tendency to marginalize indigenous languages through technology and our own privilege as readers and writers of dominant languages.
3. I include Jean Anderson's translation of this novel (*Island of Shattered Dreams*) in a course I teach in English entitled "Francophone Environmental Literature." In a course taught in French, I would suggest reading this novel prior to reading Tahitian writer Titaua Peu's *Mutismes* (2002), which takes place after the 1995 riots in Papeete, well after the publication of *L'Ile des rêves écrasés*.
4. In my Pacific Ocean literature class taught at Quest University Canada, I set up a debate centered on the question "Can we consider this novel a feminist work?" I gave students time to list their arguments (with passages to support their claims) before reconvening to debate. As they had previously read Chandra Talpade Mohanty's essay "Under Western Eyes: Feminist Scholarship and Colonial Discourses," their arguments were grounded in intersectional feminist ideas, as well as differing definitions and understandings of the word "feminist."
5. French Polynesia is considered a "pays d'outre-mer au sein de la République," which maintains significantly more autonomy than France's DOMs such as Martinique, Guadeloupe, and La Réunion.
6. Matamimi means "eyes of a cat" in reo mā'ohi.
7. One of the criteria for assessment in this graduate seminar was the preparation of questions to lead in-class discussions. Each day one student was responsible for preparing one to three questions regarding the day's reading.
8. A list of supplementary readings can be found on my syllabi located on the accompanying website.
9. The translated version of this story is located in *Nights of Storytelling: A Cultural History of Kanaky-New Caledonia* (2011), edited by Raylene Ramsay.
10. Gorodé has a wide array of novels, short stories, and poetry collections from which to choose. The short story "Affaire classée" in the collection *L'Agenda* works particularly well for the undergraduate level. A "ghost story," it depicts the clash of European and Kanak culture in three different periods of New Caledonian history, demonstrating how Kanak voices have been repeatedly silenced. The recurring haunting figure, typical of Gorodé's cyclical writing style, is a woman, which enables a "gendered" reading of the anticolonial work.
11. For more advanced courses, Homi Bhabha's theoretical notions of hybridity from *The Location of Culture* is useful secondary reading material to accompany this or any of Gorodé's novels.
12. Tahitian writers Rai Chaze and Titaua Peu are also notable (women) contributors to the Oceanian corpus. Chaze's *Avant la saison des pluies* (2011) is a stylistically straightforward novel that I can imagine would work well in an undergraduate course; Peu's more violent and audacious *Pina* (2016) would be more appropriate for the graduate level.

References

Bhabha, Homi. *The Location of Culture*. Routledge, 1994.

El-Dessouky, Dina. "Activating Voice, Body, and Place: Kanaka Maoli and Ma'ohi Writings for Kaho'olawe and Moruroa," in *Postcolonial Ecologies: Literatures of the Environment*, ed. George B. Handley and Elizabeth M. DeLoughrey. Oxford University Press, 2011, 254–272.

Gorodé, Déwé. *L'épave*. Madrépores, 2005.

Gorodé, Déwé. *Tâdo, tâdo, wéé! ou "No More Baby."* Au Vent des îles, 2012.

Gorodé, Déwé. *The Wreck*, trans. Raylene Ramsay and Deborah Walker-Morrison. Little Island Press, 2011.

Mohanty, Chandra Talpade. "Under Western Eyes: Feminist Scholarship and Colonial Discourses." *Colonial Discourse and Post-Colonial Theory: A Reader*, ed. Patrick Williams and Laura Chrisman. Columbia University Press, 1994, 196–220.

Plumwood, Val. *Feminism and the Mastery of Nature*. Routledge, 1993.

Ramsay, Raylene. "Indigenous Women Writers in the Pacific: Déwé Gorodé, Sia Figiel, Patricia Grace: Writing Violence as Counter Violence and the role of Local Context." *Postcolonial Text* 7. 1(2012): 1–18.

Ramsay, Raylene, ed. *Nights of Storytelling: A Cultural History of Kanaky-New Caledonia*. University of Hawai'i Press, 2011.

Richard-Vivi, Ari'irau. *Matamimi, ou La vie nous attend*. Au Vent des îles, 2006.

Spitz, Chantal T. "L'Ecrire colonisé," in *Pensées insolentes et inutiles*. Editions Te ite, 2006.

Spitz, Chantal T. *L'Ile des rêves écrasés*. Au Vent des îles, 2003.

Spitz, Chantal T. *Island of Shattered Dreams*, trans. Huia Publishers, 2007.

11

MAKING THE CASE FOR FRENCH STUDIES

Strategies for Teaching Gendered Multiculturalism in Contemporary French Literature

Rebecca E. Léal

In the twenty-first century, multiculturalism is well integrated into the American educational curriculum across a wide range of disciplines. In the context of French-language classrooms in the United States, many instructors introduce multicultural concepts using American methodology, commonly through Francophone themed self-contained units or courses which celebrate the diversity of French-speaking countries. While this approach may be insightful in increasing awareness of the great expanse of the French-speaking world across the continents, it may ignore the highly gendered colonial/postcolonial melting pot which occurred and is still occurring in many Francophone countries, including France.

Through interdisciplinary lenses incorporating civilization, intercultural, and gender studies to literary studies, this study will propose new, creative pedagogical strategies for university educators to introduce French multiculturalism by focusing on the lived experiences of minority women of North African origin in France. The immigration literary genre in contemporary France has its origins in Beur literature, a largely masculine genre in which male authors and narrators give their perspectives of *banlieue* life. More recently, texts written from female perspectives provide more complete accounts of minority experiences. Female voices fight not only against male patriarchy in the family and towards the dismantling of the colonial apparatus, but also against the patriarchy of a French Republic that seeks to protect minorities through the erasure of difference. In the proposed course, "Multicultural Identities and Gender in Contemporary French Literature," students will read literary texts and analyze cultural supports from a variety of perspectives in order to understand that multiculturalism in contemporary France is a highly gendered experience and problematize its effects.

Teaching gender in multicultural France can be both a pedagogical strategy for linguistic and cultural capital acquisition at the intermediate and advanced language levels as well as a critical component in French studies courses taught in English aimed at attracting new French students. Although many of the concepts and activities could easily be adapted to an English-language classroom, it is important to recognize the limits of the availability of English-language versions of the literary texts proposed in this course; to date, only Faïza Guène's *Kiffe kiffe Tomorrow* is available in translation. This study does not seek to be an all-inclusive approach to teaching French multiculturalism or encapsulate the experiences of female minorities in France in all their diverse forms past and present; rather, it provides one possible approach that may be used as a framework in intermediate or advanced studies in French-language university classrooms. It is one example of how reorienting a unit, a course, or even an entire program towards a multicultural view of France which takes into account its gendered nature can help move toward a more complete, inclusive understanding of the micro-communities and diverse experiences that constitute the French nation.

Teaching Images of Multicultural France

"Rethinking the French Classroom" first involves rethinking how the French portray themselves to each other and to the world in order to bring students to an understanding of the uniqueness of French multiculturalism. The American model is often the most familiar to students in the United States, however, it is not a universally accepted concept and remains a site of contestation. Students will learn how multiculturalism is very much dependent on the specific conditions present both in the host country and the countries of origin.

Although scholarly and creative work in French studies increasingly centers around the representation of minorities who have been historically absent from the master narrative, the knowledge and experience that recent high school graduates bring to the university setting does not always reflect current trends in research. Stereotypical, clichéd images that students may have of France can be quite limiting. Learning activities tied to teaching and problematizing images of French multiculturalism might include internet image searches of keywords such as "French" or "français" with follow-up discussion or student-generated word clouds listing connotations of the word "France." Both tasks are useful pre and post-course activities to informally and comparatively assess student understanding. Such activities also encourage discussion about gaps between the real and imagined French community, especially when juxtaposed with statistics about diversity in contemporary France. Students may also be asked to critically analyze the French national self-image through popular mythology (the introduction to *Astérix le Gaulois*, for example) or satirical clips such as *Cliché* (Villain), both available in translation, and compare it with their own understanding of France. As a learning activity, students might make a list of French heroes (referring to the *Cliché* short film, if necessary), then make a list of American heroes. Discussion prompts might include: Compare and contrast the two lists; what do the similarities and differences reveal? How is a hero identified? In framing the discussion, students should be able to analyze trends they observe in gender, race, ethnicity, social class, and accomplishments that qualify someone as a "hero" in both cultures. An alternative activity may include asking students to make a list of the most famous celebrities in the U.S. and then provide them with a list of the 50 most popular people in France using the bi-annual *Ifop* [1] "Top 50 Celebrities" poll. Students could critically observe both the gender distribution as well as the percentage of celebrities in each country that are minorities.

Another useful learning activity for introducing a discussion about comparative multicultural studies is Vanessa Schwartz's assertion in *Modern France* that France is "a nation of immigrants that lacks a proud poetry about tempest-tossed seekers of golden doors" (81). Assigning a critical reaction to the quote as homework or as a five-minute pre-write at the beginning of class allows students to inventory their prior knowledge of immigration in France as well as juxtapose it with the American experience ("tempest-tossed seeker" and "golden doors"): Do you agree? Where do immigrants in France come from today and historically? Does the U.S. have a "proud poetry" about immigrants? Give some examples. A follow-up discussion should help guide students to an understanding that the quote recognizes that until the late twentieth century most minorities in France did not choose to or were not able to document their presence through literature. Despite this perception of absence, and in contrast with the well-documented narrative of European emigration to the New World, France has been home to more immigrants than any other European country for nearly 200 years. The cultural productions that come out of these immigrations have led to characters, plots, and themes that change in tandem with changes in conceptions of French identity and can reveal much about what French society values at a given historical period, including gender-inclusive (or -exclusive) perspectives. A learning activity that illustrates this point may include providing students with a list of the titles, authors, and publication dates of early Beur novels, widely recognized as the first significant immigrant genre in French literature, and asking students to make observations. Students should be able to recognize that such a list includes largely male authors writing about the male experience in the *banlieue*. A short summary of key novels might also be included in order to expand the discussion even further, asking students to identify what experiences were documented and therefore perceived as valuable by authors, publishers, and intended audiences.

The shifts that have occurred over time in the French's own conception of the nation are also illustrated by national symbols, such as Marianne, the feminine emblem of the French Republic, whose image has, as Gilles Asselin and Ruth Mastron write in *Au Contraire! Figuring out the French*, undergone a series of "relookings" from Delacroix's original 1830 depiction in order to reflect the multicultural reality of France today (10). In 2003, the French National Assembly in collaboration with Fadela Amara and the association Ni Putes Ni Soumises organized an exhibition to recognize the multicultural realities of France in which 14 women were selected to pose as the "new" Mariannes. These included black women, Arab women, white women, and women from France's poorest urban neighborhoods who were photographed as Marianne and their portraits were hung on the façade of the National Assembly (Asselin and Mastron 10). National Assembly president Jean-Louis Debré's remarks at the opening of the exhibit in which he spoke of "the values of a liberating and protecting Republic to which the women of the projects wish to pay tribute"[2] could be read and critically compared with short excerpts from Amara's essay *Ni Putes ni soumises*, in which Amara categorically refutes any sort of protectionist notion from a patriarchal state.

These visual redesigns and reconceptions of the symbol of the Republic can provide an additional learning activity for students in which they can observe and critically analyze the shifts that have taken place in the image of Marianne over time; the activity might also be expanded to include comparing the fluid nature of Marianne to the permanent nature of America's Lady Liberty. Students might create and present to the class hashtags to accompany the Mariannes and thereby give contestatory voices to static images that might otherwise be objectified or exoticized through visual art.

Although it is important to point out and critically analyze such examples of public recognition of a multicultural society in France today, students should be aware of the official state policy of centralization and its effects on expressions of diversity through forced homogenization. The refrain in Black M's 2016 hit "Je suis chez moi" can be used with students as an example of questioning the limits of France's commitment to diversity and inclusivity: "I'm French/They don't want Marianne to be my fiancé/Maybe it's because they think I'm too dark."[3] From its birth as a modern nation state, France has continuously redefined its meaning of citizenship and nationality in order to unify rather than fracture an imagined community under the singular label French. Understanding the history and cultural heritage of modern France means coming to terms with the denial of the existence of minorities within the country; such minorities including slaves, blacks, Jews, and colonial subjects, both male and female, were among those who sought to affirm their rights and identities and, in the process, helped to redefine the French nation culturally, socially, legally, politically, and economically, while the Republic repeatedly sought to deny their existence as French citizens. The roles, places, and representations of minorities in France have shifted significantly according to historical conditions, and multiculturalism in contemporary France is the legacy of its past struggles and evolutions towards national unification and homogenization.

Defining French Multiculturalism

A comparative study of American and French perceptions of multiculturalism is a further entry point into critical inquiry in the classroom. Using American society as a natural comparison, students will learn that because of the specificity of the French historical context, multiculturalism in France has evolved differently. Although as Raymonde Carroll (*Cultural Misunderstandings*) and Ruth Mastron and Gilles Asselin (*Au Contraire*) assert in their respective studies of Franco-American relations, referring back to an American point of view reinforces inherent cultural bias. It is necessary to recognize that the connotations of multiculturalism for American undergraduate students are based on the American model. As a preliminary learning activity, students might first individually propose their own definition of multiculturalism as they understand it (using low-tech whiteboards or high-tech online polling programs), which will likely be similar to *Webster's Dictionary*, "of, relating to, reflecting, or adapted to diverse cultures; a multicultural society, multicultural education, a multicultural menu." Then, students might research and analyze the term's denotations in French, revealing a fundamental difference from the American concept. In *Larousse, multiculturalisme* is the "1. Coexistance of several cultures, often encouraged by a voluntarist policy. 2. Current of American thought that questions the cultural hegemony of white rulers towards minorities [ethnic, cultural, etc.] and calls for full recognition of these minorities." Are the terms synonymous? What do the definitions reveal about how each society views multiculturalism? As an additional learning activity, students might interview French nationals asking them to define the term. Students should be able to recognize that the French definition is politically charged and directly refers to an American model, inferring that it is not French by nature. Americans connect multiculturalism with practices, such as education and culinary styles, while the French link it with politics and Americanism.

It is also imperative to clearly define and develop the specificity of French multiculturalism independent of the American model. Although comparisons may be made with experiences in the U.S., the concepts of *laïcité* (the French version of secularism) and *Républicanisme*, which define and confine the multicultural experience, should be clearly defined within the French context. Key terms to critically analyze with American students include assimilation, multiculturalism, and integration. How a nation chooses to establish equality differs between the United States and France. While the American model celebrates public displays of difference and has a federalist, decentralized system which allows for regional variation, the French notion of equality focuses on the erasure of difference. This is illustrated through French *laïcité* as well as a fear of *communautarisme* (preferential treatment of one religion or ethnicity), which, for the French, could lead to identity-based politics and fractures in the nation's unity. Students may be asked to reflect upon Mastron and Asselin's explanation of why the headscarf ban exists in France in the context of *laïcité* and gender: "In other words, whatever a woman's origins may be, she is first and foremost a citizen of the Republic—this is her primary identity and characterizes what is shared among all French people" (10). As *laïcité* is currently a buzzword in the French media, a learning activity might include students posting and commenting upon news articles to a collaborative current events blog, which would curate authentic materials for later use in student research projects.

The French model is also unique in the strong relationship between the absence of assertion of multiculturalism and the development of a sense of civic unity through the national education system. Students will analyze the link between multiculturalism and education as well as its relationship to *laïcité*. In late nineteenth-century France, policies which centered around nation building through assimilation focused on the establishment of free, mandatory, and secular education through the Jules Ferry laws (1881–2). This national education system transformed nineteenth- and early twentieth-century Patois-speaking peasants into French republicans and successfully integrated European immigrants into the nation. Consequently, education themes are prominent in literary representations of immigrants and their descendants, including Beur novels which question the notions of a single, unified *francité* (Frenchness) and propose multicultural identities within the national education system. Although Azouz Begag's *Le Gone du Chaâba* (1986) has been most often used as a typical example of a Beur novel depicting the childhood experience in a shantytown, other lesser-taught works by female authors provide additional perspectives. Novels that address these themes and could be assigned for intermediate or advanced language learners include Farida Belghoul's *Georgette!* (1986) and Soraya Nini's *Ils disent que je suis une beurette* (1993), which problematize the triangular relationship between parents, school, and child, as well as the unique pressures on young girls from the North African community in France.

In contemporary France, the national education system remains one of the key institutions in the transmission of *francité*, and the multiple ethnic groups that are visible within the French republic can be considered by authorities a result of a failed assimilation and the building up of a feared *communautarisme*. French media responses to terrorist attacks in January 2015, for example, focused on the perceived failures of the national education system in transmitting French Republican values. Contemporary French citizenship requirements still include the vague and subjective requirement of the candidate to justify his/her "assimilation to the French community" in addition to a "good understanding" of the French language, of the rights and duties of French nationality, and of the essential principles and values of the Republic ("Comment devient-on citoyen français?"). For native-born French, these citizenship requirements are to be acquired through the national education system.

In order to understand the nuances of multiculturalism in France today, it is important to help students understand such concepts as *l'unité civique*, which, as Schwartz reminds us, has its origins in the ideals of a single, unified, Republican culture set forth by the 1789 French Revolution (83). Assimilation in France comes from the feeling that the French Republic is one people, one language, and one law, in contrast with the preferential hierarchy of the *Ancien Régime*; it is feared that any break from this homogeneous model of society may threaten the stability of the Republic (Schwarz 83). A critical writing or discussion prompt might include questions such as: Are the assimilationist model and its sister concept for spreading Frenchness abroad *la mission civilisatrice* (civilizing mission) incompatible with a multicultural society?

Such a discussion can also be used to remind students that the term "contemporary France" is a key notion in understanding French multiculturalism; the definition of who is considered a foreigner or an outsider to the nation has varied significantly across time. Definitions of who is popularly considered to be French may not always correspond with the strict legal definitions of French nationality, as pre-1962 Algeria or the DROM-COM today clearly show. A follow up discussion of how identity terminology is used to show the incompatibility of ethnic minorities with Frenchness include such examples as the lack of usage of hyphenated and thereby hybrid identities and the persistent usage of terms such as "first" and "second" generations. In the media and public opinion, how is one determined to be French? And legally? To whom and to what does the term multiculturalism most refer in contemporary French culture? Who and what are ignored by these restricted definitions?

Representing Gender in Multicultural Productions

Beginning in the late 1990s and early 2000s, additional cultural productions written by and about women began to be added to the critical discourse. These productions problematized the representations of North African women in French society with a particular focus on adult females, rather than young Beur males. Yamina Benguigui's cinematographic corpus in both fiction (feature length *Inch'Allah dimanche*, 2002 and television miniseries *Aïcha*, 2009) and documentary (*Mémoires d'immigrés*, 1997) is an excellent point of departure for analyzing representation in film. Her work highlights in particular the highly gendered notions of multiculturalism in Maghrebi-French contexts which are linked to stereotypes associated with countries of origin and those specific to Maghrebi-French women. These highly gendered, racist stereotypes may include remnants of colonial-era exoticism in art and literature or connotations of terrorism dating to the Algerian War. Women are also stigmatized as the "reproducers" of the Maghrebi community in France, both in a biological sense and in the transmission of non-French cultural values. Because of their non-Frenchness, they are perceived as barriers to assimilation. The stereotypical representation of first-generation Maghrebi-French immigrant women is that of a female who remains exclusively within the closed space of the home. After viewing Benguigui's *Inch'Allah Dimanche*, students might analyze how the film is a response to the predominately male perspectives on female postwar immigration; examples of male perspectives can be found in sociologist Abdelmalek Sayad's interviews with North African immigrant males, one of whom in 1958 explained why he did not invite his wife to join him in France: "She would lose her freedom. It would simply make her unhappy, lonely; she would be imprisoned in one dirty, dark, damp room. That is all there is for her. She would very much want the sun, she would miss the sky" (*La Double absence: des illusions de l'émigré aux souffrances de l'immigré*, 156). Students might read and critically analyze Sayad's interview in comparison with protagonist Zouina's experience in *Inch'Allah Dimanche*.

In contrast with the masculine-centered, often homogeneous *Beur* and *banlieue* genres, the heterogeneous nature of female experiences in Benguigui's corpus argues against the homogeneous female Maghrebi-French experience of a woman who stays confined to the domestic sphere under male authority as the stereotypes suggest. Students might be asked to keep a list of female characters and profile their diverse personal and professional paths. Benguigui's interviews in *Mémoires d'immigrés* also demonstrate that immigrant women's contacts with and roles in French society could vary widely. Some women were indeed victims of domestic violence or afraid to go out of their homes. In contrast with Sayad's interview of males in 1958 who imagined what a female experience might be, Caitlin Killian's research interviewing 45 Maghrebi immigrant women in France reinforces Benguigui's notion of heterogeneity and freedom. Students may read and critically analyze excerpts from Killian's study in juxtaposition with that of Sayad in order to understand the effects of and variations in gendered representations across time and space.

Cultural productions also directly engage in a dialogue expressing the sharp division between feminine and masculine points of view. In contrast with the public and often violent actions of protest and activism engaged in by the sons of Maghrebi immigrants, Dalila Kerchouche's narrator Leïla in the introduction to *Mon Père ce Harki* (a short excerpt that might be read aloud in class) acknowledges that it is through pacifist female voices in literature and diplomacy, novels and public speeches, that awareness, acknowledgement, and understanding of multicultural communities in France occurs. Guène also explores the sharp contrasts in behaviors and societal expectations for young male and female narrators as well as gender expectations for adult parents in *Kiffe Kiffe Tomorrow* (narrated by a young female, Doria, who speaks of her mother) and in *Un Homme ça ne pleure pas* (narrated by a young male, Mourad, who speaks of his father). Students may read the two texts or excerpts from them to create critical comparisons.

Maghrebi-French communities still remain strongly associated with the politically charged and divisive Algerian War of Independence, and there has been a recent increase in discourse about the war in cultural productions and the media. In addition to the stereotypes associated with terrorism, both historically and in the present, these strong connotations of violence reinforce the perceived dangers of multiculturalism as leading to *communautarisme* and a fractured society. Approaches to teaching French multiculturalism can also lead to discussions about lost history, such as the Harki narrative or Paris massacre of October 1961, and a nation's construction of a master narrative through the use of independent and state media. In addition to Kerchouche's novels *Leila* and *Mon Père ce Harki*, which question France's republicanism in the context of the suppression of minority voices, several other key texts may be included in a final unit exploring the suppression of multiculturalism, postmemory, and silence and the relationship of these concepts to gender. Works that might be studied include Alan Hayling's independent documentary *Drowning by Bullets* and Leila Sebbar's novel *The Seine Was Red*. These works document the participation of women in the Algerian independence movement in France as well as the highly gendered racial profiling which associated all veiled women with the emblematic *porteuses de feu* (bomb carriers) of the Algerian War era.

For further study there might be a more general analysis of representations of multicultural France in the media to help students understand public perceptions and the processes in recognition of a pluralistic society. Early portrayals of Maghrebi immigrant populations in France on television, images which shaped the development of highly gendered stereotypes depicting women in the domestic sphere under the authority of French social workers, are still available through the online archives of the Institut National de l'Audiovisuel (INA.fr). For example, Kerchouche began her career as a journalist, and chose journalism as the profession for the fictional character Leila in order to unearth and publicly disseminate Harki narratives. The media, including popular television, is also a means of denouncing racism and discrimination against minorities, especially in regards to women in contemporary French society, as Benguigui documents through the *Aïcha* telefilm series. Media sources, both traditional and innovative, continue to provide important spaces for voices of dissent against French assimilation policies.

Although a semester-long study of gendered multiculturalism in France as suggested by this study would be ideal, it is also possible to integrate aspects of this "rethinking of France" into other courses as well. Discussion and explorations into French multiculturalism within survey courses in literature or civilization help bridge the gap between what is perceived as French and what is set aside as Francophone or "the Other." The concepts, examples, and texts in this study have also been successfully taught across a wide range of courses in English, including honors program courses, interdisciplinary seminars, first-year seminars, and general education courses in history and literature. There is a need for more dissemination of "multicultural France" and the gendering that occurs within these spaces as a means of introducing students from a variety of disciplines to an alternative narrative of France and of showing the relevance of French to other fields.

Notes

1 French Public Policy Institute.
2 All translations are my own.
3 The song refers to the iconic Marianne, the national symbol of the French Republic.

References

Aïcha. Film. Dir. Yamina Benguigui. France Télévisions, 2009.
Amara, Fadela, with Sylvia Zappi. *Ni Putes Ni Soumises*. La Découverte, 2009.
Asselin, Gilles and Ruth Mastron. *Au Contraire: Figuring Out the French*. Nicholas Brealey Publishing, 2010.
Belghoul, Farida. *Georgette!*. Barrault, 1986.
Carroll, Raymonde. *Cultural Misunderstandings: The French-American Experience*. University of Chicago Press, 1994.
Cliché! Film. Dir. Villain, Cédric. France, 2010. www.cedric-villain.info
Debré, Jean Louis. *L'Assemblée nationale, ultime étape de la Marche des femmes des quartiers contre les ghettos et pour l'égalité*. Assemblée Nationale, July2003. www.assemblee-nationale.fr/evenements/mariannes.asp
Drowning by Bullets. Film. Dir. Alan Hayling. Icarus Films, 1995.
Guène, Faiza. *Kiffe kiffe demain*. Hachette littératures, 2004.
Guène, Faiza. *Kiffe Kiffe Tomorrow*, trans. Sarah Ardizzone. Harcourt, 2006.
Guène, Faiza. *Un Homme, Ça ne pleure pas*. Fayard, 2014.
Inch'Allah dimanche. Film. Dir. Yamina Benguigui. Film Movement, 2002.
Kerchouche, Dalila. *Leïla: avoir dix-sept ans dans un camp de harkis*. Seuil, 2006.
Kerchouche, Dalila. *Mon père ce Harki*. Seuil, 2012.
Killian, Caitlin. *North African Women in France: Gender, Culture, and Identity*. Stanford University Press, 2006.
Nini, Soraya. *Ils disent que je suis une beurette*. Fixot, 1993.
Sayad, Abdelmalek. *La double absence: des illusions de l'émigré aux souffrances de l'immigré*. Seuil, 1999.
Schwartz, V.R. *Modern France: A Very Short Introduction*. Oxford University Press, 2011.
Sebbar, Leila. *The Seine was Red*. Indiana University Press, 2008.

12

TEACHING ALGERIA THROUGH THE LENS OF FEMINISM

Florina Matu

Francophone literature has given a privileged place to the works of writers from the Maghreb during the past 20 years. Little by little, this interest has increased and included the cinematographic creations of the North African directors whose productions are making their way in a very dynamic industry. Algerian national literature has evolved slowly but promisingly within the field of Francophone North African literature, characterized by its variety, originality, and need to evolve. Transnational and hybrid, it occupies a solid place in postcolonial literary production.

Sinuous, the journey of women in this lively literary field has often encountered multiple obstacles. Writing, as a way of expressing one's thoughts and creativity, proves incompatible with the modesty and reserve that must characterize female behavior in the Maghreb. Daring to write and above all to publish is synonymous with the shame of revealing oneself in public, as these women writers express themselves valiantly and completely outside the values of the traditional Muslim society. As for their themes, contemporary Francophone Algerian works address subjects that escape the ideological temptation. The path taken by their authors was difficult, primarily because of the limitations of the Algerian publishing houses, the censorship, and the shortcomings of a specialized press that could promote them.

Many female writers have been forced to write under pseudonyms (e.g., Assia Djebar and Maïssa Bey) in order to protect themselves and their family from the authorities. The 1990s, deeply marked by Islamist violence and terrorism, represented a real challenge for the writers of this country. Women were the first victims of the Islamists' atrocities, an aspect that explains the impact that the violent regime has had on their literary creation. Threatened with death, many Francophone writers fled Algeria because of the climate of insecurity and fear. While in exile, especially in France, they have set themselves up as witnesses of the crisis that was tearing their country apart. Thus, their works have insisted on the themes of terror, anguish, and chaos. Paradoxically, this crisis situation gave rise, according to the findings of Najib Redouane, to "a vigorous creation characterized both by its extreme diversity" and "a certain uniformity through points of convergence"[1] (12). This last aspect of contemporary Algerian writing confirms its coherence, coupled with "a great desire to refuse and reject any totalitarian ideology" (Redouane 12). While Algerian society has continued to favor the communal way of life, characterized by immutable values, literary creations promote the individual, their quest for identity, their needs outside the norms imposed by the society. In her anthology of Francophone Algerian literature, Christiane Achour remarks that after the 1980s Algerian literature became the expression of history as experienced by its characters, described in their private lives and thus marking the transition from a collective consciousness to an individual consciousness in the contemporary Algerian literary space.

Women have embraced this trend by adding taboo subjects including the naked body, the liberation from her father, and confinement. In the majority of texts by Algerian writers, social observation accompanies the feminine perspective. This chapter includes several approaches to teaching literary and cinematic works by contemporary Francophone Algerian women writers and directors. It emphasizes how women characters articulate and express concerns regarding identity and resistance, gender roles and family dynamics, sexuality and difference, marriage and womanhood. It incorporates examples of reading guides, activities, and assessment tools. It explains the professor's choice of materials, her methods and attempts to educate her students to free themselves from the abundance of stereotypes associated with colonial and postcolonial Algeria, and to discern Algerian women's challenges, as portrayed in three contemporary literary and cinematic works: the movie *The Battle of Algiers* (1966), Maïssa Bey's novel *Bleu blanc vert* (2006), and Leïla Aslaoui's short stories included in the volume *Coupables* (2006).

The relevance of teaching contemporary Francophone Algerian literature and cinema from a feminist perspective can be explained in multiple ways. Firstly, it is important to establish the audience for this course content. In addition to students who made a firm commitment to the French program by declaring a minor or major in the target language, the content attracts international students whose native language is French. French students (from France) have the opportunity to learn about a culture whose natives represent an important segment of the immigrant population in France. Such a course broadens French students' cultural understanding of their neighbors and potentially contributes to disrupting stereotypes associated with the Maghrebi population, in particular women, their bodies, their behavior, and their struggles in a patriarchal society. Francophone students from North African countries might also express interest in such course content knowing that their cultural values are validated and important as they represent the focus of an academic course. These students stimulate intercultural exchanges and energize the classroom atmosphere as they share their own experiences. In her article pertaining to women's presence in college-level language and culture courses, Miléna Santoro relies on statistics regarding faculty gender dynamics in academia in order to emphasize how women educators and the feminist research interests reflected in their course materials generate enthusiasm among a predominantly female student population: "What is even more certain is that the increase in the number of women pursuing their interest in French, even in teaching, as well as the overwhelming proportion of female students in the French course, contribute significantly to the pedagogical atmosphere of college-level courses" (430).

Secondly, it is important to justify the relevance of this pedagogical content in the academic curriculum. The following arguments pertain to academia in the United States though they could most likely be present in other countries. Where does a course that focuses on Francophone Algerian literature and cinema fit in the broader frame of an American university? Regardless of their major, students are expected to develop an understanding of the global community and be prepared to articulate their responsibilities within this community. At a minimum, such courses help students to acquire a basic understanding of cultural behaviors within a global context, as well as to compare social practices from their own culture relative to those from another culture. In his article entitled "The New Francophonie: Teaching French from an African-Centered Perspective," Isaac Joslin insists on the importance of including the Francophone literary production of African authors in the French studies curriculum: "The enormous growth of the world's French-speaking population within Africa, inasmuch as it depends on the sustained cooperative development of educational resources and infrastructure consider a corollary shift in the focus of instruction, which more closely reflects the reality of the French-speaking world" (Joslin 129). The author highlights several themes among which are economic inequality, social justice, as well as the issue of contemporary female oppression and liberation in postcolonialism.

Jane Alison Hale, whose article enumerates the challenges one faces when teaching introductory Francophone literature courses, reveals important criteria that need to be taken into consideration when selecting course materials. She suggests incorporating:

> about 200 pages, written in an authentic French but not too difficult, written by a woman, dealing with the past, the present and the near future, telling an individual's personal experience in a cultural and historical context that is at the same time something very different for the students and something with which they can identify in some respects.
>
> *(426)*

In addition to the above mentioned criteria and its rich thematic content, in a course focused on Francophone Algerian literature written by women students examine and produce coherent analyses of literary/cultural topics through research and critical thinking, by using textual evidence and documentation as well as demonstrating an understanding of the diversity of the Francophone world within the broader framework of multicultural communities and global perspectives.

The task of teaching Francophone Algerian women's literary and cinematic productions presents various challenges, among which the most difficult is breaking stereotypes associated with Muslim women, often seen as oppressed in their patriarchal societies, victims of cultural and religious norms that delegate them secondary roles in all aspects of life. In her volume on teaching Assia Djebar's works, Anne Donadey argues against imposing rigid theories of colonialism and women's place as they pose a serious obstacle to the articulation of a coherent feminist pedagogical approach:

> Feminist texts from Muslim cultures inscribe themselves in an overdetermined context because the so-called plight of the Muslim woman has been a mainstay of colonialism ideology in the West at least since the nineteenth century ... How to teach Djebar (or any feminist writer from a Muslim or Arab background) in North America or Europe, especially post-9/11, in ways that resist the dominant, imperialist, pseudo-feminist paradigm effectively is a difficult task indeed.
>
> *(17)*

It is precisely for this reason that the following course materials could be used to disrupt stereotypes associated with Algerian women. Starting with the independence war illustrated in the documentary-style movie *The Battle of Algiers* (1966), continuing with the transition period between 1962 and 1992 which serves as the time frame for Maïssa Bey's novel *Bleu blanc vert* (2006), and concluding with the sinister "décennie noire" (the dark decade) examined in Leïla Aslaoui's short stories included in the volume *Coupables* (2006), students understand Algeria through the lens of feminism.

First, students watch the film *The Battle of Algiers* and then write a short essay in which they analyze the role played by women characters in the Algerian revolution. They determine how women characters in *The Battle of Algiers* play a vital role in the Algerian revolution with their courageous and clandestine actions, while remaining behind the scenes. In the course of the film one observes these feminine figures draped in white like angels of death, who slip silently into the crowd without arousing the suspicions of the French officers. Students realize that, paradoxically, the strength of these women is due to their modest social status because no one seems to believe that a woman could be an accomplice in such acts as the assassination of an officer. Viewers question this ironic misconception in the scene where an officer seizes an Algerian woman walking with a weapon hidden under her dress, and she starts screaming in Arabic. One of the French officers in proximity brings him closer, explaining that he should never touch Algerian women. In reality, it is they who facilitate much of the violence that leads to manifestation and independence, and without the help they bring, the revolution would have been unsuccessful. It is also interesting to note the contrast between French women and Algerian women, which would generate interesting cross-cultural dialogues. Their Western outfits and hairstyles are perhaps the mark of the colonial oppressors, but they are also the disguise that allows them to endure in their efforts of freedom.

In another scene from this film a journalist poses the following question to the leader of the Front de Libération Nationale (National Liberation Army) following his arrest by French paratroopers: "Do not you find it rather cowardly to use the bags and baskets of your women to carry your bombs?" Indeed, the film contains two scenes in which a completely veiled woman holds a revolver in her basket and gives it to a man, a member of the revolutionary group, so that he can accomplish a mission. However, this question reduces the woman to a submissive character and implies that she has no choice. On the contrary, women who take part in the Algerian revolution seem as motivated as men. One of the most important scenes illustrating the role played by female characters is that in which three women place three bombs in places frequented by Westerners. Their preparation is symbolic because they remove their veils, put on make-up, and wear a skirt and jewelry, to disguise themselves as "French" in order to avoid police checks. Thus, the emphasis of their femininity serves the Algerian revolution. The final scene is also symbolic because we see two women at the head of a group of protestors pushing past soldiers, one with the Algerian flag in hand. Learners can interpret this image as a willingness to show that women are also engaged in the struggle for independence. Students are able to observe one surprising aspect of the film, which is, according to Danièle Djamila Amrane Minne, the complete absence of speaking roles for women activists: "Women are almost totally silent throughout the whole film. This is all the more striking because, in fact, the atmosphere within resistance groups was usually characterized by a close camaraderie between men and women, sustained by lively debates" (347).

Women's underrepresented role in the construction of postcolonial Algeria is seen in Maïssa Bey's novel *Bleu blanc vert*. Born in 1950, Bey is deeply rooted in the phenomenon of postcolonialism, characterized by faith, hope, and bitter disillusionment. The fact of having witnessed tumultuous historical episodes of Algeria is noticeable in her work in which languages and cultures cohabit harmoniously. In the unstable political climate in Algeria since 1990, under the shadow of anonymity given to her by her pseudonym, her choice to write the unspoken, to expose the taboos of Algerian society and breaking silence have become vital for Maïssa Bey, whose writing reveals several inconvenient truths. Torn between the obligation to make concessions as a mother and professor, and the pleasure of debating political facts with men, Maïssa Bey found from her youth the means to balance the impositions of the Algerian patriarchal society and her desire to express herself freely. Without falling into the temptation of idealism, Bey promotes women characters in her writing, with flaws exposed.

In her narratives, Maïssa Bey uses children's perspectives consistently in order to raise the delicate questions that adults no longer ask, out of fear or duplicity. The particularity of her approach relies upon allegorical representations as well as an emphasis on the individual in the face of colonization. Beyond the historical content found in the majority of her stories, Maïssa Bey expresses a deep concern for the sociological function of her writing. She highlights the effectiveness of literature in social space and uses it to accentuate the role of Algerian women. Divided in three parts, *Bleu blanc vert* is particularly appropriate for the Francophone literature classroom given its clear structure. The time frame is spread over a period of 30 years, from 1962 to 1992, and is characterized by a perfect conjunction between Algerian history and the life stories of her characters. In addition, students can easily delve into historical references to both colonialism and postcolonialism, as well as a multitude of interesting topics: societal and family dynamics, gender roles, family values, maternity, virginity, education, and violence. The division of the book into three decades harmonizes with the double focus through the two main characters. The writer gives voice to Ali and Lilas from the moment they are 12 years old, allowing them to narrate their own evolution in the form of two balanced diaries. By inserting interesting episodes from the characters' lives in their apartment building, Bey focuses on a microcosm of Algerian society. At first infantile, full of humor and innocence, then deeper and sometimes bitter, the observations of the two narrators, while relating to their lives, do not omit the dramas of an entire society in transition, the ebb and flow of hope, and pessimistic resignation.

Moreover, considered as autofiction, students can consider new perspectives on events that mark the private and social life of the narrator, from childhood to adulthood. *Bleu blanc vert* covers, in a fictional setting, past moments, sometimes very distant, in the author's life. She insists upon them because these episodes have not yet exhausted their meaning and therefore demand to be justified, analyzed, and clarified. Serge Doubrovsky's definition of this theoretical approach could serve as a basis for analysis of the female protagonist's evolution which mirrors the writer's struggle as a child after her father died during the Independence War. Doubrovsky's characterization in "Les points sur les 'i'" (*Genèse et autofiction*) helps students to understand the value of Bey's narrative discourse which cannot be reduced to a simple autobiography but rather represents "the means of trying to catch up, recreate, reshape in a text, in a writing, lived experiences, of one's own life that are in no way a reproduction, a photograph" (64).

Furthermore, students have the opportunity to understand the relationship between generations from a feminist perspective and, in particular, how the narrator and her mother perceive being a woman. In one classroom activity students reflect on whether their points of view reflect the Moroccan sociologist Soumaya Naamane-Guessous's statement:

> Women often have only maternity to fill the void of their conjugal life; having a child is, moreover, an integral part of this duty as a wife, and we know that this duty is the foundation of the marital bond in our society. The position of the wife is reinforced during pregnancy, childbirth, and especially when the child born is male.
>
> *(105)*

Students also analyze the text and learn how the pressure on women to maintain their purity and fulfill their responsibilities as a housewife and mother of sons entails a fear that invades all dimensions of life. Indeed, Lilas deplores that, "this terror of women is present everywhere. The terror of being abandoned. The terror of losing her virginity. The terror of not satisfying the multiple desires of men. The terror of not being able to attain the rank of 'mother of sons'" (Bey 129). This recurrent terror is due to the omnipresent notion that woman as a human being exists solely in relation to male desires. If she fails at her womanly duties, she becomes tainted by an indelible shame. For some, this terror leads them to a frenzy of activity, and they strive to achieve all tasks without failure, without pause for reflection or rest. Furthermore, women characters in *Bleu blanc vert* bear the burden of certain Maghrebi traditions, including modesty, women's honor, and shame. Often presented as oppressed by the patriarchal society which preaches honor, that is, the dignity and respectability of an individual, women are forced to fulfill their obligations while ignoring their own desires. In *Bleu Blanc Vert*, the female body is highly commodified, emptied of individual identity so that it can better serve male desires. This total possession of women is reinforced by certain rituals that mark them (literally and figuratively) with an imprint that affirms the domination of men. The protagonist, Lilas, is subjected to an unwritten ritual that seeks to protect her virginity, and in order for the remembrance of the ceremony to be visible, a slight incision is made on the upper part of the thigh in order to print a horizontal scar. This ceremony remains in her memory "to such an extent that despite her training as a psychologist and her high level of culture, the protagonist has struggled to overcome the apprehension and anguish of her first premarital sex" (Soler 139). The scar serves to remind the protagonist that her body does not belong to her nor her desires, that her commitment is to her feminine duty and the honor of the family.

As they examine the impact of education on women characters' destinies through the lens on feminism, students reflect on how Lilas's success highlights the power of education in postcolonial Algeria as a path to self-discovery. Recognizing that a generation ago literacy was forbidden to women, Lilas describes the completion of her education as a privilege. This openness allows her to pursue a path previously forbidden to women like her mother-in-law and to obtain a level of independence that was once unthinkable. However, there is a price to pay for this academic success and the subsequent professional insertion: a psychologist, Lilas is now confronted by numerous accounts of the women who confide their secrets and their pains to her. Faced with these dark revelations, Lilas undergoes an identity crisis as an Algerian woman. It is true that progress has been made in education and that women now have the right to choose their husband, but expectations of submissive behavior and religious obligations remain a deleterious force in women's psychological make-up.

While the first two works mentioned in this chapter focus on filmic and textual analysis, Leila Aslaoui's short stories in the anthology *Coupables* reveal a tight connection to the author's professional occupation with justice, politics, and women's rights in Algeria. Her works, inspired by the Algerian social and political climate of the 2000s, resist oblivion, and will help future generations understand the devastating consequences of terrorism. Her books seek to denounce the flaws in the Algerian judicial system which neglects the rights of women while promoting hope for a worthy life free of suffering. In the stories of the *Coupables* collection students analyze through women characters' testimonies the causes of intolerance towards women in contemporary Algeria. If polygamy, the difficulty of obtaining divorce, and illiteracy still numb efforts towards modernity, it is because there are many complex reasons including the judicial system. In *Coupables*, divided into 12 narratives, every narrator, every "I" who embodies an aspect of female guilt, bears a name, and therefore has a precise identity. In the pages of the collection, the students become familiar with the destinies of Bédira, Chérifa, Safia, Yasmina, Khadidja, Hanifa, Nabila, Nafissa, Mériem, Alya, and Souhila.

In a country where censorship infiltrates the smallest spheres, Aslaoui uses her work published in France, thus accessible beyond national borders, to illustrate the status of minor of

Algerian women, before the law and in their private life. This is a double-edged subordination of which Arab feminists have already spoken. Before exploring representative narratives from this collection, students become familiar with the Moroccan sociologist and writer Fatima Mernissi's inquiries. Mernissi explains how the legal system that establishes the rights of Muslim women is built on both the immutability of the Koran and the timelessness of the sacred and archaic values of society. Muslim law originated in the Shari'a designates first of all the path traced by God but also a set of rules resulting from a human interpretation by Muslim jurists. It would therefore be impossible to dissociate the law from the sacred, concludes Mernissi in her study *La Femme et la loi in Algeria*: "In a society deeply imbued with Islamic culture, Koran and the immutability of the Sacred Text, but also in the other founding sources of the law and especially the Shari'a" (21). Each short story in Aslaoui's work illustrates women characters' legal struggles in contemporary Algeria and could be perceived as purely fictional without a proper context. Students benefit from exposure to the precepts included in the 1984 Family Code ("Code de la famille") which serves as a basis to Aslaoui's stories. In addition, they establish comparisons between the above-mentioned document and its most recent and improved version from 2015 which includes more protective rights for Algerian women in case of divorce and domestic violence, to name only two aspects reflected in *Coupables*.

Taught through the lens of feminism and from a chronological perspective, Algerian cinematic and literary works such as *La Bataille d'Alger*, *Bleu Blanc vert*, and *Coupables* reflect topics of interest for students interested in meaningful societal issues such as identity and resistance, gender roles and family dynamics, sexuality, marriage, and womanhood. Through the study of these works students will acknowledge the continuous transformation of Algerian society, the progress women made in order to consolidate their status in their private and social lives, as well as the power of contemporary fictional works to disrupt stereotypes associated with women in Maghreb. Beautifully written, these works are remarkable for their objective and yet compassionate tone, as well as for their courageous denunciation of taboos and misconceptions that continue to exist in their societies.

Note

1 All translations are mine unless otherwise indicated.

References

Achour, Christiane. *Anthologie de la littérature algérienne de langue française. Histoire littéraire et anthologie*. Entreprise algérienne de presse, 1990.
Aslaoui, Leïla. *Coupables*. Buchet-Chastel, 2006.
Bey, Maïssa. *Bleu blanc vert*. Aube, 2006.
Donadey, Anne. *Approaches to Teaching the Works of Assia Djebar*. MLA, 2017.
Donadey, Anne. *Recasting Postcolonialism. Women Writing between Worlds*. Heinemann, 2001.
Doubrovsky, Serge. "Les points sur les 'i'," in *Genèse et autofiction*, ed. Jean-Louis Jeannelle and Catherine Viollet. Academia-Bruylant, 2007, 53–66.
Hale, Jane Alison. "Cours d'introduction de litterature francophone: Quels objectifs?" In *North–South Linkages and Connections in Continental and Diaspora African Literatures*, ed. Edris Makward, Mark Lilleleht, and Ahmed Saber. Africa World Press, 2005, 423–428.
Joslin, Isaac. "The New Francophonie: Teaching French from an African-Centered Perspective." *French Review: Journal of the American Association of Teachers of French* 88. 4(2015): 127–139.
Minne, Danièle Djamila Amrane and Alistair Clarke. "Women at War: The Representation of Women in the Battle of Algiers." *Interventions: International Journal of Postcolonial Studies* 9. 3(2007): 340–349.

Naamane-Guessous, S. *Au-delà de toute pudeur: La sexualité féminine au Maroc: Conclusion d'une enquête sociologique menée de 1981 à 1984 à Casablanca.* Karthala, 1991.

Nouredine, Saadi and Fatima Mernissi. *La Femme et la loi en Algérie.* UNU/WIDER, 1991.

Pontecorvo, Gilles, dir. La Bataille d'Alger [The Battle of Algiers]. Criterion Collection, 2004.

Redouane, Najib, ed. *Diversité littéraire en Algérie.* L'Harmattan, 2010.

Santoro, Miléna. "La Présence des femmes dans l'enseignement de la langue et des cultures francophones au niveau universitaire en Amérique." *Jeunesse et langue française: Créer, partager, entreprendre: Langue française au Canada et en Amérique du Nord.* Biennale de la langue française, 2002, 427–437.

Soler, Ana. "Maïsa Bey, Bleu blanc vert." *Nouvelles questions féministes* 27. 3(2008): 138–142.

13

TEACHING HÉLÉ BÉJI, POSTCOLONIALISM, AND THE ARAB SPRING

Perspectives from Baudrillard, McClintock, and Giroux

Eric Touya de Marenne

More than ever, higher education needs to offer alternative ways of thinking, challenge ways of knowing, interrogate sources of information, and create a context for counternarrative. Overcoming the postmodern and utilitarian challenge implies the realization that education through teaching and learning can shape and transform society. This is particularly true if we consider that it entails a reflection and decision about what counts as knowledge, which curriculum content is worthy of attention and research, and how to approach it pedagogically. Henry Giroux and bell hooks, among others, have argued that knowledge is socially produced and determined by strategies of exclusion or containment. They discussed in particular the importance of acquiring critical consciousness through education, and the sociopolitical relevance of literature and criticism. In the words of bell hooks: "We need educators to make schools places where the conditions for democratic consciousness can be established and flourish ... The future of democratic education will be determined by the extent to which democratic values can triumph over the spirit of oligarchy that seek to silence diverse voices" (17). A challenge for educators in recent years has been to reconcile theoretical writing and the need or interest of the public at large. Wrongly perceived within and outside the academic world as a self-involved endeavor driven by abstraction, postmodernist and deconstructionist approaches did not explicitly engage with broad audiences on pertinent issues outside the university.

Aware of this perception, Jacques Derrida argued that ethics or the attainment of virtue could be conceivable in a deconstructionist or postmodernist world. He underlined deconstruction's ethical importance, arguing that it did not necessarily have hyper-relativistic or nihilistic implications and that it rested, above all, on the primacy of critical thinking:

> I am referring to the right to deconstruction as an unconditional right to ask critical questions not only to the history of the concept of man, but to the history even of the notion of critique, to the form and the authority of the question, to the interrogative form of thought ... The university should thus be the place in which nothing is beyond question.
>
> *(13)*

Shifting his attention from purely theoretical issues to the realm of human praxis, Derrida contended that "the university should remain the ultimate place of critical resistance." Such an "unconditional resistance" was needed to oppose the university to state, economic, media, ideological, and cultural powers, "in short, all the powers that limit the democracy to come" (13). This questioning thus has pedagogical and political implications.

It is in view of these considerations that I explored new approaches to teaching French and Francophone women through the work of Hélé Béji, a Tunisian author born in 1948. Over the past 30 years, Béji has written books and essays on the subjects of decolonization, cultural pluralism, feminism, and the problems of democratization in Tunisia's postcolonial era. I will discuss how teaching Hélé Béji's *Désenchantement National* (1982), and her more recent articles on the Arab Spring (2011–13), enabled me to develop new pedagogical strategies which sought to expand theoretical and interdisciplinary perspectives on colonial and postcolonial concerns and issues pertaining to historical and civic progress.

Through her work, Béji notably questioned the notion that Tunisia's postcolonial era or the Arab Spring increased opportunities for women, democracy, and the development of human rights. In light of her inquiries, I will examine further three new different approaches I adopted recently to teaching the work of Hélé Béji in a college senior seminar: first, Baudrillard's postmodern perspective on technology and the production of reality; second, McClintock's critique of the systematization of postcolonial theory; and third, Giroux's call for critical pedagogy and civic engagement. The objective of the seminar was to analyze and rethink how Francophone women writers challenged and reinvented the political, cultural, and critical discourse of their time and place through a broad range of critical approaches including the relation between literary creation, media, history, and society in feminist and postcolonial contexts.

Béji and Baudrillard on History

In her 1982 book entitled *Désenchantement National*, the Tunisian writer Hélé Béji contended that things and events in the postcolonial era had given way to *facticity*. Decolonization, she argued, limited everyone's existence to *simulations*, a fictional reality through which nothing materialized:

> To be decolonized is the most static version of the unhappy consciousness. Things and experiences merge in giving the impression of a facticity inherent in the movement of their very existence, producing in each one this unfulfilled need of foundations of all kinds. To be decolonized is neither a thought, nor an experience, nor a fact properly speaking. It is a hollow, gratuitous intensity, fed by simulations of acts or thought, where nothing adheres or sedates.
>
> *(147)*[1]

I explored with students how reading these lines brought Baudrillard to mind. The feeling of hollowness that transpired in Béji's account ("une intensité creuse") seemed to echo the philosopher's take on the fictitious self-referential nature of "reality." Béji's commentaries lead us to re-examine a variety of issues pertaining to rethinking the French classroom. As she alluded, they concern matters that are central to human experience in a democracy: justice, freedom (*liberté, égalité, fraternité*), and along with them, the ability of humanity to shape its own destiny. They also entail a reflection on the possible facticity of all forms of ideals and absolutes, and the deep uncertainty surrounding reliance on values, systems, ideologies, and/or grand narratives.

In our technologically driven world, Baudrillard has sought to examine the relationship between reality and fiction and the extent to which different modes of news and information that impact our lives are involved in constructing an understanding of what constitutes reality. From this perspective, the students analyzed how the French philosopher's reflection could shed light on Hélé Béji's disenchantment and vice versa by exploring two questions: to what extent were the more recent Tunisian Revolution and Arab Spring real or virtual events? Were their unfolding narratives technologically fabricated?

Addressing these challenging questions, the Béji-Baudrillard distant dialogue revealed parallels and contrasts about postcolonial and feminist approaches to literature and history that enabled students to grasp the complexity of the recent events of the Arab Spring, a revolutionary wave of protests in North Africa and the Middle East for social justice and democracy, which began in December 2010 in Tunisia with the Tunisian Revolution.[2]

First, Hélé Béji highlighted how a new form of repression had been born in the years that followed the independence of her country in 1956. This renewed absence of freedom implied a contradiction: the authority that had brought liberty was the very one that now dominated and perpetuated people's oppression and alienation. It was as if the new political leadership had attained its independence to deny it altogether for its citizens. The anticolonial movement thus hid within itself the existence of a hegemonic nature. It called at once for struggle to achieve autonomy, to in turn become an instrument of domination. In this respect, Béji's testimony paralleled Baudrillard, for whom history provides neither progress nor resolution, only an indefinite recurrence of old forms, recycled and illusory.

According to this vision, time has stopped in the age of media and technology. As there is no longer a forward or backward, we are speeding through "hyperreality," a world without a real origin in which all is stagnant and eternal: "There is a major difference between an event that happens (or that happened) in historical time and one that occurs in the real time of media information" (L'Yvonnet 239–40). Equipped with smartphones and immersed in the age of mass communication and information technology, the students were asked, in light of this proximity of views, whether "decolonization" and/or the "Arab Spring" have really occurred.

Two lessons emerged for students. They concern first the notion that experience and praxis may precede theory. Béji's "facticité" and "simulations" relative to her "désenchantement" evoked, like in Baudrillard, the virtual nature of contemporary culture. When I contacted her, she confirmed: "In fact, I had not read Baudrillard when I wrote my book *National Disenchantment*. So it's an unplanned affinity between himself and myself" (message of April 15, 2013). Second, they address the formidable impact of information technology. Are students measuring the role technology and social media is playing in their lives and altering their perception of reality?

It has been alleged in the first decade of the twenty-first century that technology could have a positive impact, leading to civic engagement. Calling on the honor and dignity of common people, Asma Mahfouz posted a video on social networks in January 2011 in which she called for a massive demonstration in Tahrir Square. Modern communication technologies, mobile phones, and satellite television play a significant role by facilitating the spread of information. The fact that dictators around the world attempt to counter these means of communication by cutting networks supports this view.

However, in light of Baudrillard's argument, students were able to measure the potential misuse of technology when information is produced according to models and norms controlled by governments or media conglomerates. Through this perspective, Béji's writing on postcolonial Tunisia and the collusion between media and the political hierarchy in *Désenchantement national* led them to rethink the complexity and uncertainty of social and political progress from a feminist and postcolonial perspective.

McClintock, Feminisms, Postcolonialism, and Dichotomies

In a parallel way, students were asked in a take-home assignment to deconstruct the Eurocentric interpretation of feminism, introduced earlier in the semester, which aimed at a comprehensive approach to the female condition worldwide. They read Béji's "Amina, ou l'histoire en marche," a newspaper article published in *Le Monde*, in which the author analyzed how Middle Eastern and North African women sought to escape socio-political barriers and alleviate their condition. Taking an active part in the Arab Spring, they played a leading role in street protests from Tunisia to Egypt and Yemen. It is estimated, for example, that 10 to 15 per cent of the protesters in Tahrir Square in Cairo were women even though the place of women in the public domain remained restricted in that society.

Yet, their hopes fell into disillusionment when several cases of sexual assault were reported during the protests. In Tunisia, rapes were committed when women were detained at the Interior Ministry on the night of January 14–15, 2011. Special brigades of Ben Ali were later found guilty of heinous crimes committed against minor girls raped in front of their families.[3] In light of these reports, one can legitimately question whether the events triggered by the Arab revolutions truly advanced the empowerment of women.

Could a new Hélé Béji emerge in 2050 and write a book about how the aspirations of Tunisian women in the aftermath of the Arab Spring were but illusions? Would she describe how the fate of common people was still marked by the seal of "facticity"? Has the Arab Spring increased opportunities for the development of human rights and democracy? Even as women in the Arab world have paid a high price in their continuing struggle for freedom, the path leading to emancipation and equal rights remains uncertain. Tunisian intellectuals made public a manifesto in which they expressed concern about the subsistence of democracy in their country.[4]

The students could assess to what extent these queries bring us back to Béji's postcolonial disenchantment validating the idea that revolution and the posture of opposing tradition did not necessarily bring about actual change or progress in social justice. Anticolonialism hid the birth of a political movement that was at once a symbol of autonomy and an instrument of domination through which the elite of the nation would replace the colonizer.

They explored here how Béji does not necessarily undermine aspects of postcolonial criticism embraced by authors such as Aimé Césaire who condemned the collusion between "colonization" and "civilization," or Edward Said who examined how the Western interpretation and invention of the Orient was determined by a presumed superiority of European values. They measured, however, the extent to which her analyses revealed how the systematization of postcolonial theory and the basic dichotomy it implied (oppressor versus oppressed) should be questioned when it runs the risk of perpetuating the Western compulsion to define and dominate through a process of recolonization.

Anne McClintock provides, in this respect, important insights about how postcolonialism reduced the history of people around the globe to a particular event: "Other cultures share only a chronological, prepositional relation to a Euro-centered epoch that is over (post-) … Can most of the world's countries be said, in any meaningful or theoretically rigorous sense, to share a single 'common past', or a single common 'condition' called the 'post-colonial condition', or 'post-coloniality'?" (1187–8). Using McClintock's argument, students reflected on how looking at the Tunisian Revolution and the Arab Spring from a constructed postcolonial standpoint is problematic when it embodies a continuation of Western thought and perpetuates the process of "colonization."

Coming to terms with the production of a postcolonial's perceived reality also challenged in theory and practice the students' understanding of historical events. As Hélé Béji lamented, independence led "through unexpected mechanisms" ("mécanismes inattendus") to the transfer ("reconvertit") of colonial oppression and alienation into the new political regime:

> National consciousness led after its genesis to Independence ... Here, another story has opened up for national consciousness, through which a form of colonial oppression was renewed. By what unexpected mechanisms? The permanence of alienation is not a duplication of the colonial occupation, something like its vibratory extension. Neo-colonial dependence did not determine the entire political situation that we experience.
> *(1982, 15)*

Shedding light on the ambiguous nature of reality and history, Béji stressed the impossibility to grasp or control the complex unfolding of world events. Writing *Désenchantement National*, she foretold the implications of McClintock's arguments concerning the uncertainty surrounding the reliance on the grand narrative of progress through the systematization of postcolonial theory and the basic dichotomies it implies.

Giroux and Béji's Arab Spring

Naoufel Brahimi El Mili was one of the first intellectuals to break the "myth" of the Arab Spring: "The story of the Arab Spring is transformed into a modern mythology, in the pure Anglo-Saxon story telling tradition" (14). Referring to the coverage of the Arab Spring as a "soap-opera" and a "once upon a time télé-révolution," he described how "the emotional register, anger, indignation and revolt replace any informative content [and the extent to which] Al-Jazeera is the knitting instrument of a custom story, from which are expurgated all foreign interference and economic objective" (15).

Bypassing nepotism, foreign interference, and the problem of widespread poverty and inequality as possible causes of the rebellion, television networks orchestrated the dramaturgy of the uprising in a way that hid its socio-economic reality. For El Mili, "Speaking of the Arab Spring can become a serious counter sense, as some Arab countries are entering a great winter, where presumed change would paradoxically lead to the maintenance of the old system" (211). Overthrowing a dictatorship did not necessarily lead to a substantial transformation of the social order.

Considering the media construction of the event as a custom-made reality (the "tricotage ... sur mesure"), I submitted the following questions to Hélé Béji in March 2014: "Can one hope or wish that the Arab Spring may contribute to improve the condition of women, the state of economic and social justice, or individual liberty? Or must we conclude that any affirmation pertaining to the latter would be relative or uncertain?" In her reply, she stressed the complexity of human action in the face of a simulated reality. She indicated, however, that Baudrillard would not have been insensitive to the events surrounding the Tunisian Revolution and Arab Spring, in particular to the dignity of its actors' aspirations: "As he was someone very humane, I believe that the Tunisian revolution would still have captivated him. He would not have passed over in silence the most important thing in my view ... the notion of dignity, in the name of which this revolution was made."[5]

The word "dignity" refers here to the economic condition needed to survive. We recall how economic hardship led Mohamed Bouazizi, a market vendor, to set himself on fire, an event that triggered the first waves of protest leading to the Arab Spring. Béji was skeptical in this regard about the advancement the revolutionary movement could achieve: "We know that modern economic life, as well as being an agent of progress, is a destructive agent of civility, and that it produces incivility, even violence."

Béji's remarks fostered a class reflection about the aims of education and its socio-economic but also political ramifications for society. Giroux notably argued that knowledge is socially produced and determined by strategies of exclusion or containment. In this context, a desired pedagogical outcome was to enhance students' critical consciousness: "A critical pedagogy for democracy does not begin with test scores but with questions. What kinds of citizens do we hope to produce through public education in a postmodern culture?" (2005, 74).

This critical teaching and thinking on the Arab Spring led students to question what constitutes economic justice, political rights and responsibilities, and thus democratic life. It significantly broadened students' understanding of pressing issues of our time, including globalization, economic ends, inequality, poverty, and the marketization of societies.

From a feminist approach, students also read Julie Nelson, who challenged the notion that economics was a positive science, and contended that its research was founded on constructed narratives resulting from power relations. Feminist approaches to economics have major pedagogical ramifications that pertained both to course content and students' perceptions and understandings. They also concern the preponderant question of the relation between knowledge and power—specifically how theories, norms, and values are constructed, introduced to, and acquired by the future participants and decision makers of society.

In this context, Giroux's call on educators and students promoted the questioning of accepted knowledge and authority pertaining to given norms and values. Through a new critical pedagogy asserting the importance of ethics and of responsibility toward others, "Darwinian Casino Capitalism [could] be resisted and defeated by instilling in students an ability for independent thinking, and a passion for the freedom of speech and critical analysis" (2010, 21).

Beyond its socio-economic dimension and the attributes of respect and honorability, the term "dignity" can also refer to the "self-ownership" and worthiness of each individual. To illustrate her view, Hélé Béji discussed in her article published in *Le Monde* newspaper the example of Amina Sboui, the Tunisian feminist activist who posted topless images of herself online to protest against the lack of women's rights in the Arab world: "One of the things that will remain, in my opinion, is the word of the teenage girl Amina, 'my body belongs to me and it is nobody's honor' ... If anything remains [of the Tunisian Revolution], it is this totally free act, which goes far beyond the popular uprising." Something profound had occurred with this event, whose echo would in her view have a lasting effect.

Following Amina Sboui's "acting out," women could claim the innocence of their body and rip away the physical or metaphoric veil of their culpability, even though, as Béji noted, the Tunisian political class appeared more "religiously correct" than ever in its response, and this reaction exposed the long and uncertain path toward women's emancipation: "But deep down, what does Amina say? That oppression does not end with revolution, and that care must be taken so that women may not become again the perpetrators of their own misfortune ... In Tunisia, women have altered, and not broken, traditions, so that the latter have remained in the moral landscape" (2013). Amina Sboui's action confronted the Tunisian people, conservatives and liberals, with the contradictions of their revolution, most having condemned what was for them unacceptable for women.

Reading Béji in light of Giroux's critical pedagogy helped students to formulate questions and carve out paths of inquiry. It led them to achieve a more careful and detailed reading beyond conventional boundaries in historical, political, societal, feminist, and postcolonial contexts. Béji provided a rich terrain for examining the Arab Spring from these expanded perspectives that are permeable and overlapping. Finally, the reading strategies brought students closer to the author's experience within and beyond their own contemporary epistemologies and sensibilities.

Amina Sboui's attempt to break away from tradition echoed Béji's disenchantment with postcolonial Tunisia. The independence of the 1960s had given way to facticity and reduced everyone's existence to simulations. It was marked by a continued monopolization of power and absence of freedom. A few years later, she argued in *Nous, décolonisés* (not translated into English) that the Tunisian population was freed from outside colonialism but not from the colonization of Tunisians themselves.

We have seen how the pedagogical ramifications of Béji's questioning through Baudrillard, McClintock, and Giroux renew, problematize, and expand the interdisciplinary nature of French studies and the French and Francophone classroom. From existential, political, and economic perspectives, Amina Sboui's decisive action affirmed with insistence the power that individuals possess to escape from the television plasmas, the multiple cellphone devices, and the veil of prejudices. "Mon corps m'appartient [My body belongs to me]" could well be a metaphor for Tunisia itself, above all its people, and the hopeful active participants of the Arab Spring. This claim could also prompt a reflection for our students living in advanced technological societies, yet ever fragile democracies, about whether or not this ownership can become real.

Notes

1 The book has not been translated into English. All translations from French into English are mine. "What is neo-colonialism? Why was democracy not born with independence? Why did nationalism and anticolonialism not constitute a force of freedom?" (13–14). For additional reference to this work, see Béji 1982.
2 For more information about the Tunisian Revolution and the Arab Spring, see Gana and Haas and Lesch.
3 See Mandraud et al.
4 See www.petitions24.net/manifesteintellectuelstunisiens-en
5 Hélé Béji sent me these comments and the ones that follow on March 16, 2014.

References

Béji, Hélé. "Amina, ou l'histoire en marche." *Le Monde*, June 15, 2013.
Béji, Hélé. *Désenchantement national. Essai sur la décolonisation*. François Maspero, 1982.
Béji, Hélé. *Nous, décolonisés*. Arléa, 2008.
Derrida, Jacques. "The Future of the Profession or the Unconditional University," in Peter Pericles Trifonas and Michael A. Peters, eds, *Deconstructing Derrida: Tasks for the New Humanities*. Palgrave Macmillan, 2005.
El Mili, Brahimi Naoufel. *Le printemps arabe: Une manipulation?* Max Milo, 2012.
Gana, Nouri. *The Making of the Tunisian Revolution: Contexts, Architects, Prospects*. Edinburgh University Press, 2013.
Giroux, Henry. *Border Crossings: Cultural Workers and the Politics of Education*. Routledge, 2005.
Giroux, Henry. *Zombie Politics and Culture in the Age of Casino Capitalism*. Peter Lang, 2010.
Haas, Mark L. and David W. Lesch. *The Arab Spring: The Hope and Reality of the Uprisings*. Routledge, 2016.
hooks, bell. *Teaching Critical Thinking: Practical Wisdom*. Routledge, 2010.
L'Yvonnet, François, ed. *Jean Baudrillard*. Editions de l'Herne, 2004.
Mandraud, Isabelle, Benjamin Barthe, Béatrice Gurrey, and François-Xavier Trégan. "Les révoltes arabes font-elles progresser la cause des femmes?" *Le Monde*, April 29, 2011.
McClintock, Anne. "The Angel of Progress: Pitfalls of the Term 'Post-Colonialism,'" in Julie Rivkin and Michael Ryan, eds, *Literary Theory. An Anthology*. Blackwell, 2004, 1185–1196.
Nelson, Julie. *Economics for Humans*. University of Chicago Press, 2006.
Said, Edward W. *Orientalism*. Vintage Books, 1978.

PART IV
Interdisciplinary Approaches to French Studies

14

BREAKING DOWN JAIL AND CROSS-DIVISIONAL WALLS

Teaching Simone de Beauvoir and Existentialist Writers in the Twenty-First-Century French and Criminal Justice Classroom

Araceli Hernández-Laroche

Introduction

Porous borders separate my teaching, scholarship, service, and community engagement. In this chapter, I expose why such fluid borders are of critical support for the growth of our French and Francophone studies program and world languages in general. I am the only full-time French faculty at my institution, a public regional university in the southern United States with approximately 6,000 students. Many colleagues throughout the country can probably relate to my situation; we adapt and retool to be generalists in order to carry the program forward and grow it. Thanks to collaborative, innovative partnerships throughout the university, community, state, and within my department (consisting of English and world languages), we created twenty-first-century opportunities for students interested in pursuing the study of the French language and Francophone studies that involve civic engagement. In this chapter, I showcase the critical importance of teaching cross-divisional courses which resulted in the creation of an award-winning service-learning program, *Operation Educate*. Interdisciplinary innovation brings visibility to French studies inside and outside the university. Most disciplines can benefit by integrating robust language and cultural literacies.

According to a much cited 2007 MLA report ("Foreign Languages and Higher Education: New Structure for a Changed World"), language is indispensable. Studying French literature, in the original language or in translation, plays a critical role in understanding our complex world which is—dare I say—existential. The 2007 MLA report explains that "[in] the context of globalization and in the post-9/11 environment, then, the usefulness of studying languages other than English is no longer contested." Hence, terrorism studies, to name one example, gains with the integration of languages, cultures, and world literatures.

The Value of Language and Cultural Skills in Terrorism Studies

Louise Richardson, a political scientist born in the Republic of Ireland, referenced a French existentialist play in her book, *What Terrorists Want: Understanding the Enemy, Containing the Threat*. Albert Camus's play, *Les Justes*, on terrorism and ethics, is based in czarist Russia during the first years of the twentieth century. In postwar France, when the play was written, intellectuals such as Camus debated ethical and philosophical questions related to violence and war as the world polarized during the Cold War and as decolonization movements spread. According to Richardson, Camus:

> beautifully captures the sense of morality of the nineteenth century anarchists, the precursors of many contemporary terrorists. He describes how Kaliayev, seeing two children seated in the carriage next to his intended target, the grand duke, could not bring himself to hurl the bomb. He subsequently does kill the grand duke and is executed, but he could not justify to himself killing children. Many contemporary terrorists, of course, have no trouble justifying the killing of children. There are generally a number of defenses offered for the resort to terrorism.
>
> *(16)*

In terrorism studies it is essential to understand the point of view, the motivations of those who decide to commit terrorist acts. Without careful attention to those perspectives—however alien they may seem—the task of dissuading potential individuals from carrying out murderous plots is made even more difficult. Literary studies sharpen our critical learning skills to explore various points of view.

Camus's play is of particular value because its main character echoes the thinking of the real-life terrorists that terrorism experts interview and study. These individuals, who carried out terrorist acts or intend to do so, believe they are saving society from specific types of tyranny and that their acts are for a greater good, motivated by a just cause: "A key legacy of the French Revolution to contemporary terrorism has been this notion of the killer as the self-appointed guardians of the will of the people" (Richardson 29). Terrorists perceive themselves as compassionate, as protectors, and this type of reasoning seems counterintuitive. And that's exactly the point; to dissuade such individuals, it's important to understand their opaque, incongruent worldview.

Hence, the study of literature can shed light on some of our most pressing contemporary ills. Moreover, by including the study of languages and cultures to our toolbox, we are better equipped to understand diverse worldviews, not just from the extreme minority of individuals who commit violent acts, but from the majority of (peaceful) peoples from around the world. Our worldview becomes more nuanced and more *empathetic*. Richardson emphasizes that we need to close the gap of perception amongst cultures to defeat terrorism. In our increasingly globalized cities and nations, the necessity to coexist more peacefully will persist with greater urgency. After the 2015 spike of terrorist attacks in France and around the world, French society revived its public debates on "le vivre ensemble" (coexisting) within a republic that is secular and inclusive of minorities, including religious ones. Abd Al Malik wonders, in his 2015 book on secularism and spirituality, "if it is normal that Muslims sense that France wants to rebuild itself by including them but with the condition that their religious identity be placed aside" (10). To combat marginalization in our increasingly polarized world, our youth, in particular, need to feel included, valued, and not perceived as foreign, as outsiders, in their respective societies.

In a 2007 interview at the University of California Berkeley, Richardson was asked about her recommendations for students interested in national security careers. Perhaps not surprisingly for educators in language and cultural studies, Richardson offered two main recommendations: to learn other languages and to travel to other regions of the world, especially to those in most critical need of expertise by government agencies. Likewise, this chapter seeks to encourage educators of French studies to build bridges with other disciplines. Our twenty-first-century students lead with global, interdisciplinary skills. Articulating to diverse audiences the relevancy of our field is paramount.

Criminal Justice and French

French needs cross-divisional partners and other disciplines need world-language linguistic and cultural literacies. According to a 2016 Forbes article, criminal justice, a popular major, has one of the highest unemployment rates. In an age of increasing "glocal" diversity, criminal justice majors (and others) can better serve increasingly non-English-speaking communities if they gain proficiency in French or another world language. To prepare our students for twenty-first-century challenges and a rapidly changing interconnected world, let us embrace the teaching of globalization-related material through a multilingual and multicultural perspective. With a criminal justice professor, Dr. Samantha Hauptman, I co-taught *The Twin Ills of Terrorism and Torture: A Global Perspective* in an active learning classroom, which allowed for the implementation of interactive, collaborative principles and activities. We taught French existential literature (along with sociological and criminal justice theory) and engaged our class in critical analysis of the dynamics of terrorism and torture through French existentialist philosophers such as Jean-Paul Sartre, Albert Camus, and Simone de Beauvoir, which especially for students of sociology and criminal justice was, according to one student, "initially terrifying and eventually wholly captivating." Students successfully engaged with French literature and in their final projects displayed a philosophical understanding of the complexities of terrorism and torture in our modern world.

We explored important representations of moral dilemmas in prose, theater, and film that plagued war-torn Europe and France during World War II and the Algerian War (1954–62) and how some important ethical questions related to terrorism, torture, and truth still haunt the United States today in post-9/11 society and around the world. The American response to 9/11 was informed by France's own failed counterterrorism strategies involving torture during its militarized effort to safeguard French Algeria, which was mostly populated by a Muslim majority. Utilizing criminological and sociological theory, we analyzed the complexities and divergences of existential writers as they grappled with the evils of war that often involved both terrorism and torture. The relevant documentaries and films, such as *The Battle of Algiers* (which was used by the Pentagon in 2003 as training material after the invasion of Iraq), helped us frame the sensitive debates on war censorship and national security.

It is important to place great focus on Simone de Beauvoir's *The Blood of Others*, as this 1945 novel explores ethically thorny issues such as debating the justification of terrorism as a means for social justice. In addition, reexamining Beauvoir's highly visible engagement against state-sponsored torture during the Algerian War allows us to focus on how French and Francophone women shaped ethical debates during war-torn conflicts on both sides of the Mediterranean during world wars and decolonization; their voices are often less studied. What lessons can we derive from Beauvoir's work which asks who has the right to decide for the life of others? As terrorism grips our cities and imaginations, what is the relationship between the study of literature and empathy? Can literature allow for the nuanced consideration of marginal perspectives in society?

When we think of existentialist writers, Jean-Paul Sartre and Albert Camus come to mind. Perhaps because these two writers largely embodied the debates—from the Cold War to decolonization—that galvanized postwar French society. However, new generations of students stand to gain when introduced to a critical reflection of Beauvoir's works, philosophy, life, and contribution to women's rights and human rights in general, especially in the context of war and decolonization. Not only is her work relevant to today's twenty-first-century globalized societies, her thought can reframe new frontiers of engagement.

As educators teaching during this age of social media, we can explore with our students how Beauvoir's focus on women, agency, power, and the "curation" of the self to others relates to our time. For example, the 1967 short story, *La femme rompue* (*The Woman Destroyed*), explores questions of identity and authenticity in a patriarchal society that relegates women to irrelevancy as they age. Monique, a middle-aged woman, resists facing the prison she created for herself, and largely with the complicity of her husband, the unfaithful Maurice. We learn through her journal entries the most intimate details of her contorted justifications to avoid recognizing that the world around her has changed. With each passing year, Monique chose to close herself off from the world in the dutiful care of her domestic space as a means to fortify her marriage. Her faithful submission to societal beliefs regarding the role of a bourgeois mother and wife could not shield her from the alienating torment of her husband's infidelity. Monique lost herself in playing gendered roles and in the process distanced herself from the making of authentic choices. As readers, we can only imagine what Monique's next chapter will entail. She barricades herself in her home, fearing the other side of her apartment door and walls, which signal a future alone; freedom is at this point too overpowering for a woman who perceives that her desires, family, education, upbringing, and patriarchal society have all failed her. Yet, she ends recognizing to herself, in her intimate journal, that no one can come to her rescue. Only she can overcome her existential paralysis. Thus, Monique reminds us of the transformative potential of action once we identify our prisons—from those imposed upon us to those we inadvertently build on our own.

A novel from 1966, *Les Belles images (same translation in English)*, probes our comfort and complacency with the world we inhabit. It raises ethical questions on the limits of technology and modernization. Our spiraling, alienating consumption of media seeps into our unconscious in order to deflect from our individual responsibility and collective complicity with human rights violations. The protagonist, Laurence, a successful woman living a privileged yet empty life in Paris, begins to question her lack of engagement with societal issues. She comes to a realization that gives her hope (and fear). Her daughter, Catherine, may not be as successful in her studies; yet more precious and rare, Catherine's "sensitivity was ripening" and "she was learning things that are not taught at school—learning to sympathize, comfort, give and take [and to] catch the fleeting shades of meaning in voices and expressions" (100). Hence, this novel by Beauvoir, which is often less studied, allows us to reflect on the transformative potential of empathy and its place in our Western, consumeristic societies and educational systems.

In Jean Paul Sartre's short story, *The Wall*, which our students loved to discuss in class, the existentialist dilemma resides in the stark life-or-death choices of its protagonists who face arbitrary state execution during the Spanish Civil War. Beauvoir's characters, especially in works that come after *Le Sang des autres*, published in 1945, confront existential crises that arise from women's limited freedom in society. They occupy a more nebulous, grey zone in which roles are gendered and expectations too oppressive. One of Beauvoir's key existential contributions is to expand Sartre's *situation-limite* to a realm of more ethical ambiguity which is in itself is a source of gnawing existential angst.

To give a quick example, Beauvoir won the Prix Goncourt with the 1954 novel, *Les Mandarins*, which is based in postwar France. Its main characters struggle with a world in which choosing between good and evil is not as clear cut as in the time of war and Occupation. One of the main characters, Anne Dubreuilh, commonly interpreted as Beauvoir's alter ego, summarizes the sense of disorientation, of malaise in the aftermath of the war, "cette paix qui nous rendait à nos vies sans nous rendre nos raisons de vivre" (that peace which gave us back our lives but not our sense of purpose, 112). Rather, their impasse is based on the overwhelming challenge of constructing a future free of war and oppressive governance. Should the world align with the Free World and thus accept American hegemony? Or, do communism or socialism hold the key to a more equitable (global) society? In our twenty-first century, questions of freedom, governance, and living a prison-like existence continue to challenge us. If we can motivate our students to analyze related issues outside of the classroom, we make our disciplines even more relevant and attractive.

When our class visited a men's prison, some of the inmates gave us a tour and then shared their life stories. We were struck by the very existentialist language used to describe the anguish felt with not only the loss of freedom but the moral consequences of acts, crimes that profoundly affect many others in devastating ways. Furthermore, through the service learning carried out at a local jail, our students heard again existentialist language as both female and male inmates described the poor choices that led them to detention. Education, however, transforms.

Operation Educate: Award-Winning Service-Learning Component of Cross-Divisional Courses

Our innovative, cross-divisional course integrated a service-learning program that we created. We believe that existential literature helped our students better prepare to work with incarcerated individuals at the local detention center. Our students studied literature that exposed marginalized perspectives and how individuals internalize a negative, paralyzing gaze of society.

Our university nominated us for the South Carolina Commission on Higher Education Service Learning Competition. The title of our project is "*Operation Educate*: A Cross Disciplinary, Service-Learning Community Service Partnership." To date, approximately 60 college students have been involved. *Operation Educate* is an educational, training, community-engagement program that involves several local and state public service agencies, including adult education, the local community college, and our public university; we all collaborate to support the county detention center inmates in successfully reintegrating into the community and we focus on reducing recidivism. Our students and faculty participate in this collaborative enterprise by leading a pre-GED tutoring program for inmates. Our program positions our students to help female and male inmates improve their math and English skills and prepare them to obtain a GED while incarcerated or shortly after their release. This project has since become a service-learning opportunity in additional classes including an interdisciplinary course in criminal justice and child advocacy called *Childhood Trauma: Potential Pathway to the Criminal Justice System*, a school of education course called *Foundations of Education*, and an interdisciplinary course in English, French, and African American studies called *Global Existentialist Literature*.

Our students cultivate a community-minded outlook and also actively empathize with vulnerable and underserved populations who may lack the social and economic resources and supportive networks to attain higher educational opportunities and have greater access to upward social mobility. They must grasp the dynamic experiences and life choices made by individuals who they serve and mentor through *Operation Educate*. Thus, they gain lasting and invaluable lessons in empathy and leadership as they sharpen their sense of responsibility in making an impact on their own community. This was clearly displayed by one of the student tutors who shared: "Being in the jail is like being in a whole other world. But once I met student inmates and worked with them, I saw how focused they were on seizing this opportunity to achieve their goals, and everything felt normal after that." Regardless of what our graduates do with their degrees, their jail-tutoring experience will have a lifelong impact as their community engagement impacted the lives of underserved community members.

An honors student, who tutored both female and male inmates at the jail, invited me to co-present on her research related to our service-learning class at a national conference. Her essay, "On the Other Side of the Wall: Mentors, Prisons, and Existential Literature," was published in the peer-reviewed quarterly magazine. One of the takeaways from her experience was that "students expanded their horizons in this program while gaining critical thinking skills to bring empathy and awareness to inmates, the university, and the outer community in the importance of connecting without labels or stigmas, together with hope and acceptance to create better lives for all." Our course transformed her perception on the women and men who face incarceration and on the concrete actions students can undertake to bridge some educational gaps for this underserved population.

Another honors student stated in an interview, "Being locked in a jail for a few hours every week has changed my perspective on how the accused and convicted are perceived." As educators we encourage our students to examine their own perceptions of societal challenges; we create opportunities for them to engage with communities different from their own and visualize concrete, innovative solutions for a more equitable future. Similarly, one of the tutored inmates, a 27-year-old woman and one of the first inmates to have obtained her GED in July 2016, emphasized the transformative power of mentorship. She shared in the same interview, "Outside of here, I never would have thought of participating in a program like this. I always depended on other people, the wrong people, to get me through life. I want to be a better person, a more knowledgeable person when I leave here."

Several entities have celebrated and honored the effectiveness of our service-learning program in both our county and state. For brevity, the following is one example. In July 2016, *Operation Educate* won the J. Mitchell Graham/Barrett Lawrimore Memorial Award in a state competition. The award recognizes:

> innovative projects completed by South Carolina's counties during the past fiscal year. Winners represent the best qualities of local governance—attention to details, service to citizens, efficient use of tax dollars, and improvement in the quality of life. They demonstrate how creative problem-solving and collaboration can achieve impressive results, and offer new ideas for other counties to consider.

Operation Educate has also garnered media attention by local television stations, the city paper, and university communications. We believe that *Operation Educate* received positive media attention because it fills an education gap targeting vulnerable communities. For future expansion, it would be beneficial to offer women at the detention center an opportunity to take creative writing courses based on literary works in translation by Simone de Beauvoir and other diverse women writers as a means to give voice to their experiences. As more women in the United States are incarcerated (or held in immigration detention centers), it is important to bring attention to this growing problem that remains largely invisible. What role do gender, race, class, language, national origin, and legal status play in mass incarceration and what challenges need our engagement now?

Conclusion

French and the study of world languages and cultures matter too much as we grapple with local, national, and global existential crises. How can this innovative course encourage French educators to establish bridges of collaboration with other disciplines and community partners to wrestle with societal issues from interdisciplinary, feminist perspectives? Already in the mid- to late 1940s, existentialism had gripped the imagination of its contemporaries, especially the youth in postwar France. In the years that followed, existentialist thought resonated with new generations of free thinkers, activists, non-conformists, and revolutionaries throughout the world. Freedom, or the quest to attain it, has been an inquiry that fascinates and mobilizes. French existentialist thought and literature is also a weapon of engagement that can attract more students and colleagues to the timely relevance of our field. Beyond our university walls, we can choose to tackle together, from various interdisciplinary perspectives and through our actions, what Beauvoir would call "the ethics of ambiguity" posed by our diverse, multilingual, twenty-first-century communities that still lag in inclusivity, power, equity, mobility, and freedom for all.

References

Al Malik, Abd. *Place de la République. Pour une spiritualité laïque* [*Place de la République. for a Lay Way of Spirituality*]. Indigènes éditions, 2015.
Beauvoir, Simone de. *Les Belles images*. Flamingo, 1966.
Beauvoir, Simone de. *La Femme rompue*. Gallimard, 1967; trans. *The Woman Destroyed*. Pantheon, 2013.
Beauvoir, Simone de. *Les Mandarins*. Gallimard, 1998; trans. *The Mandarins*. Harper Perennial, 2005.
Beauvoir, Simone de. *Le Sang des autres*. Gallimard, 1945; trans. *The Blood of Others*. Penguin, 2002.
"J. Mitchell Graham and Barrett Lawrimore Memorial Awards." *Sccounties.org*, www.sccounties.org/j-mitchell-graham-and-barrett-lawrimore-memorial-awards. Accessed June 9, 2018.
MLA Ad Hoc Committee on Foreign Languages. "Foreign Languages and Higher Education: New Structures for a Changed World." *Profession* (2007): 234–245.
Pontecorvo, Gillo, dir. *The Battle of Algiers*. Criterion Collection, 2004.
Richardson, Louise. *What Terrorists Want: Understanding the Enemy, Containing the Threat*. Random House, 2006.
Sartre, Jean-Paul. *The Wall*. New Directions, 1939.

15

FRANCOPHONE WOMEN WRITERS OUTSIDE THE FRENCH CLASSROOM

An Integrated Approach to Exploring Women's Voices

Shira Weidenbaum

The U.S. presidential debates of 2008 and 2016 demonstrated the continuing pressure on women to be pleasant. Barack Obama backhandedly complimented Hillary Clinton as "likeable enough," and Donald Trump's insult, "nasty woman," turned into a feminist rallying cry.[1] The same conventions that expect women to be agreeable and that label assertive women as bossy or pushy also extend to women writers and the female characters they construct. One need only consider the tradition of women justifying their writing as instructive or exemplary to appreciate that women writers might hesitate to portray characters outside a narrow frame of likeability. But just as "well-behaved women seldom make history," neither do well-behaved women generally make for interesting fiction.[2] In my course, *Women's Voices*, I choose works of literature with complicated and not entirely sympathetic—even unlikeable—female characters. I do so both for the quality of the works themselves and for the opportunities to challenge expectations about women writers and the characters they create. In this chapter, I discuss my eclectic choice of texts for this course on women writers and explain how I combine the curriculum with feminist pedagogy aimed at fostering student autonomy and creativity.

Before commencing, a few caveats seem essential. First, *Women's Voices* is a literature course taught in English. While the course includes some works originally written in French, the goal of the course is not an introduction to French literature nor to French women writers. Therefore, this chapter, rather than justifying the inclusion of these works in such courses, assumes that teaching them is valuable and presents some strategies for doing so.

Second, the students and the course structure differ in many respects from other university courses. At Quest University Canada, all courses are 18-day intensive seminars ("blocks"), meeting three hours a day, five days a week, for a total of 54 hours of class time. Faculty and students have only one course at a time, which, along with small class sizes (no more than 20 students), creates a close-knit community and an immersive experience. Furthermore, students at Quest do not have majors but instead pursue interdisciplinary "questions." Students do not necessarily enroll in my course because of an interest in literature but because the themes of the works we read intersect with their questions. The objectives in all classes at Quest aim at process and critical thinking. Because I offer this course outside the structure of a traditional French or literature major, I have less pressure to include canonical texts. I help students develop skills of close reading and textual analysis, but I also want students to think about their own reading choices, their familiarity with the work of women writers, and the challenges that come with writing as a woman or as a member of other marginalized communities.

Third, Quest's mission and teaching philosophy create a culture that allows me to take significant risks in the type of in-class activities I run and the kind of homework I assign. In addition to giving mini-lectures and facilitating discussion, I also decenter the classroom so that students take more responsibility for their own learning. In almost every class session I run "break-outs," where students leave the classroom to work in small groups (three–four students) for up to 30 minutes. While the activities may vary (from a single set of questions to separate but interlocking tasks), small group work ensures that all students engage and contribute to the learning of the whole class. I also ask students to lead activities and discussion once during the course. Giving this amount of autonomy to students creates space for their curiosity and questions and ensures their engagement with the material.

These strategies for empowering students coincide with scholarship on feminist pedagogy that envisions a liberatory environment, a "participatory, democratic process in which at least some power is shared" (Shrewsbury 167). In a course with the inevitably political goal of increasing knowledge and understanding of women's experience and writing, it is important to build in course practices that harmonize with feminist pedagogy. Carolyn Shrewsbury identifies "community, empowerment, and leadership" as "central" for the "transformation of the academy" that feminist pedagogy seeks to enact (166–7). In addition to these concepts, I add creativity as an essential element to my feminist pedagogy. Research makes clear that creative practices offer alternate ways of knowing, often not judged as sufficiently scholarly in an academic setting.[3] By allowing students to explore and express ideas differently, invitations to creativity also contribute to the liberatory environment envisioned by Shrewsbury. Students learn not only to appreciate the plurality of women's voices but to enrich and appreciate their own voices as well and to overcome feelings of their own unlikeability.

Creativity is most explicitly invited at the final class, when students present their own creative pieces. I leave the form and length open with this prompt:

> The creative writing may be any of the following: an original story written in the style of one of the authors studied this block; a re-writing of a story studied this block from a different perspective, in a different style or context; a supplement to a text studied, in the form of a "missing" scene or a continuation, for example. (Other ideas are welcome, too!)

The structure of a storytelling day, with discussion after each student's reading, was inspired by Marguerite de Navarre's *Heptameron* (1558). In this course storytelling appears in "Her Lover's Slave," from Maria de Zayas y Sotomayor's *Disenchantments of a Love* (1647), a collection of Spanish Golden Age tales presented within a frame story of pre-wedding celebrations during which several women tell tales of amatory disillusionment. The range of creative works that arise from this assignment suggests how differently students respond to and internalize the literature. Students demonstrate sensitivity to style, bring new meaning to easily overlooked details, and apply questions raised in the readings to their daily lives, proving their learning and providing a meaningful conclusion to the course. Most importantly, the opportunity for original creative work invites students to empathize with even the most unlikeable characters.

The works we read in *Women's Voices* contain many complicated female characters, to whom students often respond with frustration because the characters challenge their preconceptions about "fair" or "feminist" portrayals of women. Margaret Atwood's *Penelopiad* (2005) retells the story of the *Odyssey* from the perspective of Ulysses's long-suffering wife Penelope and of 12 anonymous maids. Although Penelope portrays herself sympathetically, she comes off as petty and petulant, and her account is undermined by the maids' interspersed commentary and burlesque. While students are initially excited with the idea of a feminist retelling of a Greek classic, they become perturbed by the fact that the narrators reinforce stereotypes and do not portray female characters in a good light, prompting discussion of the qualities we expect to see in work that is truly feminist. Similar questions arise when we discuss Zayas y Sotomayor's "Her Lover's Slave," in which a Moorish slave, Zelima, reveals herself to be a Christian noblewoman. Zelima explains how, after being raped by a suitor, she fell in love with her attacker (since marriage with him was the only way to restore her honor) and sold herself into slavery in order to follow the ungrateful and duplicitous lover. Students are primed to pity this narrator as a victim but have trouble accepting her determination to marry and find her actions and narration suspect and self-serving. *Mrs. Dalloway* (1925) by Virginia Woolf also tests students' tolerance of characters they see as too conformist for their twenty-first-century values, characters who embody the kinds of class privilege and stereotypical gender roles students are eager to critique and reject. Clarissa strikes many students as too shallow and frivolous to deserve respect. Although Clarissa, Zelima, and Penelope are not villains or antagonists, each character forces students to confront some of their stereotypes about how women writers should represent women and the extent to which students expect to find female role models in works by women writers. These first three works prepare students to encounter Gladys Eysenach, the least likeable protagonist of the course.

Gladys is the creation of Irène Némirovsky (1903–42), a French author of Jewish Russian heritage, best known today for the *Suite Française*, discovered by her daughter years after her death in Auschwitz. As in her unforgiving portraits of many characters in the *Suite Française* and of the eponymous miser of *David Golder*, Némirovsky excels at painting unlikeable characters whose unhappy situations are of their own making. *Jezebel* (1936) tells the story of a beautiful socialite, Gladys, who has clung to her youthful appearance at all costs. The novel begins at the end of her story, with Gladys on trial for murder. Gladys speaks too softly for the courtroom to hear and it is the judge who summarizes her life, including the death of her husband and her daughter and her many love affairs, while Gladys offers only the briefest affirmations of the account's veracity. After this prelude, the novel turns to the beginning of Gladys's life and recounts events chronologically, revealing along the way Gladys's own thoughts and feelings. In other words, the novel places the reader first as a fascinated and disgusted voyeur; only later can the reader begin to understand, though never find complicity with, Gladys. Obsessed with her beauty and with the power it brings, Gladys arouses little sympathy; her treatment of others provokes outrage. While it is hard to dispute the "facts" of the story, which detail Gladys's selfishness and lack of maternal feeling, students can identify the ways in which her actions are understandable within her milieu's constraints, where women have little power beyond their ability to charm. Students also recognize, without excusing Gladys, a logic in her actions and reactions: she does not see herself as strong enough to survive without pleasure and love, yet she also has a powerful impulse toward self-preservation.

Student presenters have found unusual ways to explore Gladys's character. At the beginning of one class, the presenters asked us to reflect on what aspect of ourselves we take pride in, i.e., in what way we might be a little vain. This prompt to recognize our own areas of vanity helped us better grasp Gladys. Although we might not value our appearance above all else and although we might not go to the lengths Gladys does, it was an important step for us to realize that we might react in seemingly irrational ways if a core part of our identity were threatened. The student presenters also organized a debate, asking their classmates to consider whether Gladys deserved pity. In addition to preparing arguments for an assigned side, students had to perform a pertinent scene for the class and use theatrical interpretation as a part of their argument. The activity forced students to consider how they wanted to represent Gladys, and took us to the heart of an interpretive question: was Gladys simply a monstrous human being, or was she the result of a society that only valued women for their beauty, not their agency? The creative final assignment also allowed for new perspectives on Gladys, as one student rewrote the story in the form of a modern-day "mommy blog," complete with readers' judgmental comments. This transposition of Gladys into the context of a society where maternal behaviors are scrutinized and where women may feel a loss of identity once they become mothers highlighted how Gladys's story might concern generalized restrictions on women. From this perspective, Gladys is not so different from Clarissa Dalloway, who also tries to find meaning and value in the roles imposed upon her by society. *Jezebel* not only pairs well with *Mrs. Dalloway* but also can work with Edith Wharton's *Age of Innocence* (1920) and Nella Larson's *Passing* (1929), other excellent novels that show women navigating the expectations and norms of societies where they do not comfortably belong or where they must hide aspects of themselves in order maintain their status.

Studying a truly unlikable woman, such as Gladys in *Jezebel*, provides an opportunity to practice empathy and to consider the ways that even the most despicable behavior may result partially from the roles imposed upon women. No matter how much students are able to identify societal conditions at work in the novel, they still see how Gladys errs in her thinking and are frustrated by her narrow perspective. Claire Clamont, the first-person narrator of *Amour* by Marie Vieux Chauvet (1916–73), challenges students even more than Gladys. While the third-person narrator in *Jezebel* allows the reader to maintain some distance, *Amour* is written as a journal and pulls the reader into Claire's point of view. Rather than inviting the reader's sympathy, the accessibility of Claire's most intimate thoughts proves disturbing.

The story of *Amour*, the first novel in the trilogy *Amour, Colère, Folie*, is set in an unnamed Haitian village suffering from environmental degradation, natural disasters, and the terror of a despotic police commissioner, Calédu. Although the novel takes place in 1939–40, the situation is widely understood to mirror the violence and repression Vieux Chauvet and her family experienced in Haiti in the 1950s and 1960s under the rule of François "Papa Doc" Duvalier. Vieux Chauvet lost members of her family to political violence and was forced into exile. The trilogy, originally published in 1968, was only reprinted and translated in English in 2009 after years of keeping the book out of print for fear of retribution.[4] Against this backdrop of a country in turmoil is Claire's intensely personal story of desire, unrequited love, and family drama.

From the very first moments, Claire reveals a conniving character: "I am the lucid one here, the dangerous one, and nobody suspects … I'm savoring my revenge in silence. Silence is mine, vengeance is mine" (3). She is in love with her sister Félicia's husband Jean-Luze, but she is an "old maid," "thirty-nine years old and still a virgin" (3), and instead pushes her younger sister Annette into seducing Jean-Luze and lives their affair vicariously. Claire's story gives us many reasons to sympathize with her: she is born in a bourgeois Haitian family where her dark skin color "went off like a small bomb in the tight circle of whites and white-mulattoes with whom [her] parents socialized" (4); she is so convinced of her ugliness that she rebuffs those who actually love her; her parents die while she is still young and she is left to run a household bankrupted by her father's profligacy and political ambition. Claire has been forced by circumstance and choice into the role of the responsible, sober oldest sibling, unattractive and unappreciated. Claire's story is an unhappy one; were it told differently, the reader might be her ally. Instead, students wonder about Claire's sanity and find the voice of her journal distasteful. While we clearly see how lonely Claire is, the journal makes explicit her harsh judgment, her jealousy, and her violent inclinations.

Students revise their initial impressions of Claire when they consider the novel's form, a journal, and conduct close reading to distinguish Claire's public actions from her private thoughts. Student discussion leaders have asked their peers to spend a few minutes writing a journal entry about their own day to prompt reflection on the form—in private, how did they express themselves, and what did they record? The activity helped us appreciate the extent to which we were seeing a much larger story from a narrow perspective and consider why Vieux Chauvet chose to present the story thus. Paradoxically, we found more empathy for Claire when we recognized the ways in which she was a biased observer of her own life. We noticed how little of her own speech and actions in public were recorded and how much of the action was purely in Claire's mind. We realized that Claire seems unlovable to us because she sees herself as unlovable.

After students complete reading *Amour*, I ask them to imagine Claire's very next journal entry. This exercise produces a large range of responses and illuminates how the students interpret Claire's character and the final scene in which she stabs Commandant Calédu. They must decide whether and how Claire is changed by this act, but they must also capture Claire's voice and respect Vieux Chauvet's style. When students share their endings in class, the creative writing inevitably leads back to an examination of the final scene, a discussion of Claire's evolution, and consideration of the nature of reader responses and our desire for certain outcomes.

Although issues of race and class arise in most of the works we study, *Amour* introduces more explicitly problems of intersectionality. Claire suffers not only because she is a woman, not the son her father wanted, but also because she is dark-skinned. Claire feels marginalized within the upper-class society because of her skin color, but is despised by those currently in power because she is from a Francophile family who has exploited Haitian peasants. The sense of Claire's unlikeability therefore arises from a combination of factors of gender, race, and class. The topic of intersectionality is also relevant to the final book in the course, *The Break*, by Canadian Métis Katherena Vermette.

The Break has no single character that is particularly unlikable, but plenty who are troublesome in their imperfect humanity. Published in 2016, *The Break* is Vermette's first novel and her work has received many awards, including selection as a finalist for the CBC's 2017 Canada Reads competition. The novel presents the perspectives of ten characters spanning four generations largely through a shifting third-person voice. Although a few of the characters seem to be central, the book's main character is the community itself—the collective story of abuse, poverty, drug use, imprisonment, and broken families—and a group of women who form a strong and supportive sisterhood. The multiple perspectives portray each character's private thoughts and experiences, but the reader also comes to know the characters through the ways that others see them. These perspectives are not necessarily in opposition, but reveal instead how well the women know each other and how their deep love gives them compassion and patience with one another's foibles. The reader appreciates how the characters make mistakes but have the best of intentions.

For two of the characters—Phoenix, a teenage runaway, and Tommy, a young police officer—the opportunity to read the story from their perspectives is especially important. Tommy and Phoenix are the two outsiders to the rest of the family group and they intersect in the lives of the other characters in difficult ways. Phoenix seems nothing more than a ruthless delinquent, hurting all those around her and deserving her eventual punishment. The chapters from her perspective, however, explain the trauma of her own past and her isolation from the very kind of family support system on which the other characters can depend. Tommy first appears as a bit inept, as other characters judge him as a representative of a police system that has failed to protect indigenous women. The reader discovers that Tommy is himself Métis, and he struggles with insensitive treatment from his colleagues, disconnection from his Métis heritage after years of trying to pass as white, and the casual racism of his white fiancée.

The Break presents opportunities and challenges in the classroom. The multiple perspectives provide an easy formal element for students to analyze. Students consider the effects of and possible reasons for the narrative choices, particularly the occasional use of the first person. We explore the order in which events are described and appreciate how the past trickles in through interspersed memories. An analysis of these structural components provides material for debates about the novel's story, main characters, and message. Because there are so many characters in the novel, it also works well to assign single characters to small groups that consider a larger question; for example, what does "support" look like for this character? How do they give and receive support? After the students have finished the novel, they listen to a recording of the CBC 2017 Canada Reads debates, which provides more than enough impetus for a vigorous concluding discussion.

In this annual battle of the books, five celebrities champion one Canadian work apiece and during four evening broadcasts they discuss, debate, and eliminate one book a day. The 2017 competition drew controversy for its tie-breaking procedures, which led to the elimination of *The Break* on the first day.[5] Of more interest to our study, however, were the arguments offered both for and against the book, none of which resisted scrutiny. *The Break*'s champion argued tautologically that the book's bestseller status meant that all Canadians should read it, and its detractors decried the lack of positive male figures and the focus on a small portion of Canada's population. After students finish yelling in rage at the radio, they are highly motivated to collect textual evidence to argue for a more nuanced view of the male characters. With knowledge of Canada's history with indigenous and Métis populations, a history of broken treaties, residential schools, and governmental failures to investigate the cases of missing and murdered indigenous women, students can also articulate how the novel is indeed important for all Canadians to read, how the very Canadians who don't see themselves represented in *The Break* need to understand the experiences of these women as part of an ongoing effort at reconciliation.

Although the novel contains plenty to discuss and students engage quickly with the characters and the issues, *The Break* is not an easy book to teach. Unlike a work set in seventeenth-century Spain or twentieth-century Haiti, *The Break* concerns modern-day Canada. We cannot absorb and understand the story without also recognizing the ways in which white colonizing forces continue to harm indigenous populations and without noticing that our own classrooms in an elite private university built on unceded Squamish Nation territory reflect this same marginalization. *The Break* disturbs the mostly white student body in my classes because they must confront the invisible advantages they enjoy, but students may also be triggered by the story's violence for intensely personal reasons. I found it helpful to teach the book at the end of the course, when the students had had time to get to know and trust each other and we had created as safe an environment as possible. In addition to acknowledging from the start the difficulty in discussing some of these issues, I try to destigmatize displays of emotion in class, using examples of how the strong characters in the novel give each other space to feel and cry. I make it clear that I understand and accept if a student is triggered and needs to leave class temporarily, but I nonetheless invite them to stay present if possible and to make tears, even in the classroom, an acceptable response.

In its modernity and treatment of a community rather than a single character, *The Break* is an outlier on the syllabus of *Women's Voices* and, more generally, a work that has yet to find its place in scholarly discussions. The novel does, however, pull together many themes of the course and the very fact of its inclusion is worth considering in the larger scope of women's writing. While *The Break* is an award-winning bestseller in Canada, we cannot overlook how easily it can be dismissed as a story just for indigenous and Métis women. This critique of the novel provides an opportunity to review the history of literature by and about women and to appreciate the pattern of confining women's writing to smaller spaces than men's. The assumption of a narrow audience and exemplary content underpins the criticism heard on Canada Reads and demonstrates how women's writing—really, any writing from a marginalized population—functions under and reacts against societal conventions. Whether it is in the refusal to portray likeable women or in the decision to represent the world as it really is, even if it unsettles many readers, the literature in this course expands the space for women—authors, characters, and readers—to exist in all their complexity.

Notes

1 Obama's comment occurred at a debate on January 5, 2008; Trump's on October 20, 2016.
2 See Thatcher Ulrich, who originated the phrase in 1976.
3 See, for example, Kerr and Nettelbeck's work on "fictocriticism" and Richardson on writing as a method of inquiry.
4 For the publication and censorship history of Vieux Chauvet's work, see Spear.
5 *La Ligne Brisée*, the translation by Mélissa Verreault (Québec Amérique, 2017), won the 2018 French equivalent, Le Combat des Livres. Recordings of the discussions could provide some excellent supplementary material in a French classroom. https://ici.radio-canada.ca/premiere/emissions/plus-on-est-de-fous-plus-on-lit/episodes/406711/audio-fil-du-mardi-8-mai-2018

References

Atwood, Margaret. *The Penelopiad*. Canongate, 2005.
Kerr, Heather and Amanda Nettelbeck, eds. *The Space Between: Australian Women Writing Fictocriticism*. University of Western Australia Press, 1998.
Larson, Nella. *Passing*. Dover, 2004.
de Navarre, Marguerite. *The Heptameron*, trans. Paul A. Chilton. Penguin, 1984.
Némirovsky, Irene. *Jezebel*, trans. Sandra Smith. Vintage International, 2010.
Némirovsky, Irene. *Suite Française*, trans. Sandra Smith. Vintage International, 2007.
Richardson, Laurel. "Writing: A Method of Inquiry," in *The SAGE Handbook of Qualitative Research*, 3rd edn, ed. N.K. Denzin and Y.S. Lincoln. SAGE, 2005, 959–967.
Shrewsbury, Carolyn. "What Is Feminist Pedagogy?" *Women's Studies Quarterly* 25. 1/2(Spring–Summer, 1997): 166–173.
Spear, Thomas C. "Marie Chauvet: The Fortress Still Stands." *Yale French Studies* 128(2015): 9–24.
Ulrich, Laurel Thatcher. *Well-Behaved Women Seldom Make History*. Vintage Books, 2007.
Vermette, Katherena. *The Break*. House of Anansi Press, 2016.
Vieux Chauvet, Marie. *Love, Anger, Madness*, trans. Rose-Myriam Réjouis and Val Vinokur. Modern Library, 2010.
Wharton, Edith. *The Age of Innocence*. Dover, 1997.
Woolf, Virginia. *Mrs. Dalloway*. Harcourt, 2005.
Zayas y Sotomayor, Mariade. *The Disenchantments of Love*, trans. H. Patsy Boyer. SUNY Press, 1997.

16

PUSHING BOUNDARIES

A Feminist Interdisciplinary Approach to Team Teaching French and American Women's Lives during World War II

Courtney Sullivan and Kerry Wynn

A historian and a French professor, we decided to collaborate on a course that would expose students to the diverse histories of women during World War II (WWII), a period in which women's lives tend to fade into the background of a popular culture our students know and love. Six years ago we began teaching the course, "Women in WWII: Agents of Change or Victims of Circumstance?" to explore the history and myth of women's roles during WWII in French and American fiction, film, autobiography, and history. Frequently cast as victims, resistors, collaborators, patriots, and protesters, women were expected to play many roles during WWII and the postwar period. However, the varied experiences of these women are often erased from contemporary war films and overlooked in history texts, TV shows, and popular fiction. Our course investigates WWII representations of women as agents or victims of change—the overarching theme grounding all assignments. Drawing upon diverse sources to examine women's memories of their own experiences, as well as their portrayal in popular culture, this course provides a model for an innovative interdisciplinary approach bringing the complexity of French women's experiences to an expanded audience.

By creating a "conceptual interdisciplinary course" using women's writing to explore WWII in France and the United States, we have encouraged students to reexamine their assumptions about gender, war, and nation.[1] Through the use of literary analysis and historical study, the course interrogates the boundaries of popular and academic representations of the past. In its feminist approach, our course provides a model for "challeng[ing] traditional notions of knowledge and scholarship," since it shifts the story of WWII from the often recounted tale of the exploits of men and their battles to a more nuanced exploration of the many experiences of French and American women (Lattuca 3). We encourage students to ask "big" questions about sexuality, social class, labor, race, and ethnicity to address how women experienced their lives during the war and how these experiences were perceived both by themselves and others. Due to its subject, the course attracts a variety of students who may not have otherwise studied French women's literature. As language programs and liberal arts face contemporary trials, our interdisciplinary course demonstrates that instructors can reach a diverse audience by team teaching across the curriculum on subjects with vital importance.[2]

The War and the Humanities

The course is deeply rooted in the humanities, and as scholars who are invested in experiencing texts as a way to understand past and present, we began with sources that would approach the war from differing perspectives. Through the study of literature, memoirs, and film, students learn about the specific injustices of the past and in the process develop a capacity to identify and prevent current crimes against humanity. In reading memoirs and in watching films, students place themselves in the role of the narrator or character and as a result, develop empathy and a respect for human lives. For example, after reading Simone Veil's harrowing account of life in extermination camps, students should "experience a moment of epiphany asking themselves how could such a thing happen, how could it be avoided in the future, and what is their responsibility before others" (Touya de Marenne 107). The combination of literature, film, and historical writing pushes students to reconsider the neutrality of historical work and gives life to academic studies. In his defense of the humanities, Touya de Marenne argues:

> reading literature helps students question the meaning of their existence in a historical and political context. It inspires the imagination, enhances one's ability to think critically, and constitutes the foundation for all future learning. Essential to the welfare of society, it enhances empathy and a better understanding of people who are different from us. It strengthens our emotional intelligence and creates a common bond between cultures and communities.
>
> *(113)*

This process is not always comfortable for students, as students trained to view history as impartial may initially struggle with using fiction to shed light on historical events; likewise, students accustomed to analyzing literature and film as art may strain to consider the historical context of a fictional work.

The course is framed around a roughly chronological structure, alternating focus between France and the United States. The first week establishes historical contexts for both nations, using historians' accounts and American women's reporting on Europe before the war, and then moves quickly to France, examining the portrayal of the exodus in Irene Némirovsky's *French Suite* over the subsequent two weeks.[3] To complement her portrayal of the exodus and life in France during the Occupation, students watch Jean-Paul Rappeneau's *Bon Voyage*.[4] The class focuses more on France in the beginning because events of WWII unfolded earlier than in the U.S. Explaining the rationale for what appears to be an initial imbalance on the first day of class will address concerns about the early French focus from students who are drawn into the course due to their interest in U.S. history.

After the discussion of the Exodus, the class moves to the mobilization of American women early in the war, and we are careful here to analyze not only the difference in women's experiences within and between the two nations, but also to probe contrasts in the way these experiences are remembered. The focus of the course is still heavily on France, however, as we explore Simone Veil's *A Life*, in particular her recounting of her childhood in the south of France, the anxiety leading up to the war, and her hellish experiences in Birkenau. We also examine anti-Semitism and the "Winter Velodrome" round-up of 1942 that was portrayed in the novel and film version of De Rosnay's *Sarah's Key*, since the Holocaust and its portrayal in memoir and fiction constitute the heart of week 5 of the semester. Immediately after Veil's work, students read the memoir of a U.S. woman imprisoned in a prisoner-of-war camp in the Philippines, which complicates their ideas about empowered American women who won the war with their rivet guns.

By the last third of the course, students are prepared to question assumptions they may have brought into the class—narratives in which the U.S. saves France and images of WWII as a "good war" fought by the "greatest generation"—in much greater depth. After discussing the end of the war and the liberation of Paris, students read Marguerite Duras's depiction of her involvement in the Resistance in *The War* [5] and Jeanne Wakatsuki Houston's *Farewell to Manzanar*, a memoir about a young girl's life in an internment camp for Japanese Americans. They also view portions of the film *Cigarettes and Nylons*, which briefly addresses the cover-up of rapes committed by U.S. soldiers in the European theater. In reading Duras and Wakatsuki Houston, and in considering American war crimes, students confront the idea that women, soldiers, and allied nations were not always heroic.

Most students finish the class with a more nuanced view of the complicated events and situations the French faced during the war and Occupation and perhaps a less romanticized view of the U.S. war effort. Students also question legacies of the war, such as the popularity of the "fatal woman" in U.S. films such as *Double Indemnity*, which stood in contrast to women's empowerment and roles outside of the household during the war. The conclusion of the class with *Hiroshima, My Love*, and the harsh reprisals against women who slept with German men during the Occupation, inspires students to contemplate questions of agency, empowerment, and memory.

Throughout the course, we return to complexities in the experience and the memory of the war. One prompt that generates interesting essays asks the student to explain why filmmakers keep returning to WWII stories and revising them for contemporary audiences. What about the roles women played in WWII do the filmmakers find compelling and why and to what extent do they revise them? The midterm and final exams for the course ask students to reflect on the diversity of women's experiences and the perception of women's roles in the past and present. For example, one final exam question asks students to compare the legacies of WWII for French and American women, taking into consideration both the social expectations they faced and the perception of their actions during the war. Students in the course learn to integrate many types of sources into nuanced analyses of complex experiences.

Memoir, Film, and Feminist Pedagogy

The course highlights the differing experiences of women during WWII, and recognizes the impact of racism, xenophobia, class inequality, and homophobia on women's experience. The selection of readings is informed by intersectional feminism, the recognition that perspectives and systems of power are not rooted in a single aspect of identity, but that individual experience is located at a matrix of multiple categories of belonging. Memoirs are particularly situated to help students examine what Kimberle Crenshaw has labeled "intersectional subordination," the differing barriers individuals face due to their social position, "frequently the consequence of one burden that interacts with preexisting vulnerabilities to create yet another dimension of disempowerment" (1249). Crenshaw's focus, rooted in contemporary legal structures and concerned with understanding how racism and sexism intersect in the consequences of policy for women of color, reminds us that we cannot understand historical events and processes without understanding that there are differences within the category of woman that have shaped historical experience.

Memoirs, with their very specific contexts, show students that the same war held very different consequences and experiences for the many individuals included in the category of

"French women." Central to Crenshaw's theory is the understanding that intersectionality means that categories of identity and oppression are not merely additive, but that the intersection defines unique experiences. Crenshaw writes, "The problem is not simply that both [anti-racist and feminist] discourses fail women of color by not acknowledging the 'additional' issue of race or of patriarchy but that the discourses are often inadequate even to the discrete tasks of articulating the full dimensions of racism and sexism" (1252). For instance, the difference between Catholic and Jewish French women in the war was not merely one of degrees, but one of a profoundly different context and experience. Memoirs articulate this context and experience by exploring a life at the center of the historical moment.

The structure of the class and the use of memoir and fiction, particularly those just mentioned, also upsets the pervasive privileging of rationalism in the classroom, and focuses students on the power of speaking from experience (Ellsworth 304). Feminist scholar bell hooks has argued persuasively that liberatory pedagogical approaches should recognize students and instructors as embodied individuals and empower students to speak from experience (hooks 148). Providing students with texts that are based in experience as credible historical sources gives students an understanding that their own experience is an acceptable source of knowledge and evidence, although it is not uncomplicated.

The texts we use have thus become pedagogically as well as contextually important to the course, as they move students toward claiming their scholarly voices. As hooks notes, "Coming to voice is not just the act of telling one's own experience. It is using that telling strategically—to come to voice so that you can also speak freely about other subjects" (148). Students often have very immediate and personal reactions to the memoirs they read. They express their sympathy or disgust for the people in the stories they read. They compare the historical experiences of specific women to their own experiences, and the conversations are generally very free-flowing and emotionally insightful in a way that discussions in history courses rarely are. Because the texts are nuanced, and personal, students see events from several sides at once. With this assumption embedded in the readings, students engage with differing interpretations of the war.

Assignments for the course encourage students to hone their voices by comparing memoir and film, establishing explicitly comparative questions that will not allow students to merely describe the materials, but focus them on analytical explorations of the works. For an essay that focuses on film, students may select from several topics. The first asks the students to compare and contrast films featuring female protagonists produced in the United States with those produced in France. How did the perception of women's roles during WWII differ between the two nations? Which roles were portrayed most often or most convincingly in the films of the two nations? Another prompt asks students to compare two films produced at the time of or shortly after the war (1939–50) with two films produced in a later era. How do the portrayals of women's roles differ according to the era in which they were produced? Thus, students must engage with depictions across nation or time, and consider what caused significant disparities.

Films, particularly when paired with specific memoirs, allow students to critique the manufacturing of emotion by screenwriters and producers, and essays based on these critiques produce powerful explorations of historical events. For example, students read excerpts from Lucie Aubrac's war memoir, paired with a portrayal of her in the eponymous film by Claude Berri. One essay question that students write about (as one of the four required response papers) this pairing asks them to compare and contrast the ways both portray a key raid scene. Students are directed to consider historical analyses they have read about Nazi oppression in France when interpreting the director's artistic choices. These considerations continue to influence discussions, as students compare French women's activities in the resistance with U.S. women's paid employment in war work, raising questions about the differing positions of the two nations in the war.

Team Teaching and the Shared Classroom

Our approach to the history of women in WWII is shaped as much by our style of team teaching as by the texts we have chosen. Because each faculty member specializes in a different nation, the reminder of both regions is present in the classroom at all times. This makes the weaving of two national stories much more coherent, and it keeps both national experiences and the contrasts between them in the minds of students. Pedagogically, we use a mixture of two approaches—the interactive and the participant-observer models. Both models require the presence and engagement of both faculty members, but in differing roles. In interactive team teaching, both teachers lead the class, "commenting on most or all of the scheduled discussion topics, with lively interactive dialogue and debate" (Helms et al. 30). In the participant-observer model, although both faculty members are in the room, one is responsible for leading the class, and "alternate views are not actively given but are available if students ask questions or if the observer professor offers a viewpoint" (Helms et al. 30). Although one of us takes the lead in each class, depending on whether the subject of the day is the United States or France, we are always clearly both engaged, and for the most part, learning from each other. Our students see that we respect each other as experts in our respective fields, and that we enjoy and are consistently intrigued by the material that is new to us.

Students find this model useful as it increases student engagement with the various topics. The professor who is serving as observer, asking questions of the leading faculty member, will often encourage students to ask their own questions about the material. This approach is helpful when students are uncomfortable with the interdisciplinary nature of the course or the material itself. Interdisciplinarity lies at the heart of the course, and using history to teach literature and literature to teach history challenges students to break out of their comfort zones. The presence of faculty trained in two different fields and our comfort with expressing surprise or alternate understandings help students understand that it is a valued experience to engage across disciplines.

We share the classroom in other ways as well by including whenever possible guest speakers who either lived through the war or who have academic expertise on it. The incorporation of guest speakers has served to broaden the topics of discussion for students and show them that there are many interpretations of the war and women's experiences. Although it is relatively rare, we have experienced among some students the expectation that we cover more military events, which are not the main focus of the course. In response, we have invited guest speakers to speak about military history, as well as on the topics of American pacifism, work in the French Resistance, and Japanese American internment.[6]

Over the years, we have learned a great deal from teaching with each other, and one of the greatest rewards of team teaching has been the engagement with a peer in the classroom. As psychologists Jessica Lester and Katherine Evans have noted, collaborative teaching can lead faculty to develop deeper insights about material due to the work with another scholar in the classroom, and together, co-teachers can "build something bigger" in the classroom than they might alone (378–9). There are realities to team teaching that can complicate the process, however. Truly collaborative teaching requires a significant time commitment in planning and learning the style of the other professor, and at many universities, the structure of teaching loads and department boundaries might make it difficult for faculty members to pursue team teaching (Lester and Evans 376). We are lucky to be at an institution that is supportive of this practice and focused on innovation in teaching.

Bringing French Women's Literature to a Larger Audience

The interdisciplinary offering of the course has attracted many students who would not normally have the opportunity and/or desire to take a course invested in French women's literature and experience. Overall, 63.5 per cent of the students enrolled in the course for credit in social science or history, meaning that they sought and received credit in French history, which is not otherwise available at our institution, as we do not employ a French historian.

The possibilities for adapting this type of course to the particular strengths of a campus are numerous. Offering a travel component to the course could attract a healthy number of students. Ideally, students would first spend a few weeks studying and reading the material before travelling to France over a winter or spring break to visit sites in and about Paris, such as the Deportation Memorial, the Shoah Memorial, and the Holocaust Center, and the Leclerc Memorial and Liberation of Paris-Jean Moulin Museum. In Normandy, the Memorial in Caen, the American Cemetery, and the museums and beaches of D-Day also pay witness to all the men lost to their mothers, sisters, and wives.

Yet another possibility, although it would mean losing the interdisciplinary nature of the course, would entail a course taught entirely in French and focusing uniquely on the experiences of French women. Those teaching such a course could examine Marceline Loridan-Ivens's *But You Did Not Come Back* (2016), the letter to her father with whom she was deported to Auschwitz and who later perished in the camps, as a complement to Veil's autobiographical *A Life*. Loridan-Ivens and Veil were in the same convoy to Auschwitz and subsequently interned together at Birkenau. The two remained life-long friends and film director Loridan-Ivens's *The Birch-Tree Meadow* (2003) evokes the same tragic internment experiences in a semi-autobiographical film in which a camp survivor travels back to Auschwitz and Birkenau to relive and confront her past. Her film, which is not currently subtitled in English, is an autofictional account she wrote and directed about the deportation and internment in Birkenau she revisits in *But You Did Not*. In this memoir, she recounts the toll the loss of her father and her captivity have taken on her life since the war. Moreover, Claude Chabrol's *Story of Women* (1988) captures the grim and difficult existence of poor French families during the Occupation and recounts one enterprising woman's reinvention as an abortionist (based on the true story of Marie-Louise Giraud) to make her life and that of her children more comfortable.[7] The film could prove an interesting addition to the course, particularly as a work students could analyze in the final paper. Finally, although due to our specialties we have thus far focused on the experiences of French and American women, the rich and varied expertise of historians and literary scholars on individual campuses present infinite possibilities for collaboration. The lives of Canadian, English, Russian, Japanese, Italian, or Polish women during WWII provide fascinating comparisons, and all have been mentioned over the years by our students as subjects they wished they could study. Why not pair these experiences with those of French women? Moreover, specialists of the literatures and histories of African nations, of Oceania, and of the West Indies,[8] to name a few, could focus on the way the war impacted women's lives outside of the European theater and would bring the specter of imperialism to the fore with greater immediacy.

Conclusion

Each time we teach this course we include some different material, and we expand or shift our focus, but we always come back to the central question that motivated this interdisciplinary course: were French and American women during WWII agents of change or victims of circumstance? By coming back to a question about women's agency, both in practice and in perception, we ask students to see not only the factors influencing women's experiences, but also limitations in the ways scholars ask questions about history and literature. True to the interdisciplinary nature of the course, we ask students to push the boundaries of disciplines and categories. We challenge them to scrutinize the contemporary novels and films they will encounter the rest of their lives through a feminist lens. With a sharper eye, they will be able to employ what they learned about the historical realities women faced during the war when considering the ideologies proposed in representations of WWII. Exposing them to women's writing, particularly French writers they might not have studied otherwise, should make them more empathetic, globally aware, and thus better citizens who are hopefully eager to study more works of French literature in the future.

Notes

1 Lisa Lattuca defines conceptual interdisciplinary courses as classes that "assume that a variety of perspectives must be brought to bear on a particular issue or problem" (96).
2 The College of Arts and Sciences at Washburn University, where we both teach, is supportive of team teaching, and this three-hour course counts as three hours in each of our regular teaching loads. The course is capped at 25 students and is cross-listed as upper-division French, foreign language, and history electives; and as a lower-division general education course in our university honors program. The team-taught and cross-listed nature of the course allows us to attract the minimum number of students necessary to teach the course.
3 New work on Némirovsky can add complexity to this discussion, as Susan Suleiman addresses critiques of Némirovsky's position and perspectives in *The Némirovsky Question* (10).
4 An eponymous film adaptation of *French Suite* exists but had not yet been released in the U.S. the last time we taught the course.
5 We read pages 3–141.
6 See Goossen.
7 A special thanks to Annabelle Dolidon who suggested this addition and to Nancy Arenberg who recommended the course devote more time to examining the Shoah by incorporating Elie Weisel's *Night*. We are grateful for Dawn Cornelio's recommendation of *Résistance* (2014), a French miniseries. *A French Village* has also recently won acclaim for its depiction of Occupied France and could be another excellent source.
8 See *Rose and the Soldier* (2015), a film that focuses on the ways the conservative and racist policies of the Pro-Vichy government in Martinique negatively impact a young patriotic woman and her family the first few years of the war.

References

Aubrac, Lucie, Konrad Bieber, and Betsy Wing. *Outwitting the Gestapo*. University of Nebraska Press, 1995.
Bon Voyage. Dir. Jean-Paul Rappeneau, Sony Picture Classics, 2004.
Cigarettes and Nylons. Dir. Fabrice Cazeneuve, Arte France and France 3, 2010.
Crenshaw, Kimberle. "Mapping the Margins: Intersectionality, Identity Politics, and Violence against Women of Color." *Stanford Law Review* (1991): 1241–1299.
De Rosnay, Tatiana. *Sarah's Key*. St. Martin's Griffin, 2008.
Double Indemnity. Dir. Billy Wilder, Paramount, 1944.
Duras, Marguerite. *The War: A Memoir*. 1985. Reprint, New Press, 2008.
Ellsworth, Elizabeth. "Why Doesn't This Feel Empowering? Working through the Repressive Myths of Critical Pedagogy." *Harvard Educational Review* 59. 3(1989): 297–325.

Goossen, Rachel. *Women against the Good War: Conscientious Objection and Gender on the American Home Front, 1941–1947*. University of North Carolina Press, 1997.

Helms, M., J. Alvis, and M. Willis. "Planning and Implementing Shared Teaching: An MBA Team-Teaching Case Study." *Journal of Education for Business* (2005): 29–34.

Hiroshima, My Love. Dir. Alain Resnais, Criterion Collection, 2015.

hooks, bell. *Teaching to Transgress*. Routledge, 2014.

Lattuca, Lisa R. *Creating Interdisciplinarity: Interdisciplinary Research and Teaching among College and University Faculty*. Vanderbilt University Press, 2001.

Lester, Jessica N. and Katherine R. Evans. "Instructors' Experiences of Collaboratively Teaching: Building Something Bigger." *International Journal of Teaching and Learning in Higher Education* 20. 3 (2009): 373–382.

Loridan-Ivens, Marceline and Judith Perrignon. *But You Did Not Come Back*, trans. Sandra Smith. Atlantic Monthly Press, 2016.

Lucie Aubrac. Dir. Claude Berri, USA Films, 1999.

Némirovsky, Irene and Sandra Smith. *Suite Française*. Vintage Books, 2007.

Rose and the Soldier. Dir. Jean-Claude Barny, Lizland Films, 2016.

Sarah's Key. Dir. Gilles Paquet-Brenner, Studiocanal, 2011.

Story of Women. Dir. Claude Chabrol, MK2, 1990.

Suleiman, Susan Rubin. *The Némirovsky Question: The Life, Death, and Legacy of a Jewish Writer in Twentieth-Century France*. Yale University Press, 2017.

The Birch-Tree Meadow. Dir. Marceline Loridan-Ivens, Mascaret Films, 2003.

Touya de Marenne, Eric. *The Case for the Humanities*. Rowman & Littlefield, 2016.

Veil, Simone. *A Life*. Haus Publishing, 2009.

Wakatsuki Houston, Jeanne. *Farewell to Manzanar*. 1973. Reprint, Ember, 2012.

17

WOMEN NOVELISTS AND THE MUSIC OF PARIS

Arline Cravens

Introduction

The reciprocal nature of literature and music has long fascinated authors, philosophers, and theorists. Viewed as sister arts, they have been historically linked through their common emotive powers of persuasion and expression of human passion. The relationship between language and sound forms the core problematic in a growing field of literary criticism which considers the narrative aspect in musical works and the role of music in literary texts. The conceptualization of literature in musical terms has also brought about innovative approaches in the study of language and raised the question of gender in texts. Delia da Sousa Correa writes in her introduction to *Phrase and Subject: Studies in Literature and Music*:

> As the field of literary studies progressively embraces interdisciplinarity, there have been signs of a burgeoning interest in the role played by music within literary culture. This has frequently been accompanied by a desire to understand how these interactions have engaged with other cultural developments such as ideologies of gender.
>
> *(1)*

Other critics in the field of word and music studies, such as David Powell, Eric Prieto, and Leo Treitler,[1] have also explored the interdisciplinary relationship of music and literature. Their works, such as Powell's *While the Music Lasts* and Prieto's *Listening In*, explore the possibility of literary signifiers evoking music and capturing its essence, thereby providing a definition of music, and music's ability to encapsulate literature. This course provides a wonderful opportunity to introduce students to the interdisciplinary conception of the arts. Despite their different approaches, both nineteenth-century and contemporary novelists and musicians cross boundaries through narrative and sound. Evident in the novels of George Sand, Marguerite Duras, and Virginie Despentes, students explore this reciprocal relationship in their novels through the contemporary musico-literary approach. In addition, students learn about the vital role these authors played and continue to influence in the important evolution of gender identity. Introductory assignments on the interdisciplinary conception of the arts include listening to short music selections, such as Frederic Chopin's *Piano Preludes* and Claude Debussy's *Piano Preludes*, while focusing on the representation of literature in music. In addition to music and literature, the relationship between image and sound as portrayed in film provides another facet in the inquiry of the communicative role of music. Of particular interest for my course "Women Novelists and the Music of Paris" are film adaptations of literary texts, such as Marguerite Duras's *Moderato Cantabile*. Specific assignments focus on how music shapes perception, advances the film narrative, and even changes one's initial reaction to the literary text.

Literary-Musical Milieu of the Parisian Salon: Writers and Musicians

Musical and literary sensibilities of the nineteenth century were influenced by the changing aesthetic responses by the public to music and literature. One of the impacts on this development was the perception of music which shifted during the course of the century, ultimately affecting the writing style of the period. A transformation took place not only in the behavior of audiences, which became increasingly silent, but in the perception of music by the listener. Examining this phenomenon in *Listening in Paris: A Cultural History*, James Johnson writes: "Set in the stream of time, listening becomes a dialectic between aesthetic expectations and musical innovations … Change occurs when music accessible enough to meet listeners' criteria for meaning is at the same time innovative enough to prod them into revising and expanding those assumptions" (3). This change in degree and depth of engagement while listening corresponds to the perception of instrumental music as dramatic and expressive, specifically piano music, and the development of the miniature form. This genre, best exemplified by the piano works of Robert Schumann, Frédéric Chopin, and Franz Liszt, illustrates the nineteenth-century theory of musical expression: a representation of sentiments and emotions, with music interpreted as language.[2] The innovations that Romantic composers made in harmony would ultimately lead to the polytonality of late nineteenth-century and early twentieth-century composers of piano compositions, such as Claude Debussy and Maurice Ravel. Students discover these evolutions in music composition by listening to the *Piano Preludes* of both Chopin and Debussy, as well as the solo piano version of *Pavane for a Dead Princess* by Ravel.

Representations of Music in Literature and Literature in Music

George Sand (1804–76) was exposed to both classical and popular music from a young age. While her father had a love of opera, played the violin, and composed music, her mother enjoyed singing simple popular melodies. Music likewise permeates and influences her novels and short stories which are filled with the description of musicians and their education, and her philosophy and commentary on music. Her novels contain a verbal depiction of the "experience" of music: the profound effect that music has on both the listener and the performer. Later in life she writes in her memoirs: "I only truly loved literature and music" (433).[3] Her unique writing style is evident in novels such as *Spiridion, A Woman's Version of the Faust Legend: The Seven Strings of the Lyre, The Master Pipers*, and *Consuelo*, which strive to enrich these two arts, the one with the other. Her novel, *Spiridion*, first appeared in five installments in *La Revue des deux mondes*, between October 1, 1838 and January 15, 1839. It was first published in book form in February 1839 and later rewritten in a second version published in 1842. To summarize briefly, this novel describes a search for true religion. Alexis, an aged monk, is the narrator and central figure of the novel. As he nears death, he decides to tell his story to Angel, a young novice monk. Inserted into this dialogue are the mysterious apparitions of a dead monk named Spiridion, from whose name is derived the title of the novel. He is the founder of the monastery where Angel now lives and Alexis previously resided. Music makes a very brief, yet poignant, entrance two thirds of the way through the novel where Alexis is admiring the natural setting of the monastery. Contemplating the perpetual movement of the waves against the shore, the calm is disturbed when he hears a fisherman singing. Alexis remarks: "I was listening to the sound of the sea waves as they reached the shore, similar to the steady rhythm and eternal harmony of the cosmos, when I heard a fisherman singing to the stars" (229).[4] From the beginning of the monologue, we see that nature and music are intertwined. Sand paints a picture of a fisherman singing to the stars while surrounded by water. Nature, which is personified, is imbued with intellectual and timeless qualities. Alexis continues with the description of the song, which does not contain any intelligible words. We notice that it is the sound of the untrained peasant's voice and the expressiveness of the melodic line that charm him. It is not the interpretative ability of a trained singer in the concert hall, nor the poetic beauty of the words, as there are none; but rather the sonorous quality of expression, which is unique to music that so moves Alexis. He observes:

> I noticed that the fisherman's song instinctively followed the rhythm of the sea, and I thought that perhaps he was one of those great true artists, educated by nature itself ... The astonishing beauty of his melody, like that of the waves, struck me so vividly that the music was suddenly revealed to me.
>
> (230)[5]

This "natural" or "folk" music is so powerful that it suddenly brings an awareness to Alexis that there is a higher form of communication, one which does not require words. As Sand will similarly write of the music of the lyre in *A Woman's Version of the Faust Legend: The Seven Strings of the Lyre*, published in 1840, and Albert's violin music in *Consuelo*, published in 1842, here in *Spiridion* the fisherman's melody seems to convey meaning and his music appears to communicate to Alexis.

This passage on music also highlights Sand's choice of male narrators and dialogue in her novels. Her extensive use of male narrators is well documented in Françoise Massardier-Kenney's work *Gender in the Fiction of George Sand*, where she demonstrates the crucial aspects of their use as a means of questioning masculinity and femininity, thereby articulating Sand's conception of gender. Sand's use of the male narrative voice provides an opportunity for students to explore gender positions and the empowering effect on her readers, both male and female. Sand's choice of the male voice for this dialogue on music begins what will become an evolving theme of transcendence through music in her novels. Male characters undergo transformation through music and/or contact with women, both enlightening them to the communicative capacity of music. Though Sand's focus is on male dialogue in this novel, Sand will later use this narrative structure to allow a feminine voice to emerge in *A Woman's Version of the Faust Legend: The Seven Strings of the Lyre* and *Consuelo*. The choice of a male narrator in this novel also serves as a tool that gives voice to a critique of traditional values. By exposing her readers to the motivation and process of change in the male character Alexis, Sand offers a revised vision of authority and identity. She will later voice the crucial role of women in the transformation and education of male characters through dialogue, thereby allowing Sand to cross boundaries and challenge the oppositions upon which the sense of identity and ultimately the traditional conception of gender are built. Sand's numerous representations of gender, as well as her deconstruction of the hierarchal binary opposition in gender, allows the reader and students to further explore the construction of gender identity. Classroom activities include discussions of gender identity and gender representation.

George Sand was familiar with the evolving musical styles of piano music in the nineteenth century through her relationships with the famous pianists Franz Liszt and Frédéric Chopin. She was first introduced to Chopin in the fall 1836 through their mutual acquaintances Liszt and Marie d'Agoult. Sand's relationship with Chopin is one of the first where she experiences first-hand the creative process of music and the struggle to communicate through a language without words. Marie-Paule Rambeau writes: "He is the first artist she observed in her continuous struggle to comprehend the language of the incommunicable" (161).[6] Unlike other nineteenth-century composers, such as Robert Schumann and Franz Liszt, Chopin's creative process is conceived and written exclusively for the piano. His unique style makes use of the acoustical properties of the keyboard instrument and new harmonic patterns that are now possible. In addition, his long melodic lines are influenced by the *bel canto* style of Italian opera and the French *romance*, resulting in a melody that is imitative of an ornamental aria. Compositions in this genre which George Sand would have heard performed by Chopin include Opus 15 nos 1–3 written between 1830 and 1832, Opus 27 nos 1–2 written in 1835, and Opus 32 nos 1–2 composed in 1837.

To this body of work must be added his set of 24 piano *Preludes*, finished during their stay in Mallorca and published in 1839. The *Prelude* No. 15 in D-flat Major has often been programmatically titled the "Raindrop" *Prelude*. The turns and embellishments of the melody in the opening section are one of the reasons for that title. George Sand writes in her memoirs that one of Chopin's preludes, which he completed during their sojourn to the island of Mallorca, came to him "during a rainy evening" (420). However, when Sand draws a correlation between the natural phenomenon and his composition, he rejects the comparison. The style of writing in the *Preludes*, distinctly Chopinesque, prompts Franz Liszt to label them poetic preludes rather than merely introductory pieces intended to be played before another, as the title suggests and is understood in the early nineteenth century. Jeffrey Kallberg notes the challenge that Chopin issues to his audiences through his concept of the *Preludes* as a cycle of self-contained pieces:

> "By asking listeners and performers to accept a transformed genre whereby individual preludes might serve both as introductions to other works and as self-standing concert pieces, he challenged the conservative notion that small forms were artistically suspect or negligible" (157). Sand recounts the composition of the *Preludes* in her memoirs and writes of his musical genius: "Chopin's genius is the deepest and the fullest of feelings and emotions that ever existed. He made a single instrument speak the language of infinity, of eternity".
>
> (511)[7]

Through a comparison of the use of instrumental music in Sand's novels stated above and the description of Chopin's compositional style, as found in the *Nocturnes* and *Preludes*, we are able to explore the influence of Chopin's music on Sand's writing style. In her later work *Consuelo*, we find that music not only communicates, but leads to understanding, as well. The language of the infinite of *Spiridion* becomes the language of the divine of *Consuelo*.

Assignments include listening to Frederic Chopin's *Preludes* and discovering where the musician crosses boundaries by creating a musical narrative. Of particular interest for the classroom is *Prelude* No. 15.

Literary-Musical Milieu of the Twentieth Century

Marguerite Duras's novel *Moderato Cantabile*, published in 1958 and turned into a screenplay in 1960, is an early example of the *nouveau roman*. Music permeates the novel through the use of the Italian musical term "moderato cantabile," which refers to a moderate tempo in a singing style. Introduced during the opening of the novel at Anne Desbarsdes's son's piano lesson, the scene of the lesson will serve as a leitmotif throughout the novel when the piano lesson scene returns in chapter 5. The steady tempo of the Diabelli Sonatina that Anne's son is learning is juxtaposed against the unfolding events of the novel. Music also serves as a place of refuge in the novel. Through a focus on a style of music found in Chopin's *Preludes*, the moderate tempo and singing style of music provides balance in contrast to the murdered woman's cry. Whereas Sand uses the music of the fisherman's song to awaken in Alexis a knowledge of the beauty of nature, Duras incorporates music as a reflection of our deepest emotions. Assignments focus on the pervasive role of music throughout the text: the transformative influence of music as well as the writer's perception of music. In addition, an analysis of the role of music in the film adaptation of *Moderato Cantabile* provides an excellent opportunity to discuss the ability of music to convey meaning. Particular selections in the film include Diabelli's *Sonatina* No. 8, as well as selections from *Sonatina* No. 1 and *Sonatina* No. 6.

Virginie Despentes has been championed as a pioneer of a new wave of feminism and as an innovator in feminist literature since the publication of her first novel *Rape Me* in 1993. The novel was also produced as a film in 2000, which was written and directed by Despentes and Coralie Trinh Thi. Her novel *Bye Bye Blondie*, published in 2004, incorporates music in her critique of contemporary society and representation of female rebellion. While she was not musically trained in the classical tradition, she was a band member during her youth. She has also stated that punk and rock music were fundamental in her development as a writer and to her understanding of the world around her. Listening to music, in contrast to the nineteenth-century perception of sound, was for Despentes "a way to cling to life, to continue to contemplate existence" (Adler).[8] Similar to George Sand's statement that she could have been a musician, Despentes states that she would rather have been a singer than a writer (Poncet).

In *Bye Bye Blondie*, Despentes incorporates music as a means whereby the heroine rebels against social norms and explores meaning in life. While Despentes integrates many different types of music groups, the particular music genre highlighted in the novel is punk music. She describes it in the novel: "Punk rock was the first admission of failure of the post-war world, denouncing its hypocrisy and its inability to confront old demons" (50).[9] This critiquing of society is one of the main characteristics of the novel, focusing on the alienation and marginalization of its heroine. The heroine Gloria is addicted to this music, which has a profound effect on her: "This music that she had been listening to for several years had two contradictory effects on her: extraordinary relief and extraordinary anguish" (103).[10] Gloria's relationship with Eric is also marked by music. As he attempts to lead Gloria away from destructive choices and behavior, they both realize that punk music is not the answer for them: "In different ways, both (Eric and Gloria) would later realize how punk rock had not been a good preparation for real life … too much fun … too much utopia" (120).[11]

Despentes's use of music as a narrative tool in critiquing society in *Bye, Bye Blondie* represents the late twentieth-century *Zeitgeist*, much like Sand in the nineteenth century, which she will further explore in *Vernon Subutex*. Essay assignments probe the communicative role of music in the narrative text: how music and musical elements influence the text, and its influence on perception by the reader.

Conclusion

As current literary criticism attempts to understand literature in musical terms, analysis must explore the transposition of music or musical effects into literary expression by investigating how music and musical elements shape the form of the text and advance the narrative.

Where music serves as paradigm, music is defined as a language in the sense that music communicates both verbal and extraverbal content. David Powell probes the function of music as language in Sand's works and mentions her frustration with "the inability of verbal language to properly describe musical language" (153)[12] in his article on ""La Langue de l'infini." He points to her success, however, in presenting the two languages as not only coexistent, but also reciprocal: "For Sand, music and verbal language form a counterpoint to create a harmony that is impossible to define. However, it still illuminates the nature of musical language and verbal language" (153).[13] This harmony, portrayed in the musical novels of Sand, Duras, and Despentes, as well as in the music of Chopin, Liszt, and Ravel, enriches the life of the reader and the listener. Permeating the novels as an integral part of the narrative, music serves as a symbol that reflects at once the intimate expression of our deepest and most profound emotions, as well as the larger societal system and current *Zeitgeist*. Studying this reciprocal and interdisciplinary relationship in literature and music provides students with the ability to discover a crucial role of music: to aid humanity as a guide in attaining understanding and enlightenment by establishing connections to our world and with others ... to express and bring about harmony.

Notes

1 See Powell, *While the Music Lasts*, Prieto *Listening In*, and Treitler *Music and the Historical Imagination*.
2 In writing, language is also understood in musical terms, as has been discussed and outlined in Stamos Metzidakis and Marie-Christine Clemente's article, "Au coeur de l'esthétique baudelairienne: thyrse et caducée." This article demonstrates, among other things, the impact of Liszt's music on the poetics of Baudelaire and his entire generation of poets.
3 "Je n'aimais réellement jamais que la littérature et la musique." All translations are my own.
4 "Un soir j'écoutais avec recueillement le bruit de la mer calme brisant sur le sable; je cherchais le sens de ces trois lames, plus fortes que les autres, qui reviennent toujours ensemble à des intervalles réguliers, comme un rythme marqué dans l'harmonie éternelle; j'entendis un pêcheur qui chantait aux étoiles, étendu sur le dos dans sa barque."
5 "Je remarquai que le chant du pêcheur suivait instinctivement le rythme [de] la mer, et je pensai que c'était là peut-être un de ces grands et vrais artistes que la nature elle-même prend soin d'instruire ... le charme de sa voix, l'habileté naïve de son rythme, et l'étonnante beauté de sa mélodie, triste, large et monotone comme celle des vagues, me frappèrent si vivement, que tout à coup la musique me fut révélée."
6 "C'est le premier artiste qu'elle observe dans sa lutte obstinée avec le langage de l'incommunicable."
7 "Le génie de Chopin est le plus profond et le plus plein de sentiments et d'émotions qui ait existé. Il a fait parler à un seul instrument la langue de l'infini."
8 "[U]n moyen de s'accrocher à la vie, de continuer à envisager l'existence."
9 "Le punk rock était le premier constat de l'échec du monde d'après-guerre, dénonciation de son hypocrisie, de son incapacité à confronter ses vieux démons."
10 "Cette musique qu'elle écoutait en boucle depuis plusieurs années avait deux effets contradictoires: un soulagement extraordinaire, défoulement et soulagement. Et, dans le même temps, ça appelait une angoisse extraordinaire, sans la résoudre, ça parlait de ça, être enfermé, être terrorisé, être dans le noir."
11 "Plus tard, de façon différente, l'un et l'autre (Eric et Gloria) réaliseraient à quel point le punk rock n'avait pas été une bonne préparation à la vraie vie ... trop de rigolade ... trop d'utopie."
12 "[L]'inaptitude du langage verbal à bien décrire la langue musicale."
13 "Pour Sand, la musique et la langue verbale forment un contrepoint pour créer une harmonie impossible à définir mais qu'éclaire tout de même la nature de la langue musicale, et celle de la langue verbale, aussi."

References

Adler, Laure. "Hors-Champs," interview with Virginie Despentes, *France-Culture*, February 7, 2014. www.youtube.com/watch?v=12M9_jeOphM

Da Sousa Correa, Delia. *Phrase and Subject: Studies in Literature and Music.* Modern Humanities Research Association and Maney Publishing, 2006.

Despentes, Virginie. *Baise-moi.* Poche Revolver n°1. Florent-Massot, 1993. *Rape Me*, trans. Bruce Benderson. Grove Press, 2003.

Despentes, Virginie. *Bye Bye Blondie.* Grasset, 2004.

Duras, Marguerite. *Moderato Cantabile.* Éditions minuit, 1980.

Johnson, James H. *Listening in Paris: A Cultural History.* University of California Press, 1995.

Kallberg, Jeffrey. *Chopin at the Boundaries: Sex, History, and Musical Genre.* Harvard University Press, 1996.

Massardier-Kenney, Françoise. *Gender in the Fiction of George Sand.* Rodopi, 2000.

Metzidakis, Stamos and Marie-Christine Clemente. "Au coeur de l'esthétique baudelairienne: thyrse et caducée." *Romanic Review* 101.4(2010): 741–759.

Poncet, Dominique. "Le style cru de Virginie Despentes: portrait de Virginie Despentes," *Ina Culture*, October 28, 1998, www.youtube.com/watch?v=LOSEKN6w5wQ

Powell, David A. *While the Music Lasts: The Representation of Music in the Works of George Sand.* Associated University Presses, 2001.

Prieto, Eric. *Listening In: Music, Mind, and the Modernist Narrative.* University of Nebraska Press, 2002.

Rambeau, Marie-Paule. *Chopin dans la vie et l'oeuvre de George Sand.* Belles Lettres, 1985.

Sand, George. *Consuelo*, 3 vols, ed. Simone Vierne and René Bourgeois. Editions de l'Aurore, 1983. *The Countess von Rudolstadt*, trans. Gretchen van Slyke. University of Pennsylvania Press, 2008.

Sand, George. *Correspondance*, 25 vols, ed. Georges Lubin. Garnier, 1964–91.

Sand, George. *Histoire de ma vie*, 2 vols, ed. Damien Zanone. Flammarion, 2001. *Story of My Life*, trans. Thelma Jurgrau. Sunny Press, 1991.

Sand, George. *Les Maîtres Sonneurs*, 2 vols, ed. Joseph-Marc Bailbé. Éditions Glénat, 1994. *The Master Pipers*, trans. Rosemary Lloyd. Oxford University Press, 1994.

Sand, George. *Les Sept Cordes de la lyre*, ed. René Bourgeois. Flammarion, 1973. *A Woman's Version of the Faust Legend: The Seven Strings of the Lyre*, trans. George Kennedy. University of North Carolina Press, 1989.

Sand, George. *Spiridion*, ed. Oscar A. Haac and Michèle Hecquet. Slatkine Reprints, 2000.

Treitler, Leo. *Music and the Historical Imagination.* Harvard University Press, 1989.

18

INTRODUCING OR EXPANDING QUEER CONTENT IN THE CONTEMPORARY FRANCOPHONE CLASSROOM

CJ Gomolka

Within the past two and a half decades, interest in queer studies has been prolific on college campuses as more and more queer- and non-queer-identified students take interest in the existential debates on cultural and political heteronormativity that circumscribe their existence. Some French and Francophone departments have latched on to this important pedagogical bent through specific tenure-line hires or rotating seminars by gender and sexuality/queer specialists. Many, especially smaller and/or more frugally funded French and Francophone departments, search for ways to make their classrooms more inclusive through a targeted pedagogy invested in scrutinizing and critically analyzing the dynamic intersection of queer and non-normative expressions of gender and sexuality with literature, culture, politics, linguistics, and history.

We should not underestimate this pedagogical commitment to diversity and inclusion. Indeed, it promotes interdepartmental and intercultural connections that can be leveraged within and without French and Francophone studies to more fully understand the pluralistic modes of being of LGBTQ persons of the past, and those of today, in and outside of the Francophone world. In the following pages, I will offer several approaches and strategies that I hope are instructive for those interested in introducing or expanding queer content in their Francophone classrooms. In addition, I propose structures, methods, and content that I have found useful and engaging as well as a short *entrée* into the historical dimension of queer studies in France with, what I hope to be, useful resources for further exploration and use.[1]

Setting the Scene: Resources for Providing Background on Queer Studies in France

In his work on queer studies and France, Bruno Perreau dates the arrival of queer theory in the Hexagon to the late 1990s. Indeed, in the summer of 1996 and 1997, Sam/Marie-Hélène Bourcier, in collaboration with several other queer activists, doctorant.e.s, and LGBT militants, hosted a series of conferences at the Centre gai et lesbien de Paris under the working group Le Zoo. Imagined as a site of collective pedagogical and militant engagements against elitist and "straight" knowledges with a campy twist, the seminars, later published under the title Q comme Queer (1998) (Q like Queer),[2] offer a rich and fascinating look at France's first reactions to the arrival, or "return" (Perreau), of queer theory to France. In the classroom, this work can be presented ensemble for those interested in exploring specific interpretations of Foucault, Deleuze, Wittig, and especially film studies, or more intentionally as an introduction to epistemological orientations toward queer in France in the late 1990s. Of particular interest are the sections "D'un discours sur à un discours de" ("From a Discourse on to a Discourse about/Queer Discourse")[3] by Catherine Deschamps; "Queer Made in France" and "Le 'nous' du zoo" ("The 'Us' of the Zoo") by Sam/Marie-Hélène Bourcier, all of which provide instructors with a textual platform from which to discuss the transversal links between the identitary appeals discussed during these seminars and larger hegemonic Francophone systems such as republicanism, assimilation, and universalism. In addition to these primary sources, several queer Francophone authors have engaged with this topic and can be used to enrich discussions (Preciado; Bourcier; Revenin).

For students, an interesting exercise is to discuss what exactly is meant by "queer" in the *Zoo* seminars and how it might differ from, on the one hand, the identity politics of the Anglo-American LGBT tradition, and on the other, the universalizing tendencies of the American queer movement. Moreover, reading these "popular" expressions of queer during the seminars as possible extensions of other longstanding social discourses against racism, capitalism, colonialism, genderism, and sexism, among others, in France, allows students to consider queer's contribution to anti-racist and anti-globalist languages of justice and inclusion and their operation in a Francophone context. Another interesting and related conversation might explore the choice of the seminar's setting: Le Centre gai et lesbien de Paris versus a university space. Introducing Foucault's notion of "heterotopia" would provide the theoretical background necessary to discuss space and queerness in this context (Foucault). In addition, comparing and contrasting student-led models of activism, like *Le Zoo* seminars, with examples on their own campuses allows students to critically analyze and compare alternative examples of militancy through what Éric Fassin has called the "Transatlantic mirror" (2000).

The PaCS (1999)[4] and *Mariage pour tous* (2013)[5] debates offer professors ample material to discuss ideological and epistemological negotiations between contemporary non-normative sexual and gender identities and French Republican traditions. Because of this, they are welcome additions to courses discussing sexuality and gender in the Francophone world. The surrounding scholarship, however, can be overwhelming and could indeed provide fodder for semester-long discussions. Instead of focusing specifically on the PaCS or *Mariage pour tous*, I often orient class discussions in both my upper-200-level "Sex, Gender, and Identity in Contemporary France" (SGI) and 300-level "Queer Francophone Identities" (QFI) courses[6] toward the epiphenomena churned up by these events offering students an atypical induction into the cultural and ideological pushback provoked by the "recognition of difference" that the PaCS debate and *Mariage pour tous* decision seemed to invoke.

Shortly before and after the May 17, 2013 "*loi Taubira*," which extended legal recognition of civil marriage to same-sex couples, an array of anti-marriage-equality *manifestations* and groups[7] dotted France's geography including demonstrations against the anxiously envisioned unbinding of "traditional" French familial values, the loss of sexual and gender distinctions, and a specific piece of pedagogical legislation, *Les ABCD de l'égalité* (*The ABCDs of Equality*), by then minister of women's rights Najat Vallaud-Belkacem (Foerster; Perreau).[8] The *realia* produced in the wake of these demonstrations is an invaluable resource for classrooms wishing to engage with the necessary negotiations between sexual and gender non-conformity and "traditional" French values and Republican traditions. In addition to materials opposing the use of the program in French *écoles maternelles* and *collèges*,[9] articles against the "promotion" of gender theory more generally,[10] videos and official sites dedicated to explaining the program's relevance to French universalism and Republican values,[11] there is also a diverse array of demonstration posters that I use over the course of two or three class periods to critically examine the intertwined discourses to which protesters appealed against marriage and gender equality.[12] These posters are a particularly useful tool to employ either through written assignments, individual student-led presentations/discussions, or in-class brainstorming sessions. In my QFI course I highlight and have students critically consider how thick the network of discourses invoking communism, socialism, neoliberalism, "reproductive futurism" (Edelman), racism, postcolonialism, religion, economic liberalism, universalism, biology, "traditionalism," homophobia, transphobia, genderism becomes when trying to "other" and muzzle non-normative expressions of gender and sexuality in the French polity.

A final introductory resource that has worked well in both my SGI and QFI courses is the thematically and programmatically affiliated podcasts *Homomicro* and *Gouinement Lundi*. [13] *Homomicro* is a combination of campy and sarcastic *chroniques*, LGBT-themed literature and film reviews, health and culture segments, topical interviews with Francophone and global authors, activists, and politicians, as well as music and (homo)sex advice. *Gouinement lundi* is a feminist-inflected series of discussions on lesbian, bi, and trans culture, sports, entertainment, and politics.[14] Of particular interest for introductory units on queerness is a double program aired on *Gouinement lundi* entitled "Le Queer." Interviews with Université de Lille III professor Zoé Adam, as well as queer militant and member of GARCES Cécile Lavier, provide students with material for a fecund debate on the definitions, expressions, and material manifestations of queer in contemporary France. These two programs invite classroom discussions on the similarities and tensions between feminist and queer movements; the influence of the Anglo-American gender and feminist movements on French articulations of feminism, gender, and queerness; the effects of globalization on French thought and universities; the development of dedicated queer movements and centers in France; as well as the often necessary negotiations between appeals to communitarianism—based on an Anglo-American identity-based model—and the sacrosanct principles of universalism and assimilation of French Republicanism.[15] Useful for both listening comprehension and their cultural import(s), the *Homomicro* and *Gouinement lundi* podcasts can also be adapted for written assignments: I routinely ask students to choose current episodes, to listen, and to write critical reports to be shared with the class. And because the podcasts are topical, airing every Monday night for *Homomicro* and every fourth Monday for *Gouinement lundi*, students have the opportunity to take part in current conversations on gayness and globalization (Altman), popular LGBTQ-friendly literature and film, AIDS and HIV in contemporary Francophone culture, citizenship studies (Le Bitoux), as well as discussions with global and Francophone queer activists. Another contemporary Francophone podcast comes to mind as a useful tool for the classroom: *Les couilles sur la table* (*Balls on the Table*) on Binge Audio. This podcast features a series on masculinity in France including a particularly informative episode on black masculinities, "Masculinités noires," and trans men, "Vikken, Portrait d'un homme trans" ("Vikken, portrait of a transman"), not to mention episodes invoking men's participation in the #MeToo movement ("Après #MeToo: ce que peuvent faire les hommes"; "After #MeToo: what men can do") and an extended interview with Olivia Gazalé, author of an excellent diachronic study of the mythology of virility (Gazalé).[16]

Creating Queer Units for Upper-Level Francophone Courses

Inheritor of a grassroots genealogy, queer theory and queer studies emerged in the United States out of a feminist as well as gender and sexual non-conforming militancy dissatisfied and disillusioned with the neoliberal and commercial bent of the gay and lesbian identity-based politics of the late 1980 and early 1990s. To be sure, queer studies is an anarchist and anti-heteronormative response to the blunt, political rhetoric and mostly white activist bodies that populated the contemporary LGBT landscape. While often contentious, the relationship between queerness and academia in the Anglo-American tradition has generated complete disciplines, special departments, degrees, and certificates, as well as an ever growing body of venerated scholarship.

In France, the advancement of queer studies (or even sexuality and gender studies) has been sluggish for several reasons. On the one hand, the inherent interdisciplinarity of gender and sexuality studies poses problems for students embroiled in the competitive selection processes of France's elite *Écoles* that often favor more conventional and discrete approaches to research domains. And while departments such as modern languages, sociology, and history have slowly incorporated more diverse specialization options for interested students, there is currently a dearth of positions available for *doctorant.e.s en genre et sexualité* after graduation (Revenin). In addition, general sentiment toward gender and sexuality studies has been negatively influenced by the specter of communitarianism and Anglo-American identity-based politics raised at least in part by the gay and lesbian conferences organized in the late 1990s by *Le Zoo* and those by Didier Eribon, fears of the disastrous effects of globalization on the "traditional" *mœurs* of France (Gordon and Meunier), the PaCS debates, Najat Vallaud-Belkacem's *Les ABCD de l'égalité* programs, the publication of Frédéric Martel's *Le rose et le noir* in which the author emphatically states the danger of "ghettoization" posed by LGBT studies in France (Martel; Eribon), as well as the recent *Mariage pour tous* legislation. For Francophone classrooms, engagements with these social and cultural issues charts a highly textured, dynamic, and complex topography for students in various disciplines to explore.

After introductory material on gender and sexuality studies in the Anglo-American and Francophone tradition, I begin my "Queer Francophone Identities" course with Brahim Naït-Balk's *Homo dans la cité: la descente aux enfers puis la libération d'un homosexuel de culture maghrébine* (*Homo in the Ghetto: Descent into Hell then the Liberation of a Maghrebi Homosexual*). *Homo dans la cité* is an autobiographical work that traces the devastating and difficultly navigated network of discriminations faced by a Franco-Moroccan homosexual living in Paris's infamous *Cité des 3000* at Aulnay-sous-Bois. Harassed by jeers invoking *haram* and *chouma*,[17] as well as the bullish omnipresence of the troubled and anxious hypermasculinity of the *banlieue*,[18] Naït-Balk finds some solace in the mediatized world of community radio on *Fréquence pluriel* and the highly virilized "terrain d'expérimentation sexuelle" ("site of sexual experimentation") (Naït-Balk 19) of France's soccer clubs. *Homo dans la cité* provides a stringent examination of the actively strained intersections of (homo)sexuality with the familial Muslim traditions of filiation, marriage, patriarchy (also prominent and stifling Republican values), and religion, or what Naït-Balk calls his personal "carcan" ("straight-jacket") (15). Hints of "homonormativity" (Duggan; Naze) also circulate throughout Naït-Balk's discourse including a scathing critique of *La Gay Pride* called a "carnaval de 'folles' [qui] donne une image désastreuse des homosexuels, dont la majorité est loin d'être exhibitionniste" ("carnival of queens [that] provides a disastrous image of homosexuals, the majority of whom are far from exhibitionists") (Naït-Balk 134). In class I often ask students to be *animateurs de discussion* ("class discussion leaders") of specific chapters, far-reaching themes, or larger theoretical discourses that allow for critical engagement with queer, post and decolonial, as well as gendered, ethnic, and racial lenses. Such topics might include the space of sexuality in the *banlieue*, the queerness of the Franco-Moroccan family (Provencher, 2017), the "rules/codes" of masculinity in the *cité*, the sexualization of the *beur*[19] body (Mack), the development of "parallel lives" as a homosexual, as well as homophobia (effeminophobia) among homosexuals.

My reasons for starting with *Homo dans la cité* are pragmatic and structural: several of the works (*Homo-ghetto; Les gens normaux*) read during the semester as well as many of the podcasts (*Homomicro; Gouinement lundi*) listened to involve Naït-Balk in one way or another. I like the continuity that this brings to the course; it also allows students to see that there are specific contemporary, queer, Francophone figures doing amazing work in the diffusion and articulation of gay and lesbian interests in different literary, popular, and cultural venues. Additionally, my students question and critique this work and the cultural vehicles used in its dissemination. For example, along with its listeners in France, *Homomicro*'s 15,000 downloads per month have an expansive geographical reach, spread out among the U.S., the Maghreb, and Sub-Saharan Africa, among others. The presence of *Homomicro* in such a diverse array of geographies seems to invite investigations into the constitution and influence of the "homo" envisioned for this "imaginary (queer) listening community." Several leading questions might be asked to students: How does *Homomicro* define the ideological topography of their imagined consumer and what might analytical excavations of their content tell us about the circulation of "queerness" from a (Parisian) French perspective? How might such Western notions of queerness influence non-Western sexualities through contemporary information technologies like podcasts? How might the consumption of *Homomicro* contribute to, embolden, or butt up against local and non-local cultural understandings of non-normative gender and sexuality within but also without the Hexagon (Puar)? What influence do Anglo-American notions of queerness have both on *Homomicro*'s platform, but also on its listeners?[20]

In many ways a complement to *Homo dans la cité*, Franck Chaumont's *Homo-ghetto gays et lesbiennes dans les cités: Les clandestins de la République* (*Homo-ghetto Gays and Lesbians of the Projects: The Clandestine of the Republic*) is a collection of ethnographic *témoignages* (accounts) gathered over a period of two years that bear witness to the personal, physical, and mental "*enfer*" (hell) lived by those understood to be or openly declared gay and lesbian in Paris's *banlieues*.[21] The text paints a picture of these areas as highly virilized and patriarchal lawless zones where sexism, masochism, homophobia, and genderism reign under the supreme mandate of archaic and opportunistic religious interpretations and the omnipresent, argus-eyed pack mentality of the young (*beur*) men that police its borders. The *banlieue* inhabitants, both gay and straight, exist as perpetually active menaces to the Republican values of assimilation, universalism, and *laïcité* (secularism). Besides these themes, students quickly pick up on the double discrimination that contorts these gays and lesbians into complicated socio-cultural, identitary postures: in Paris, gays from the *cité* often perform the exoticized and eroticized roles of the rough-n-tough slum *beur*, the fetish of many white, bourgeois, gay Frenchmen; in the *cité*, they carry out ironclad displays of masculine mastery or are verbally stoned, physically accosted, victims of gang rape and forced fellatio, ultimately isolated and excluded from (homo)sociality; in the case of lesbians they are invisibilized or existentially denied materiality in the *cité* while also dangerously defying and denying the longstanding mythology and (pre)dominance of a "male-bodied" masculinity in constant threat of delegitimation. In my QFI class, students use this work to discuss the relationship between space, sexuality, and gender (Bell and Valentine; Bell et al.), questions of visibility versus invisibility, the socio-cultural and religious management of bodies and spaces, as well as the use of specific social strategies to survive and (sometimes) thrive in culturally and socially circumscribed spaces. In addition to these questions, my students are also tasked with the questioning/critique of the author's methodology in collecting this information, something he details in the introduction. This activity gets students thinking about research methods, interpretation of ethnographical findings, as well as possible epistemological bias when creating interview questions for participants. For example, we discuss how the anonymity of participants and dissimulation of city names might affect our interpretation of the phenomena described by Chaumont; how the author's use of gay meet-up sites to solicit participants could have influenced his interview sample; as well as how this work might contribute to the continual othering/exoticization of the lives it attempts to demystify.

Les gens normaux: paroles lesbiennes, gay, bi, trans (2013) (*Everyday People: The Words of Lesbian, Gay, Bi, Trans*) is a collection of ten interviews imaged as chapters of a graphic novel accompanied by five socio-cultural and political essays written by scholars and historians questioning the hegemonic, heteronormative structures and dominant (hetero)sexualities that manage the concept of "normalcy" in the French polity. In collaboration with the Centre Lesbien, Gay, Bi, Trans de Touraine, Hubert, the collection editor, stages interviews that spotlight the epistemological and existential variety with which one might approach divergent modes of being and non-normative sexualities and genders in France. Interviews interrogate sexual orientation, adoption, living as a couple while LGBTQ, the effects of the AIDS epidemic, gender-confirmation surgeries, the dangers of living as a homosexual within and without the Hexagon, ethics, morality, and the gaze of an overwhelming, assumed heterosexual majority. In my QFI course, each student is charged with the critical analysis and presentation of one of the interviews in this collection. I ask them to work specifically on appropriate language and lexicon, discouraging essentializing structures like "authentic" or "true" gender/sex or outdated and discriminatory constructions such as "sex-change operations." Instead, students learn to privilege inclusive language and expressions such as "lived or understood" gender and "gender-confirmation surgeries."[22] This collection is also a great way to introduce terms such as "cisgenre" ("cisgender"), "expression de genre" ("gender expression"), "identité de genre" ("gender identity"), "morinommer" ("deadname"), "genre neutre" ("gender neutral"), "non-binaire" ("non-binary"), and "intersexe" ("intersex").[23]

Conclusion

With the materials, methodologies, and pedagogical suggestions offered here, I hope to provide useful resources for professors and instructors of French and Francophone studies who desire to introduce or expand LGBTQ content in their classrooms. These works, while chosen because of their queer tenor, reach beyond queer studies to embrace students interested in broader axes of research including masculinity, critical race, postcolonial, media, literary, and global studies, making them especially ideal for interdisciplinary classrooms. With some modifications and guiding supplements, many of these works, podcasts, and interviews could also be adapted to advanced 200-level courses, something I have routinely done. Most importantly, perhaps, these materials orient students toward timely and critically engaging conversations playing out in the Francophone world and that should be localized and considered in the contemporary Francophone classroom.

Notes

1 I have decided to take a contemporary and intersectional approach to proposing materials for queer studies in the Francophone classroom rather than attempting a diachronic survey of gender and sexuality studies throughout French history, a daunting and impossible task for a contribution such as this. Additionally, I have decided to concentrate almost exclusively on twenty-first-century queer material because, to my mind, it seems to facilitate more seamlessly the transversal investigations into class, race, nationality, ethnicity, gender, and sexuality that I want to foreground in my classroom.

2 All translations are my own.
3 This title is a play on words as "un discours de" means both "a discourse about" but also invokes the French possessive and in turn points to a reappropriation of discourses on "queer" by queers themselves.
4 The PaCS ("Pacte civil de solidarité/Civil Solidarity Pact") is a contractual form of civil union available to two individuals in either same-sex or opposite-sex couples that gives certain formal rights and responsibilities to those couples, thereafter, known as "pacsé." See Fassin 2000, 2001 and Stychin.
5 The *Mariage pour tous* ("Marriage for Everyone") legislation, also known as the "*loi Taubira*," and "*mariage homosexuel*" ("gay marriage"), offers same-sex couples, since May 17, 2013, the juridical guaranties of civil marriage.
6 Both courses are taught in French.
7 See specifically the following groups: Les Veilleurs (www.lavie.fr/actualite/societe/mariage-pour-tous-une-soiree-avec-les-veilleurs-21-04-2013-39421_7.php); les Antigones (http://lesantigones.fr/qui-sommes-nous/); and Hommen (www.youtube.com/watch?v=_B1b9lcQqMU; https://www.facebook.com/leshommen; http://hommen-officiel.tumblr.com).
8 The *ABCD de l'égalité* is a pedagogical program instituted in France by Najat Vallaud-Belkacem that intends to provide materials to educators and students to battle sexism and gender stereotypes within and without the Francophone classroom. Adopted experimentally at the start of the 2013 academic year in 275 *écoles maternelles et collèges*, the program's mission was "la transmission, à l'école et par école, d'une culture d'égalité entre les filles et les garçons, entre les femmes et les hommes" ("the transmission, in school and by schools, of a culture of equality between girls and boys, between men and women"). For more information see: www.reseau-canope.fr/outils-egalite-filles-garcons
9 See Vigigender's website: www.vigi-gender.fr, and especially their "informational" packet "Le genre en images: Quelle société voulons-nous pour nos enfants": www.vigi-gender.fr/wp-content/uploads/2017/01/Livret-3ème-édition-1.pdf; another helpful resource is a direct anti-gender theory workshop produced and animated by Vigigender's founder and spokesperson Esther Pivet given in 2017: www.youtube.com/watch?v=f73-ueeGAl0
10 See the article by Alain de Benoist "Non à la théorie de genre": http://blogelements.typepad.fr/blog/2014/02/si-lon-en-croit-les-journalistes-samuel-laurent-et-jonathan-parienté-du-monde-la-première-escroquerie-des-anti-.html#more
11 See an explanation by Véronique Rouyer, *maître de conférences en psychologie du développement de l'enfant et de la famille*, of the importance of these teachings in school: www.youtube.com/watch?v=opBj3fL1qyA; see also the *ABCDs*' official site: www.education.gouv.fr/cid4006/egalite-des-filles-et-des-garcons.html, or Najat Vallaud-Belkacem's personal explanation of this program: www.cafepedagogique.net/lexpresso/Pages/2013/11/08112013Article635194907592747148.aspx
12 These posters can be found at: www.lamanifpourtous.fr/kit-du-manifestant/, https://genere.hypotheses.org/385, and http://leplus.nouvelobs.com/contribution/845577-mariage-gay-le-gouvernement-a-laisse-les-opposants-dire-n-importe-quoi-sur-la-filiation.html, among other sites.
13 *Gouinement lundi* is a play on the French noun *gouine* which may be translated as "dyke" and the adverbial French suffix "ment." We might understand the title of the podcast then as "Dykey Mondays."
14 All podcasts can be downloaded for free at: http://homomicro.net
15 For an extended discussion of this see Provencher 2007 and Gunther.
16 See https://soundcloud.com/lescouilles-podcast; also available on Apple podcasts. For those interested in masculinity studies and the Francophone world see also Gourarier.
17 *Haram* ("forbidden" in Arabic) and *chouma* ("shame" in Arabic; sometimes *h'chouma*) are often invoked by gay-identified Franco-Moroccan authors as weighty, culturally charged external commentaries and internalized discourses on non-conforming sexual and gender orientations.
18 Etymologically, *banlieue* refers to an area or league (*lieue*) of distance from official decree (*ban*) or the space just outside of a major city. These areas may be affluent, but increasingly the term has come to refer to and stigmatize lower-income, largely immigrant, or French born of immigrant descent-populated urbanized areas.
19 The term *beur* is French slang used to designate a young male, born in France to Maghrebi immigrant parents. The word is formed using *verlan* or backslang: taking the French word "arabe" ("Arab") and flipping the syllabic order. See Mack.
20 Besides Naït-Balk's podcast, a documentary entitled "Banlieue gay," aired on France's M6 in 2006, stages the tensions between non-normative expressions of gender and sexuality and the *banlieues* outside of Paris. Available for free online, this documentary is especially useful from an

interdisciplinary perspective documenting the lives of Emir, an androgynous, gay, black man; Brahim of *Homo dans la cité*; Mikaël, a white, gay student; and Julia, a lesbian living with a partner.
21 Brahim Naït-Balk also provides an account of his own story in Chaumont's work.
22 The terms "chirurgie de réattribution sexuelle" or "d'affirmation sexuelle" are preferred over "chirurgie de changement de sexe." In addition, "genre vécu" or "ressenti" as well as "assigné à la naissance" are preferred over "genre/sexe biologique."
23 The term "cisgender" is used to describe a person whose sense of identity and gender corresponds to the gender assigned them at birth; or not transgender. "Deadname" is the use of a transman or woman's given name rather than their preferred or chosen name.

References

Altman, Dennis. *Global Sex*. University of Chicago Press, 2001.
Bell, David and Gill Valentine, eds. *Mapping Desire: Geographies and Sexualities*. Routledge, 1995.
Bell, David, Jon Binnie, Ruth Holliday, Robyn Longhurst, and Robin Peace, eds. *Pleasure Zones: Bodies, Cities, Spaces*. Syracuse University Press, 2001.
Bourcier, Marie-Hélène (Sam). *Homo Inc.orporated: Le triangle et la licorne qui pète*. Cambourakis, 2017.
Bourcier, Marie-Hélène (Sam). "Le nouveau conflit des facultés: biopouvoir, sociologie et queer studies dans l'université néo-libérale française." *SociologieS, Dossiers, Sociétés en mouvement, sociologie en changement* (2016). https://journals.openedition.org/sociologies/5271
Bourcier, Marie-Hélène (Sam). *Zoo: Q comme Queer. Les séminaires Q du zoo (1996–1997)*. Les Cahiers Gai Kisch Camp, 1998.
Chaumont, Franck. *Homo-Ghetto gays et lesbiennes dans les cités: les clandestins de la République*. Le cherche midi, 2009.
Duggan, Lisa. *The Twilight of Equality? Neoliberalism, Cultural Politics, and the Attack on Democracy*. Beacon Press, 2004.
Edelman, Lee. *No Future: Queer Theory and the Death Drive*. Duke University Press, 2004.
Eribon, Didier. *Réflexions sur la question gay*. Champs, 1999.
Fassin, Éric. "Same Sex, Different Politics: 'Gay Marriage' Debates in France and the United States." *Public Culture* 13. 2(2001): 215–232.
Fassin, Éric. "The Politics of PACS in a Transatlantic Mirror: Same-Sex Unions and Sexual Difference in France Today." *SITES* 4(2000): 55–64.
Foerster, Maxime. *La différence des sexes à l'épreuve de la République*. L'Harmattan, 2003.
Foucault, Michel. "Des espaces autres." *Architecture, Mouvement, Continuité* 5(1984): 22–27.
Gazalé, Olivia. *Le Mythe de la virilité: Un piège pour les deux sexes*. Robert Laffont, 2017.
Gordon, Philip H. and Sophie Meunier. *The French Challenge: Adapting to Globalization*. Brookings Institution Press, 2001.
Gourarier, Mélanie. *Alpha mâle: Séduire les femmes pour s'apprécier entre hommes*. Le Seuil, 2016.
Gunther, Scott. *The Elastic Closet: A History of Homosexuality in France, 1942–present*. Palgrave MacMillan, 2009.
Hubert, ed. *Les gens normaux: paroles lesbiennes, gay, bi, trans*. Casterman, 2013.
Le Bitoux, Jean. *Citoyen de seconde zone: Trente ans de lutte pour la reconnaissance de l'homosexualité en France (1971–2002)*. Hachette, 2003.
Mack, Mehammed Amadeus. *Sexagon: Muslims, France, and the Sexualization of National Culture*. Fordham University Press, 2017.
Martel, Frédéric. *Le rose et le noir: Les homosexuels en France depuis 1968*. Points, 2008.
Naït-Balk, Brahim. *Homo dans la cité: La descente aux enfers puis la libération d'un homosexuel de culture maghrébine*. Calmann-Lévy, 2009.
Naze, Alain. *Manifeste contre la normalisation gay*. La Fabrique, 2017.
Perreau, Bruno. *Queer Theory: The French Response*. Stanford University Press, 2016.
Preciado, Paul. "Il faut queeriser l'université." *Rue Descartes* 40(May2003): 79–83.
Provencher, Denis M. *Queer French: Globalization, Language, and Sexual Citizenship in France*. Ashgate, 2007.
Provencher, Denis M. *Queer Maghrebi French: Language, Temporalities, Transfiliations*. Liverpool, 2017.

Puar, Jasbir K. "Queer Times, Queer Assemblages." *Social Text* 23. 3–4(2005): 121–140.
Revenin, Régis. "A Preliminary Assessment of the First Four Decades of LGBTQ Studies in France (1970–2010)." *Paragraph: A Journal of Critical Theory* 35. 2(2012): 164–180.
Stychin, Carl F. "Civil Solidarity or Fragmented Identities? The Politics of Sexuality and Citizenship in France." *Social and Legal Studies* 10. 3(2001): 347–375.

INDEX

ACTFL *see* American Council on the Teaching of Foreign Languages
Adler, Laure 147
Africa 33, 57, 80, 84; and the growth of the world's French-speaking population within 105; and the patterns of migration to Europe 74; politics of 85
AIDS and HIV 152
Algeria 2, 5, 27, 84, 86, 103–6, 108–9; contemporary 108–9; culture of 5; and feminism 103–9; as a patriarchal society 103, 106–7, 109; and the role of women in the revolution 105–6; and the role of writers 104
Algerian War 6, 100–101, 123
Algiers 5, 51, 104–6, 109–10, 123, 127
American Council on the Teaching of Foreign Languages 53
American experience, compared with immigration in France 96
American fiction 6, 135
American multiculturalism 96, 98
American students 30, 71, 73, 81, 98
American universities 28, 104
American women 6, 135–37, 140–41
Anglo-American 151–54; gender and feminist movements 152; identity-based models 152; politics 153
Angot, Christine 40–41
Arab 5, 29, 57, 84–85, 91, 105–6, 111–17, 156; countries 114–16; feminists 109; women 97
Arab Spring 5, 91, 111–17
artifacts 55, 57, 59
arts 6, 12, 20, 35, 41, 45–46, 55–56, 81, 100, 136, 141, 143–44; humanities-based interpretive 18; liberal 135
Asselin, Gilles 97–98
assimilation 88, 99, 101; cultural 72; failed 99; in France 98–100, 151–52, 154

Au Contraire: Figuring out the French 97–98, 102
Auschwitz concentration camp 13, 130, 140
authors 27, 41, 70, 81, 95, 97, 105; *see also* writers
autobiography 2, 6, 19-26, 32; *see also* memoirs
autofiction 3, 36, 38–42, 107, 109

banlieue (suburbs) 72, 74, 97, 153, 156
basic interpersonal communication skills 69
The Battle of Algiers 5, 104–6, 109–10, 123, 127
Baudrillard, Jean 5, 111–13, 115, 117
Beauvoir, Simonde 3, 6, 20, 25–26, 51, 64–65, 67, 123–24, 126–27
behavior 101, 104, 144, 147; cultural 104; despicable 131; ethical 36; female 103; human 13; maternal 131; submissive 108
Béji, Hélé 5, 112–17
beliefs 79, 87, 124; as social constructs 79; and the treatment of women and women's place in society 87; of women in the role of bourgeois mothers 124
benefits 11, 14, 37, 39, 41, 47, 54, 121; instructional 48; reciprocal 40; transferrable intellectual 14; unemployment 73
Benguigui, Yamina 100, 102
beur novels 95, 97, 99, 153–54
BICS *see* basic interpersonal communication skills
biographies 79n1
The Birch-Tree Meadow 140
Birkenau concentration camp 136, 140
blacks 14, 22, 65, 70, 73, 82–83, 97, 117, 152, 157; African 83; Francophone 73
Bleu blanc vert (novel) 104–10
bodies 23, 33, 73, 81, 90, 92, 116–17, 154, 157; activist 153; female 91, 93, 108; naked 104
bombs 106, 122
The Break (novel) 133
"bridge courses" (intermediate-language-level) 5

Bugul, Ken 2, 20, 23, 25
Bye Bye Blondie 147

Camus, Albert 121–23
Canada 35, 72, 79–80, 82, 132–34; history of indigenous and Métis populations 133; and the issue of race 80; and the Maritime Provinces 82
"Canada Reads" CBCs 2017 competition 29, 132–33
Catholic Church 83, 85
Chabrol, Claude 140, 142
characters 37, 39, 48, 64, 66, 80–82, 89, 97, 104, 107, 122, 124, 128–30, 132–34, 136; "blocking" 85; "conniving" 131; independent 83; male 73, 91, 133, 145; single 132–34; strong 133; submissive 106
Chaumont, Franck 154
Chauvet, Marie Vieux 131–32, 134
childbirth 81, 107
childhood 2, 20–21, 23, 26, 32, 89, 92, 99, 107, 136
children 12, 16, 24–25, 31, 48, 71, 73, 83–84, 90, 99, 107, 122, 140; assimilating to dominant new cultures 81; killing of 122; literature of 83; small 46
choices 21, 30, 33, 36–37, 39, 56–57, 70, 93, 106, 125, 132, 145, 151; active 37; artistic 138; authentic 124; destructive 147; director's 23; narrative 133; professor's 104; stark life-or-death 124; subversive language 88; women's 90
Chopin, Frédéric 144, 146–48
Cigarettes and Nylons 137
civilizations 69, 71, 73, 75, 114; Francophone 4; French 68, 74
Cixous, Hélène 15, 27–28, 47
Claire d'Albe 63–65, 131–32
class discussions 24, 32, 65–66, 153
classes 20–21, 23, 35–39, 46, 54–56, 58, 62–63, 66, 71, 73–74, 84, 123–26, 128–34, 136–39, 152–53; advanced 62; beginner-level 62, 65–67; final 129; first-semester 62, 65; graduate 27, 80; political 116; science 38; social 74, 96, 135
classrooms 2, 27–29, 33, 39, 53–59, 63, 87, 98, 125, 129, 133–34, 138–39, 146, 150–52, 155; activities 70, 107, 145; culture 88–89, 92; foreign-language 53; Francophone 6–7, 117, 150–51, 153, 155–57; graduate 88; interdisciplinary 155; intermediate 3; online 2; traditional 45–46; virtual 57
Cold War 122–23
colonial 4–5, 77, 104, 112; oppression 106, 115; and postcolonialism 5, 105, 107, 111, 113–15, 117, 152
colonialism 5, 50, 74, 107, 117, 151; French 92; ideology 105; and neocolonialism 92
communication 13, 58, 62, 113, 145; effective 38; intercultural 69; mass 113; presentational 58; spoken 58
concentration camps 13, 22, 130, 136, 140 *see also* Auschwitz, Birkenau

Condé, Maryse 17, 27, 80–82, 85–86
Cornelio, Dawn M. 3, 35–42
courses 1, 3, 6, 31, 35–36, 46–47, 58–59, 61–62, 67–71, 87–88, 101, 126, 128, 151, 156; college-level 104; correspondence 46; honors program 101; lower-level 62; on-line 46; outreach 2
Cravens, Arline 6, 143–48
creativity 19–20, 38–39, 103, 128–29
Creoles 71, 74, 81
criminal justice 5, 123, 125
critiques 91, 111, 130, 134, 138, 141, 145, 147, 154; explicit 11; masculinist 85; scathing 153
culinary styles 98
cultural 1–6, 14–16, 18–20, 27–30, 53–59, 62, 67–72, 74–75, 80–81, 86–88, 93–102, 104–6, 112, 121–23, 149–57; artifacts 55, 57, 59; awareness 54–55, 58; differences 28, 53, 58; documents 56–58; domination 80; perspectives 2, 20, 56, 62; pluralism 5, 112; self-suppression 81
cultures 1, 14, 16–17, 29–30, 53–54, 58–59, 61, 68–70, 80–82, 84–89, 93, 96, 104, 121–22, 156–57; contemporary 113; distinct 24; diverse 98; electronic 81; human 13; indigenous 82; literary 143; native 87; postmodern 116
curriculum 2–3, 5, 47, 53–54, 56–58, 70, 128, 135; academic 104; American educational 95; content 111; French 3, 53, 105; hybrid 54; online 49; undergraduate 54

Darrieussecq, Marie 16
Davidson, Cathy N. 3, 45–46, 49, 51
De l'autre côté de la Périph 72
death 24, 103, 106, 130, 142
decolonization 6, 112–13, 123
democracy 12, 14, 19, 112, 114, 116, 157; and the development of human rights 112; and social justice 113
Despentes, Virginie 143, 147–49
Diderot, Denis 90
Diome, Fatou 17, 27, 32–34, 70, 73
distance-learning courses 46
diversity 1, 2, 33–34, 53–54, 57, 59, 95–97, 105, 137, 150; cultural 5; extreme 103; global 27; teaching 2, 4, 77; unprecedented 46
Djavann, Chahdortt 28–31, 33–34
Djebar, Assia 3, 47, 103, 109
Double Indemnity 137
Drowning by Bullets 101
Drowning by Bullets (documtary) 101
Duras, Marguerite 2, 20–22, 25, 143, 146–49

e-journals 3, 53–59; assignments 58; entries 55–56, 58; interactive 3, 53; topics 56–57
e-portfolios 54–55, 58
ecofeminists 88
education 12, 17, 19, 25, 42, 46, 73, 98–99, 107–8, 111, 116–17, 124–25, 141–42, 144–45; adult 125; arts 35, 54; classes 6; democratic

111; elite 13; foreign-language 13, 25; higher 12–13, 36, 45–46, 53–54, 111, 121; multicultural 98; online 3, 45–46, 49; public 116; secular 99; themes 99
educators 13, 45, 49, 111, 116, 122, 126, 156; French 126; teaching 124; university 95; women 104
Edwards, Natalie 4, 41, 68–74
Einstein, Albert 19, 26
emotions 12, 65, 90, 133, 138, 144, 146–48
empowerment 23, 37, 129, 137; and the Arab revolutions 114; female 47, 137
English-language classrooms 95
English-language courses 5
entrepreneurs 56–57, 89
Ernaux, Annie 2, 20, 24–25, 37
essays 38, 88, 105; Cixous's 15; critical 65; political 155; short 38, 88, 105
ethics 111, 116, 121, 155
"the ethics of ambiguity" (Beauvoir) 127
ethnicity 96, 98, 135, 155
events 15–16, 21–22, 32, 74, 81, 84, 107, 112–16, 133, 136, 138, 151; contemporary 2, 4; military 139; personal 15; real-life 89; silent painful 21; unspoken 22; virtual 113
examinations 4, 23, 56, 62, 73, 132; scholarly 87; searching 79; stringent 153
existentialist writers 5, 121, 123
experiences 16, 20, 28–30, 45–46, 53, 82, 90, 92, 96, 112–13, 115, 126, 136–38, 140, 144; author's 117; educational 45; female 100, 129, 137; gendered 95; historical 137; human 3, 14, 18, 31–32, 112; individual 137; male 97; multicultural 98; personal 90, 105; violent 30
expressions 14–15, 19, 27, 30–31, 33, 38–39, 58, 81, 97, 104, 124, 143, 145, 152, 155; artistic 53, 56–57; complex 65; facial 33; female 4; grammatical 38; intimate 148; literary 147; musical 144; oral 28–29; physical 16
extermination camps *see* concentration camps, Holocaust

faculty 4, 45–46, 54, 67, 125, 128, 139; and administrative colleagues 17; full-time French 121; members 139–40; and the resistence to online learning 45
families 2, 16, 20, 22–23, 41, 69, 73, 83–85, 95, 103, 108, 114, 124, 131, 141; bourgeois Haitian 131; colonized 81; drama 131; dynamics 5, 104, 107, 109; migrant 73; resettlement policies 5; and the support systems 133
female characters 5, 73, 91, 100, 106, 128–30
feminism 5, 33, 89, 103, 105, 107–9, 112, 114, 147, 152; core principle of 47; and decolonization 5; and immigration 27; intersectional 137
feminists 20, 88, 93, 112–13, 116, 130, 138, 152; Arab 109; assertions 89; authorial strategies 85; engagements 88; pedagogical approach 105, 128–29, 137; writers 2, 6, 15–16, 20, 27–28, 30, 32–33, 70, 87, 92–93, 103, 105, 107, 144, 147
fiction 21, 26, 32, 36, 39, 41, 57, 59, 89, 109, 112, 136, 138, 145, 149; American 6, 135; biographies 79n1; characters 21, 101; "jazz" 6; popular 135; reading of 12, 35; realistic 80; works of 109, 136
films 2–3, 23–25, 50–51, 55, 58–59, 61–67, 75, 100, 102, 105–6, 123, 135–38, 140–42, 144, 147; *8 Femmes* 3; *The Battle of Algiers* 5, 104–6, 109–10, 123, 127; *The Birch-Tree Meadow* 140; *Cigarettes and Nylons* 137; *De l'autre côté de la Périph* 72; *Double Indemnity* 137; *Inch'Allah Dimanche* 5, 100, 102; *The Intouchables* 72; *The Lover* 21–23; *Rose and the Soldier* 141n8; *The Women* 61
foreign languages 13, 16, 20, 39, 54, 59, 86, 121, 127, 141; extensive training in 14; requirements for reading and speaking 13; studies 14
Foreign Languages and Higher Education: New Structure for a Changed World MLA Report 121
France 5–18, 23–24, 30–34, 57, 59–60, 68–69, 71–75, 79–80, 82, 84, 89, 95–104, 122–23, 135–41, 150–58; and relationships with America 98; and the colonial past 73; commitment to diversity and inclusivity 97; contemporary 4–5, 95–96, 98–99, 151–52; and the DOMs (Martinique, Guadeloupe, and La Réunion) 93; and images of WWII 137; and immigration 71, 96; and the interconnectedness with the Francophone world 70–71; metropolitan 72; and Moroccan families 153; nineteenth-century 99; postwar 121, 124, 127; regional 69; and the separation of church and state in 72
Francophone 1–7, 17, 19–20, 24–25, 27–28, 33–34, 40–41, 45–46, 53–59, 67–74, 79–80, 85–89, 93, 103–5, 150–57; Algerian literature 104–5; authors 27, 41, 70, 81, 95, 97, 105; autobiographies 24; classrooms 6–7, 117, 150–51, 153, 155–57; countries 56, 95; cultures 3, 57–59, 68–69, 74; departments 150; immigrants 72; literature 6, 27, 33, 40, 73, 86–89, 91–93, 103; literature courses 4; newscasts 56; newspapers 55; North African literature 103; queer activists 152; regions 70; societies 70; students 104; study programs 5, 41, 121, 150, 155; traditions 153; writers 2, 6, 15–16, 20, 27–28, 30, 32–33, 70, 87, 92–93, 103, 107, 123, 144, 147
Francophone Metronomes (website) 2, 27, 33–34
Francophone women 1, 3–4, 6, 20, 41, 85, 112, 123; authors 1, 45–46, 58, 68, 80; diverse 7; and literature 45; perspectives 3, 54; perspectives of 3; teaching texts 1; and their voices 53, 56
Francophone Women Writers outside the French Classroom: An Integrated Approach to Exploring Women's Voices 6, 89, 112, 128

freedom 55, 64, 82, 84, 100, 106, 112–14, 116–17, 124–25, 127
French: classes 65–66; courses 3, 28; culture 30, 70, 74, 100; discipline 5; existential literature 6, 123; existentialist thinking 127; families 140; history 68, 98, 140, 155; instructors 1, 6; literature 6, 45, 70, 89, 97, 123, 128, 141; media 57, 98–99; and Moroccan homosexuals living in Paris 153; multiculturalism 95–96, 98–99, 101; national self-image 96; nationals 98–99; officers 106; presidential elections 71; programs 2, 4, 6, 20, 24, 62, 67, 104; school teachers 73; settlers 82; speaking countries 95; speaking world 4, 88, 95, 105; studies 1–6, 24, 26, 35, 61–62, 67, 70, 86, 95–97, 99, 101, 105, 117, 119, 121–22
French feminists 33, 49, 73
French language 1, 29, 31, 46, 69, 88, 99, 121; classrooms 31, 95; dominant 88; pedagogical settings 34
French Polynesia 4, 87–89, 91, 93
French Republic 82, 95, 97, 99, 102
French women 89, 139; and Algerian women 106; and their literature and experience 45, 49, 140; writers 6, 29, 128, 141
Frengs, Julia L. 4, 87–94
Front de Libération Nationale (National Liberation Army) 106

gays and lesbians 153–57
Gebhart, Richard C. 39, 41
gender 1–2, 4, 23–25, 29, 61, 63, 65, 92, 95–96, 98, 101–2, 132, 142–43, 145, 149–57; differences 41; distribution 96; domination 81; equality 152; equity 4, 70, 73; expectations 101; issues 3, 16, 80–81; non-conformity 151; non-normative 154; orientations 156; racial profiling 101; representation 145; roles 5, 79, 87, 104, 107, 109; stereotypes 79, 156; studies 2, 20, 31, 49, 51, 95, 153
genres 1, 5, 31–32, 57, 63, 92, 144, 146, 153, 156
Giroux, Henry 111–12, 116
globalization 53, 69, 116, 121, 123, 152–53, 157
Goellner, Sage 3, 45–50, 52
Gomolka, CJ 6–7, 150–55
graduate-level courses 90–91
graduate seminars 88–89, 93
Guadeloupe 71–72, 82, 85, 93
Guène, Faiza 101
guest lecturers 45–47, 49–52

Haiti 79–80, 82–83, 85, 131
Hayling, Alan 101
Heilbrun, Carolyn 20–21, 23, 25
Hernández-Laroche, Araceli 5–6, 121–27
historians 135–36, 140, 155; and historical events 5, 80, 89, 107, 114, 136–38; oral 82; wide-ranging 82
history 5–6, 26, 30, 70, 72–73, 80–82, 85–86, 88–89, 101, 104, 111–15, 133–36, 139–41, 149–50, 153; Acadian erased by the British 82; censorship 134; courses 138; and the lack of awareness about women's 6; military 139; recent 16; shared human 15; texts 135
HIV and AIDS 152
Hoft-March, Eilene 2, 11–18
Hogarth, Christopher 4, 68–74
Holocaust 13, 22, 130, 136, 149, *see also* Auschwitz, Birkenau, concentration camps, World War II
Homo dans la cité 153–54
homophobia 137, 152, 154
homosexuality 157
homosexuals 153–55
honors program courses 101
human rights 112, 114, 123

identity 2, 5, 16, 23, 33, 40, 71, 85–86, 97, 102–3, 108–9, 124, 131, 137–38, 145; constructed 36; crisis 108; and gender-based themes 79; intersectional 33; multicultural 95, 99; personal 84, 108; political 151; religious 122; themes 79, 84
images 1, 21–23, 27, 33, 39–40, 55, 57, 62–65, 67, 97, 101, 106, 137, 144, 156; clichéd 96; cultural 62; exoticized 90; idyllic 91; popular 11; public 36; sexual 21; stereotyped 91; textbook 62
immigrants 28, 72, 81, 84, 96–97, 99–100, 156
immigration 1, 4–5, 17, 27–28, 33, 56, 72–73, 95–97
incest 2–3, 20, 22, 37, 40
Inch'Allah Dimanche 5, 100
independence 36, 79, 83–84, 101, 106, 108, 113, 115, 117; Kanak 90–92; national 80; protests 89; war (Algeria) 105, 107
indigenous 88, 90, 133–34; cultures 82; language 84, 89, 93, 104; Oceanian community 91; societies 4, 87; women 89, 133
institutions 1–2, 6, 13, 54, 99, 121, 140; educational 67; political 1, 4, 68; social 68–69, 72–73
instructors 2–4, 36, 39, 45–48, 54–59, 61, 63, 65–66, 84–85, 87, 93, 95, 135, 138, 142
intercultural 53–54, 69–70, 75, 95, 104, 150; capabilities 70; competence 53–54; exchanges 104
interdisciplinary 7, 125–26, 128, 135, 140–41; approaches 2, 5–6, 119, 135; conceptions 6, 143; connections 5; innovations 121; relationships 143, 148; seminars 101; skills 122; studies 1
intermediate French classes 53, 55
interviews 19, 26, 30–32, 39, 47, 51, 55, 59, 86, 98, 122, 126, 148, 155; extended 152; filmed 2, 27–28, 30–33; individual 33; original 50; with sociologist Abdelmalek Sayad 100; topical 152
The Intouchables 72
Introducing or Expanding Queer Content in the Contemporary Francophone Classroom 6, 150, 155

Al-Jazeera 115
Johnston, Joyce 1–7, 61–67

Jours sans faim 36
justice 5–6, 46, 70, 105, 108, 112–16, 121, 123, 125, 136, 151; criminal 5, 123, 125; social 46, 70, 105, 113–15, 123

Kanak 87, 90–94; and Caledonian societal problems 92, 93n1; culture 93; history 91; independence 90–92; politics 91; society 91
Kanaky-New Caledonia 87, 91, 94
Killian, Caitlin 100
knowledge 11–13, 17, 19–20, 35, 39, 48, 58, 68, 71, 111, 116, 133, 135, 138, 147; cultural 58, 88; historical 90; interdisciplinary 53
Koran 92, 109
Kristeva, Julia 27, 31, 33

La Bataille d'Alger, Bleu Blanc vert 109
La Douleur 21
language 3–4, 13–16, 24, 26, 29–30, 54–55, 59, 68–73, 80–81, 121–23, 126, 143–44, 146, 148, 157; abstract 31; anti-globalist 151; classrooms 53–54; college-level 104; courses 3–4, 62, 69, 71; curriculum 54, 69; existentialist 125; former colonizer's 80–81; human 13; inaccuracies 38; indigenous 84, 89, 93, 104; learning 53–54, 69; levels of 15; official 35, 81; Polynesian 93; programs 54, 135; skills 4, 15, 55, 58, 62, 69; studying 14, 53, 59, 69, 74, 121, 143; teaching 53, 69–70; training 18, 68
Léal, Rebecca E. 5, 95, 95–102
learning 29–30, 36–38, 41, 46, 49, 54, 59, 70, 75, 124, 129, 136, 139, 142, 147; active 38–39; activities 41–42, 96–98; advanced language 3, 61–67, 99; collaborative 3, 48; distance 49; foreign-language 35; online 45–46; self-motivated 53
lecturers 45–47, 49–52
lectures 6, 36, 46–48, 50–51; archival 46; recorded 47, 50–51; special 49
legacies, cultural 49
Les Belles Images 80, 83, 85–86, 124
Les Filles de Caleb 83
lesbians 150–55, 157
LGBT studies in France 152–53, 155
liberal arts 135
literary studies 11, 20, 26, 69, 95, 143
literary texts 7, 12, 15, 68–74, 95, 143–44
literature 1–4, 11–13, 15–20, 31–33, 39, 69–70, 79–81, 86–87, 100–101, 122–23, 127–29, 136, 139–41, 143–44, 147–50; advanced 3; analyzing of 38; autobiographical 32; autofictional 36; canonical 87; children's 83; comparative 69; existential 125–26; feminist 147; imaginative 85; postcolonial 88
love stories 21, 64, 88
The Lover 21–23

Maghreb 4–5, 17, 75, 80, 103, 109, 154; community in France 100; immigrant populations in France 101; immigrant women in France 100
Maillet, Antonine 80–82, 85
Maritime Provinces (Canada) 80, 82, 85
Marks, Elaine 46
marriage 5, 64, 104, 109, 124, 130, 152–53, 156; and anti-marriage-equality 151; gay 156; relationships 83
Martel, Frédéric 54, 59, 153, 157
Massardier-Kenney, Françoise 145
Mastron, Ruth 97–98, 102
Matu, Florina 5, 103, 103–9
McClintock, Anne 5, 111, 114–15, 117
media 5, 48, 56, 99, 101, 112–13, 155; conglomerates 113; contemporary 53; French 57, 98–99; mainstream 61; social 36, 39, 53, 56–57, 113, 124
memoirs 21–22, 25, 85, 136–38, 140–41, 144, 146
memories 23, 25–26, 36, 108, 137; interspersed 133; recent 65; repressed 92; suppressed 22; women's 6, 135
Meyer, E. Nicole 1–7, 19–26
motherhood 31, 81
movies *see* films
Mrs Dalloway 130–31, 134
multiculturalism 1, 3–4, 28, 95–96, 98–101; American perceptions of 98; French perceptions of 95–96, 99, 101; gendered 101; uses of the term 100
music 5–6, 20, 32, 46, 92–93, 143–49, 152; communicative role of 143–44, 147; composition 144; groups 147; instrumental 144, 146; and musicians 6, 143–44, 147; performances 6; piano 144, 146; representation in French literature 6; representation of 6, 149; studies 143; styles 146
Muslims 30, 72, 103, 105, 109, 122–23, 153, 157; classmates 72; cultures 105; familail traditions 153; families 72; jurists 109; society 103; women 105, 109

Naït-Balk, Brahim 153–54, 157
National Disenchantment 113
national education system 99; *see also* education
National Liberation Army 106
national security 122–23
nationalism 117
nations 17, 79, 83, 86, 96–99, 114, 122, 135–36, 138–39; allied 137; colonized 71; unity of 98
neocolonialism 92, 117; and colonialism 92
New Caledonia 4, 71, 90, 92–93
The New Francophonie: Teaching French from an African-Centered Perspective 104
novels 15, 28, 31–32, 36–38, 41, 81, 86, 89–90, 92–93, 99, 101, 143–45, 148; contemporary 141

Oceania 4, 17, 87–88, 92, 140
online courses 45–46, 49; allowing participants and instructors to become "collaborators in the advancement of learning" 46; digital 49;

education 3, 45–46, 49; on French women's literature 45, 49, 140; working in the learning environments of 46, 49
Osnabrück 15
outreach courses 2
Ozon, Francois 61–64

Papeete 93
Paris 27–28, 31, 33–34, 71, 86, 124, 137, 140, 143, 145, 147, 149–51, 154, 156; French and Moroccan homosexuals living in 153; massacre of October 1961 101; Salon 6, 144
Paris-Jean Moulin Museum 140
pedagogical strategies 4–5, 95, 112, 116–17, 138
pedagogy 6–7, 46–47, 49, 63, 150
Perreau, Bruno 150–51
perspectives 1, 3, 36, 38, 57, 59, 69, 71–72, 74, 89, 91–92, 95, 97, 113, 129–33; children's 107; chronological 109; diverse 3, 53, 57; economic 117; feminine 95, 104, 107, 126; global 5, 105, 123; interdisciplinary 5, 112, 127, 157; multiple 47, 133; narrow 131–32; new 3, 107, 131
Petrovich, Michael 46
Peu, Titaua 93
Pineau, Gisèle 4, 68, 70–73, 75
podcasts 4, 55, 57–59, 72, 152, 154–56
politics 48, 50, 52, 62, 72, 79, 86, 98, 108, 150, 152, 157; African 85; identity-based 98, 141, 151, 153; Kanak 91
polygamy 83, 85, 108
Polynesian languages 93
Poncet, Dominique 147, 149
Porter, Laurence M. 4, 79–86
postcolonial 4–5, 20, 103, 112–14, 155; Algeria 104, 106, 108; feminist writings 4, 77, 80
postcolonialism 5, 105, 107, 111, 113–15, 117, 152
poverty 74, 80, 115–16, 132
poverty cultures 17
Powell, David A. 143
power 4, 18–19, 22–23, 25, 108–9, 112, 116–17, 124, 127, 129–30, 132, 137–38; boundaries of 19–20; and control 22; cultural 112; emotive 143; heuristic 12; irrefutable 14; political 4
prisoner-of-war camps 137
prisons 82–83, 124–26
programs 1, 17, 55, 66, 96, 121, 126, 151–52, 156; foreign-language 13; language arts 13; university honors 141
projects 11, 27–28, 37, 47, 63, 97, 125, 154; e-journaling 54; student research 98
Provencher, Denis M. 153

queer 6, 61, 150–54, 156–57; activists 150; Francophone authors 151, 154; movements 152; studies 6–7, 150, 152–53, 155, 157

race 4, 20, 23, 80, 92, 96, 126, 132, 135, 138, 155
racism 28, 137–38, 151–52
readings 20, 22–25, 28, 35–37, 39–40, 47–51, 58–59, 68, 71, 81, 84, 92–93, 129, 137–38, 140; assigned 49; colonial 88; Duras 137; Gorodé 91; Matamimi 90; primary 88; supplementary 93; theoretical 90
regional universities 62, 121
religion 1, 4, 69, 72–73, 80, 84, 98, 144, 152–53
reports 114, 152; *Foreign Languages and Higher Education: New Structure for a Changed World* 121
representations 2–3, 39, 41–42, 48, 62, 71–74, 79, 96, 98, 100–101, 143–45, 147; academic 135; allegorical 107; contemporary 72; gendered 100; literary 99; of music in literature 144; stereotypical 100
republicanism 101, 151–52; culture 99; values 99, 152–54
research 24, 33, 35–38, 55–56, 67, 70, 73–74, 96, 98, 105, 111, 116, 126, 129, 155; domains 153; feminist 104; literary 19; methods 154; student projects 98
Rice, Alison 2, 27, 27–34
Richard-Vivi, Ari'irau 89–90, 92

Sand, George 6, 47, 143–47
Sarraute, Nathalie 2, 23–24
scholars 33, 45, 50–51, 61, 69–70, 136, 139, 155; literary 140; rethinking the teaching of literature 1; women 47; young 28
scholarships 85, 121, 129, 135, 151, 153
Schumann, Robert 144, 146
science classes 38
Sebbar, Leila 80–81, 84–85, 101
The Seine Was Red 101
self 2–3, 9, 12, 21, 23, 25–26, 31, 36, 38–42, 124; appointed guardians 122; fulfillment 63; private 36; representations of the 3
self-narratives 20
semesters 23, 36–37, 39–40, 55–58, 62, 69, 71, 73–74, 90, 114, 136, 154; long study 101; modeling how to use websites, newspapers, and academic resources 74
sexuality 4–5, 16, 104, 109, 135, 150–58; human 16; non-normative 155; non-Western 154; studies 153, 155
short essays 38, 88, 105
skills 11–12, 18–20, 128; critical learning 122; critical thinking 62, 65, 126; film-analysis 3; intellectual 11; interdisciplinary 122; interpersonal communication 69; language 4, 15, 55, 58, 62, 69; literary 48; transferable 38
slaves 48, 82, 97
social change 4, 7
social institutions 68–69, 72–73
social justice 46, 70, 105, 113–15, 123
social media 36, 39, 53, 56–57, 113, 124
society 11–12, 19, 23, 80, 86–87, 98–99, 103, 107, 109, 112, 114, 116, 123–25, 131, 147; consumer 124; contemporary 68, 147; fractured 101; globalized 123; multicultural 97–99; pluralistic 101; transforming 111; upper-class 132
soldiers 137, 141–42

songs 55–56, 61, 67, 102, 145; fisherman's 145, 147; popular 67; rap 72
Spiridion 144–46, 149
Spitz, Chantal T. 88–90, 92
STEM 17, 19–20, 35
stereotypes 5, 66, 89, 100–101, 104, 130; feminine 66; gendered 101; subverted historical 47
Story of Women 140
strategies 2, 5, 7, 11, 37, 88, 95, 111, 116, 128–29, 150; concrete 1; pedagogical 4–5, 95, 112, 116–17, 138; rhetorical 20–21
student 63, 65, 67; leaders 92, 132; learning of French studies and women's studies 2, 37, 54; presenters 130–31; understanding in large science classes 38–39, 96
Sullivan, Courtney 6, 135–41
Supplément au Voyage de Bougainville 90

Tahiti 71, 88–89, 93
Tahitian 88–90, 93; identity 89; language 88; origin story 88
team teaching 5–6, 135, 139–41
technology 3, 17, 20, 35, 45–46, 56–57, 93, 112–13, 124
terrorism 5, 84, 101, 103, 108, 123, 127; acts 122; contemporary 122; studies 121–22
textbooks 54, 62, 68, 71–74
topics 5, 21, 27–28, 46, 54–59, 64, 66, 72, 74, 80–82, 109, 132, 138–39, 151, 153; controversial 48, 54; cultural 56; personal 90; range of 23, 27; suggested 58; taboo 87, 89
Touya de Marenne, Eric 5, 20, 111, 111–17, 136
traditions 85, 87, 91–92, 114–17, 128; classical 147; French Republican 151; Maghrebi 108; Muslim familial 153; oral 81–83
Tunisia 113–14, 116–17; feminist activists 116; and the postcolonial era 5, 112; women of 114
Tunisian Revolution 113–17

Un Papillon dans la cité 4, 68, 71–75
unemployment benefits 73
United States 34, 104, 126, 135–36, 138–39, 152, 157; and courses concerning French civilization 68; and ethical questions relating to terrorism, torture, and truth haunt the 123; and France 98; and multiculturism in the educational curriculum of the 95; and the uniqueness of French multiculturalism 96; and the viewpoint of American students 81
universities 1, 35, 139, 152; American 28, 104; regional 62, 121

values 11, 14, 19–20, 24, 26, 39, 41, 45, 97, 99, 103, 107, 112, 116, 130–31; archaic 109; central 53; core 41; democratic 111; human 13; immutable 103; traditional French 145, 151
Vanuatu (Oceania) 4, 87
Vermette, Métis Katherena 132

victims 67, 100, 105, 130, 135, 141; of cultural and religious norms delegating women to secondary roles 105; of gang rape 154; and women during WWII in French and American fiction, film, autobiography, and history cast as 135
videos 6, 55–57, 59, 113, 151
violence 20, 22–23, 30, 52, 92, 101, 106–7, 115, 121, 131, 141; domestic 2, 20, 92, 100, 109; Islamist 103; political 131; sexual 92
voices 1, 3, 5, 24, 27–28, 33, 47–48, 51–52, 88, 123–24, 126, 129, 132, 138, 145; diverse 6, 111; eloquent 27; female 100, 145; genderless 23; male 145; mother's 21, 24; scholarly 138; untrained peasant's 145

Wallis and Futuna (Oceania) 87
war 21–22, 25, 72, 101, 109, 122–25, 135–41; Algerian War 6, 100–101, 123; censorship 123; work 139; World War I 81; World War II 6, 79, 81, 91, 123, 135–38, 140
websites 2, 27, 30, 32–33, 71, 73–74, 93
Weidenbaum, Shira 128–34
West Africa 17, 79, 82–83
women 1–2, 15–17, 27–28, 33, 47–51, 61–67, 73, 79, 85–87, 89–91, 100–101, 103–4, 106–9, 114–16, 128–42; Algerian 105–9; American 6, 135–37, 140–41; Arab 97; black 97; conceptualizations of 91; emancipation of 116; European 89; in film and literature 63; in Francophone cultures 58; French 6, 135, 138, 140; hard-working 46; historical realities of 141; images of 3, 61, 63, 65; in Kanak history and political struggles 91; minority 95; Muslim 105, 109; novelists 143–48; Oceanian 87–91, 93; rights of 73, 91, 108, 116, 123; role during World War II in French and American fiction, film, autobiography, and history 6, 135, 138; role in the past and present 6, 58, 63, 91, 135, 137–38; status of 17, 64; Tahitian 89; tattooed 23; veiled 101; voices of 54, 56–59, 89, 128–29, 134; well-behaved 128, 134; white 97
The Women 61
women authors 2–4, 6, 25, 27–29, 31, 33, 49–50, 52, 70, 73–74, 79, 86–91, 93–94, 103–4, 128–31; contemporary 28–29, 33, 104; contemporary Francophone 79; diverse 126; excellent Francophone 79; Francophone 3–4, 45, 79; lesser-known 3; Oceanian 87–91, 93; and women characters 6, 63, 66, 104–6, 108–9
"Women Novelists and the Music of Paris" 144–45, 147–48
women writers *see* women authors
World War I 81
World War II 6, 79, 81, 91, 123, 135–38, 140
writers 2, 6, 15–16, 20, 27–28, 30, 32–33, 70, 87, 92–93, 103, 107, 123, 144, 147; existential 5, 121, 123; individual 70; lesser-known 27; letter 83; male 79, 87; recognized 27
Wynn, Kerry 6, 135–41